A serious playfulness, a [...] of the world—this is w[...] sees as the essence of Fi[...] charitable and too disabused to make a satirist, he 'puts on the mask of tavern keeper and serves up the various dishes of human nature': his great successes were 'festive' books—*Joseph Andrews* and *Tom Jones*; when he attempted moralising, in *Amelia*, he lost his touch.

In this excellent book, Professor Wright examines the workings of Fielding's comic genius. He shows how realistic detail is blended with 'operatic' structure, and artificial situations arise paradoxically from naturalistic elements. He calls attention to the big, set scenes, which Fielding's experience in the theatre and his friendship for Hogarth helped him to create. There are chapters on the plotting and style of the novels and on the 'bas-relief' quality of the characters, who are at the same time round and flat.

Henry Fielding was one of the great founders of the English novel; changing fashions and new techniques, as Professor Wright triumphantly shows, have done nothing to diminish this greatness.

A native of Columbus, Ohio, Andrew Wright studied at Harvard and Ohio State University. At London University he did research on Fielding on Fulbright and Guggenheim fellowships. He was appointed associate professor of English at Ohio State University in 1958 and is now Professor of English at the San Diego campus of the University of California, at La Jolla. He is the author of *Jane Austen's Novels: A Study in Structure*, of *Joyce Cary: A Preface to his Novels* and of many articles.

HENRY FIELDING
MASK AND FEAST

A

By the same Author

JANE AUSTEN'S NOVELS
A Study in Structure

JOYCE CARY
A Preface to His Novels

HENRY FIELDING

MASK AND FEAST

By

ANDREW WRIGHT

Professor of English
University of California
San Diego

UNIVERSITY OF CALIFORNIA PRESS

BERKELEY AND LOS ANGELES

1965

PUBLISHED IN THE UNITED STATES OF AMERICA
BY THE UNIVERSITY OF CALIFORNIA PRESS
BERKELEY AND LOS ANGELES, CALIFORNIA

PRINTED IN GREAT BRITAIN

For Gina as always

ACKNOWLEDGMENTS

I want to thank the following persons, who have helped me in the study of Fielding: Martin C. Battestin, Matthew J. Bruccoli, Elizabeth Dalton, Robert C. Elliott, Robert M. Estrich, Hyman Kritzer, Agostino Lombardo, Jerome Mandel, T. J. B. Spencer, Philip T. Stevick, James Sutherland, and Virginia Wright.

I am also grateful to the American Council of Learned Societies, the John Simon Guggenheim Memorial Foundation, and the Ohio State University for financial help.

A section of the first chapter of this book has appeared in *Essays in Criticism*, XIII (July 1963), to whose editors I am grateful for granting me the hospitality of their journal.

A. W.

Lewes
July 1964

A NOTE ON THE TEXTS CITED

The most inclusive edition of Fielding is *The Complete Works of Henry Fielding, Esq.*, ed. William Ernest Henley, 16 vols. (London, 1903)—but it is neither complete nor accurate. Fortunately, the Wesleyan University Press (Middleton, Connecticut) is now on the point of bringing out an edition which promises to be more comprehensive and textually more impeccable, under the editorship of William B. Coley. In the meantime, scholars must use the Henley edition, and I have done so throughout, except where I have quoted from works of Fielding not included in Henley; and except also where textually better editions exist. Martin C. Battestin's edition of *Joseph Andrews* & *Shamela* (Riverside paperback edition, Boston, 1961) is textually superior to Henley for *Joseph Andrews*, and Henley does not include *Shamela* at all; I have therefore used the Battestin edition when quoting from these two works. And, when quoting from *The Covent-Garden Journal*, I have used the edition of Gerard Edward Jensen, 2 vols. (New Haven, Connecticut, 1915). Other exceptions to my rule of quoting from Henley are noted in the appropriate places.

CONTENTS

'I must blame you for taking so little notice of our Diversions and Amusements; tho' these may perhaps be called the best Characteristics of a People. They are, indeed, the truest Mirrors . . .'

FIELDING, *The Champion*, 1 April 1740

Chapter 1

THE FESTIVE STANCE

They'll tell you virtue is a masque:
But it wou'd look extremely queer
In any one to wear it here.

FIELDING, *The Masquerade* (1728)

JOSEPH ANDREWS: ART AS ART

TRADITIONALLY, the writer of fiction pretends to be telling the truth, to be relating actual fact – whether implicitly by establishing an air of verisimilitude so that the reader suspends his disbelief, or explicitly by masquerading in the foreword and perhaps parenthetically throughout as an editor, as an antiquarian, or even as a sympathetic and literate friend. Fielding mocks expectation, as he mocks convention, by demonstrating at once that *Joseph Andrews* is false. He thus makes more precise and at the same time makes more ample the boundaries of the world of the novel. Eschewing the extravagance of the romance, eschewing likewise and with indignation what seemed to him the indiscriminate and irresponsible serving up of detail which in massive bulk made the testament to prurience that was, for him, *Pamela* – Fielding on the one hand brought fiction within the realm of probability and on the other elevated the novel from the level of the cautionary tale, or mirror for ambitious young girls, to the level of serious playfulness. In *Joseph Andrews* the narrator masquerading as an author is the player who by his opening fanfares as well as by his preliminary gambits and interruptions reminds us that what he is telling is a story, that what he fabricates is for all its fidelity to nature ultimately and deliberately faithless to mere fact, that what he is offering is not a guide to life but the transfiguration of life which is his art. Fielding the comic observer and Fielding the moralist are united – that is to say, reconciled – in Fielding the narrator, Fielding's 'second self'.[1] Seen in proper perspective *Joseph Andrews* does of

15

course exhibit both the bad and the good life: but the artistic motive is festive rather than lenten, ideal rather than hortatory: not simply representational, but spectacular.

Two hundred years later, playfulness, however serious, may seem an unworthy outcome, but this is largely because art has for so long exhibited different motives. Yet the common denominator of eighteenth-century criticism is the assumption or argument, with Horatian warrant, that the motive of art is to give civilized and civilizing pleasure to reader, viewer, or auditor. 'From the time of the critical essays of Dryden,' M. H. Abrams points out, 'through the eighteenth century, pleasure tended to become the ultimate end [of poetry], although poetry without profit was often held to be trivial, and the optimistic moralist believed with James Beattie that if poetry instructs, it only pleases the more effectively.'[2] It may be for this reason that eighteenth-century literature sometimes appears to be a refuge from the present. Doubtless the century is attractive either to those ambitious for gentility or to those nostalgic about gentility's decline. But Fielding and some of his contemporaries, who actually lived in that largely cruel and mostly ugly era, tried in what they wrote not to rub a civilized gloss on the England in which they lived: they tried to make civilization. As a young man Fielding had been legislated off the stage. But later as pamphleteer, editor, lawyer, and magistrate he had good opportunity to make a direct assault on the evils of his day which were many and to him grievous.[3] In his view, nevertheless, fiction was not the slices of life he was to experience in Bow Street: his art was – or so he thought until he could bear it no longer – a recreation, elevating because suggestive of an order not envisioned in the Richardsonian formulation. In this connection it is well to recall Lord Kames's essay, 'Emotions Caused by Fiction', published in his *Elements of Criticism* (1762). Kames wrote precisely to this point: 'The power that fiction hath over the mind affords an endless variety of refined amusements, always at hand to employ a vacant hour. Such amusements are a fine resource in solitude and by cheering and sweetening the mind contribute mightily to social happiness.'[4] As an artist – that is, first as a playwright and then as a novelist –

Fielding for the most part aimed at neither the excoriation nor the amendment of mankind. At his best, and at the top of his form, he succeeded in writing comic novels as splendid – and, because comic, as disengaged – as any in the language. Yet in *Joseph Andrews* and in *Tom Jones* Fielding laid out plans which he could not keep to: life itself became so clamorous that his last novel, *Amelia*, failed to be the masterpiece he hoped it would be. But in 1741 – *Joseph Andrews* was published in February of the following year – it was still very possible for Fielding to maintain the supposition that art was artifice. This is not to say that Fielding endeavoured to make a merely refined art: the prefaces and narrative intrusions throughout *Joseph Andrews* and *Tom Jones* would persuade us by various appeals – to nature, to life, to the world – that his novels will provide what was later to be called the shock of recognition. ('The lawyer is not only alive, but hath been so these four thousand years.') On the other hand, to serve up life as art, to make transcripts of day-to-day experience and bind them up in book form – this, too, was wrong because false to art on his plan.[5]

Accordingly, the central fact about the famous preface to *Joseph Andrews* is that in discoursing upon the nature of the comic epic poem in prose Fielding is promising not simply a work of art different in structure from *Pamela*: he is adumbrating an ontological and thus aesthetic answer as well. Fielding and Richardson are incompatible because they inhabit different worlds. Against a world consisting of middle-class ambitions, promised, denied, frustrated, and fulfilled – against this world, Fielding puts an ampler world in which getting and spending are subordinated to civilization itself. The world of selfish prudence and the world of benign innocence are worlds apart: so the character of Parson Adams demonstrates. But that such a man as Adams can thrive even in an evil world, this is the comic and civilizing point; he thrives, however, not by applying his learning: his learning is pure, inapplicable, irrelevant to day-to-day life; he thrives by the sublime benefaction of a world created by him in his own image, a world wherein men are kindly, women are virtuous, and sermons publishable.

Fielding objected to Richardson's fiction as false to life

because inadequate to life. As Parson Oliver says in a letter to Parson Tickletext in *Shamela*,

> The instruction which it [*Pamela*] conveys to servant-maids, is, I think, very plainly this, To look out for their masters as sharp as they can. The consequences of which will be, besides neglect of their business, and the using all manner of means to come at ornaments of their persons, that if the master is not a fool, they will be debauched by him; and if he is a fool, they will marry him. Neither of which, I apprehend, my good friend, we desire should be the case of our sons.[6]

But the negative aspect of *Joseph Andrews* is all too frequently emphasized in criticism at the expense of its more important and central point. Fielding objected in *Shamela* to bad morals and bad art. The objection is sustained in *Joseph Andrews* – and surpassed: Fielding's first novel becomes a sort of jubilee book.

The Author's Preface, then, with its anatomization of the epic and of the drama, is a rationale of comic high seriousness, set forth with briskly comic self-depreciation. The new genre, 'the comic romance', the 'comic epic-poem in prose', is to be differentiated from comedy in extent and in comprehensiveness. Fielding puts spaciousness and variety first. The fable and action are 'light and ridiculous', as over against those of the serious romance, which are 'grave and solemn'. Low characters are introduced; and the diction is ludicrous – sometimes even burlesque – rather than sublime. Nothing here even hints at an exemplary intent behind the comic epic poem in prose: what Fielding does point to is a kind of spectacular immediacy.[7]

'The Ridiculous only', he writes, 'falls within my province in the present work.' And when he explains with some thoroughness what he means by the term, it becomes clear that the fangs of righteous indignation do not grow out of the ridiculous, because the subject-matter is carefully chosen and carefully handled to preclude such a response. His scope, though broad, must nevertheless on this plan make certain exclusions. The world of *Joseph Andrews* is not going to be the actual world transprosed. It is going to be a comic transfiguration.[8] 'What could exceed', he asks, 'the absurdity of an author, who should write *the Comedy of Nero, with the merry incident of ripping up his Mother's Belly?*'[9] For, although human vices will make their appearance in the following pages, because 'it is very difficult to pursue a series of human actions, and keep clear from them', they will be rendered harmless in that, among other things, 'they never produce the intended evil'. So it is fitting that Parson Adams should be the subject of the final paragraph of this preface – Parson Adams rather than the more prominently eponymous hero. The clergyman is 'a character of perfect simplicity', and thus well suited to the purposes of the planned myopias of the author's own vision. Abraham Adams is simple by nature, the author simple by choice: that is, by design. And Adams is a parson, 'since no other office could have given him so many opportunities of displaying his worthy inclinations'. The office of the priesthood, as Fielding did not need to remind his eighteenth-century audience, centres on the most important of all feasts.

In the main the purpose of the narrator of *Joseph Andrews* is twofold: first, to discuss the method of his book, that is to say the art of the comic epic romance; and, second, to establish the relationship between himself and the reader. Over all, the narrator's role thus emphasizes the artificiality of the novel as a whole. Ian Watt in *The Rise of the Novel* uses the phrase 'formal realism' as a key to his explanation of the rise of the novel in the eighteenth century. But Watt's analysis of Fielding does not explain – or rather, explains away – Fielding's use of unromantic materials for the opposite of realistic motives: thus Parson Trulliber, that avaricious hog fancier, is as a character so much larger than life as to be splendidly fabulous. The reason is that 'formal realism', possible at last in the eighteenth century, made for verisimilitude in the works of Defoe and Richardson and Smollett – but in Fielding underscored rather than effaced artifice.[10] The narrator puts at a distance and thus makes bearable the human condition: thus does Fielding bring outrage under control by a fine and flexible art of reverse telescopy. So much the Author's Preface has indicated; so much the three prolegomenous chapters assure us; so much the narrator's handling of scene confirms.[11]

Joseph Andrews does not even begin *in medias res*. The first chapter of Book I treats the reader to a disquisition on the sub-

ject of biography which, coming just after the 'Author's Preface', makes for much explanation before the action of the book
gets under way. The title of the chapter is 'Of writing lives in
general, and particularly of *Pamela*; with a word by the bye of
Colley Cibber and others'. Life as a teacher is asserted to be
superior to art, and biography is denigrated so far as to turn
itself inside out: 'the writer ... by communicating such valuable
patterns to the world . . . may perhaps do a more extensive
service to mankind, than the person whose life originally
afforded the pattern'. From the beginning the narrator wears
an ironic mask, and the reader is prepared for the mock
pedantry of his several examples, including 'the history of John
the Great, who, by his brave and heroic actions against men of
large and athletic bodies, obtained the glorious appelation of
the Giant-killer'. What he is doing here is not simply criticizing
pedantry, and – when he talks of *Pamela* and Colley Cibber's
autobiography – criticizing bad morals: he is criticizing art as
well.

Forgetfulness becomes, in Fielding's hands, a weapon against
verisimilitude: a sovereign remedy against the pain of judgment. This technique can be observed in the small scale of the
triangular relationship of Lady Booby, Joseph, and Mrs Slipslop. 'It is the observation of some ancient sage, whose name I
have forgot . . .' Fielding writes; and 'Another philosopher,
whose name also at present escapes my memory, hath somewhere said ...' – these disclaimers of erudition point to the level
at which he wants his remarks to be taken. He wants them to be
taken lightly. 'We hope, therefore, a judicious reader will give
himself some pains to observe, what we have so greatly laboured
to describe, the different operations of this passion of love in the
gentle and cultivated mind of the Lady Booby, from those
which it effected in the less polished and coarser disposition of
Mrs Slipslop' (I, 7). The irony is plain enough. The question
raised by the pretended forgetfulness of the narrator begins to
answer itself: if the moral implications of the Lady Booby,
Joseph, and Mrs Slipslop triangle begin to become insistent,
the intervention of the narrator invites us to dissociate ourselves
from them.

With equal address, Fielding poses as the scholar, anxious for exactitude. A good example occurs in chapter 15 of Book I. Joseph, recovering at the Dragon Inn from the beating at the hands of the highway robbers, is being looked after by the recently-arrived Parson Adams. Joseph is hungry, and expresses a desire for boiled beef and cabbage. 'Adams was pleased with so perfect a confirmation that he [Joseph] had not the least fever, but advised him to a lighter diet for that evening. He accordingly eat either a rabbit or a fowl, I never could with any tolerable certainty discover which; after this he was, by Mrs Tow-wouse's order, conveyed into a better bed and equipped with one of her husband's shirts.' What stands out here, and is made to stand out, is the phrase 'I never could with any tolerable certainty discover which': unquestionably he is borrowing a device common to two of his favourite writers, Lucian and Cervantes. In the course of an authoritative comparison of Lucian and Fielding, Henry Knight Miller adverts to 'the meticulous and scholarly caution with which very dubious materials – or bald lies – are presented, the reader being assured that his author offers no more than what he can be certain of as fact'.[12] Fielding's is playful and mock pedantry, as it is also in Cervantes; in Part II of *Don Quixote*, for example, appears this remark: 'first of all he had washed his face and head with five or six buckets of water – there is some difference of opinion as to the number'.[13] Defoe uses this device to achieve the effect of verisimilitude[14]; Fielding, like Cervantes before him, uses it to break the thread of the narrative, and remind the reader that this is a story, told by a story-teller. For there is a certain moral importance behind Fielding's decision to enter here in his own person, that his 'second self' should be so obtrusively in evidence. In general, what Northrop Frye says about this device is helpful.

All the great story-tellers, including the Augustan ones, have a strong sense of literature as a finished product. The suspense is thrown forward until it reaches the end, and is based on our confidence that the author knows what is coming next. A story-teller does not break his illusion by talking to the reader as Fielding does, because we know from the start that we are listening to Fielding telling a story – that is, Johnson's arguments about illusion in drama apply equally well to prose fiction of Fielding's kind.[15]

In particular, Fielding's intrusion, for all its literary forebears, helps to define the special relationship which Fielding establishes in *Joseph Andrews* between himself and his readers.

The opening chapter of Book II, which Fielding calls 'Of divisions in authors', provides a crucial demonstration of the way in which *Joseph Andrews* is to be taken. Ostensibly an essay on the 'art of dividing' a work into books and chapters, this prefatory disquisition actually exists for the purpose of beguiling the reader into reading *Joseph Andrews* as a special kind of entertainment. Significantly, the images which animate this chapter are those of eating and drinking: the two principal reasons for 'division in authors' are, first, to provide for the reader 'an inn or resting-place, where he may stop and take a glass, or any other refreshment, as it pleases him', and, second, to provide a forecast – in the chapter headings, which are like 'so many inscriptions over the gates of inns . . . informing the reader what entertainment he is to expect'. Finally, having gone with mock-sobriety through the epic argument, Fielding with superb casualness concludes the chapter with a figure of speech that shows up his other 'arguments' in the light of common day: 'it becomes an author generally to divide a book, as it does a butcher to joint his meat, for such assistance is of great help to both the reader and the carver'.[16]

In fact, the substance of this chapter lies somewhere on the journey between Defoe and Sterne. At the very beginning, Fielding announces that he will deal with the trade-secret of 'divisions in authors', for 'common readers imagine that by this art of dividing we mean only to swell our works to a much larger bulk than they would otherwise be extended to'. Surely this anticipates the skepticism which Sterne carries to the wild limit of missing chapters, blank pages, and asterisks. Fielding's figure of speech is that of a tailor's bill – 'so much buckram, stays, and stay-tape . . . serving only to make up the sum total'. Here, however lightly, he hesitates at the edge of the chaos into which Sterne would so desperately plunge nearly two decades later. On the other hand, no doubt remembering the breathless indivisibility of such a work as *Moll Flanders*, and at the same time refusing the precedent of the epistolary form, Fielding writes: 'A volume without any such places of rest resembles the opening of wilds or seas, which tires the eye and fatigues the spirit when entered upon'.

Hence the playfulness with which he speculates about divisions in authors. Having solemnly assured us that the two main reasons for divisions are to give the reader an opportunity to rest and to give him also the opportunity to see where he is going, Fielding prevents a too straightforward response to this ratiocination by anticlimactically bringing forward a third reason: 'it [division] prevents spoiling the beauty of a book by turning down its leaves'. Nor can he resist recourse to the epic parallel once again; he now calls this recourse 'the sanction of great antiquity'. Homer is said to have divided 'his great work into twenty-four books' because, as he suggests, the Greek alphabet contains twenty-four letters, and because as the inventor of publication by numbers Homer 'hawked them all separately', and so, like Fielding's contemporaries, made more money by this method of publication than by the usual method. With a glance at the modest Virgil's twelve books and the at first even more modest Milton's ten, he dissociates himself from prescriptive critics and briskly brings this chapter to a conclusion; the reader is prepared to resume his reading of the journey of Joseph and Adams, now with a renewed sense of the comic spirit that pervades their adventures.

Two questions assert themselves here. First, how straightforward is Fielding in his assumption of the nature of his audience? Second, what is the connection between Fielding's narrative management and the playful theme of *Joseph Andrews*: what is the relationship between mask and feast?

To the first question the answer is that Fielding knew himself to be addressing two classes of readers, the initiates, and the members of the reading public who did not possess a classical education. The epigraphs, the parade of erudition, mainly classical erudition, the Latin and sometimes Greek tags, the ponderous chapter headings, the jaunty and mocking scholarly air of the prefatory and interspersed comments – all of these are no doubt meant to elicit amusement at the smell of the lamp; equally they are intended to be amusing to those who have smelt the lamp. Furthermore, as Ian Watt demonstrates, the ironic posture of the Augustans stems, in part at least, from the fact of a double audience: the mob, and the chosen few.

> The chosen few – the men of wit and judgment and learning – could be assumed to have a considerable identity of attitude and understanding: to them you could speak as subtly and elliptically as you wished. But to the many, the mob – you obviously couldn't and in any case wouldn't use the same language. . . . The ironic posture, in fact, was both a formal expression of the qualitative division in the reading public, and a flattering reinforcement of the sense of superiority which animated one part of it.[17]

The *tone* of the relationship between narrator and reader is bantering: he chaffs his reader for perhaps being so provincial as not to have travelled beyond the outskirts of London (*Joseph Andrews*, II, 10); he teases the 'gentlemen at White's' (*Amelia*, VIII, 9) for their self-consequence, for their readiness to make hasty and skeptical literary judgments. But this tone proceeds from a confident awareness of the general nature of his readership rather than from the blind hopefulness that made for the patient wooing and the impatient instruction of the writers of a century later.[18]

To the second question – that of the relationship between mask and feast – the answer is that the narrator, untroubled by the necessity of making contact with he knows not whom, is free to wear his mask how he pleases. If, as I am arguing, Fielding believes that the function of the novel is to provide a paradigm of civilization which is above the level of ordinary moral imperatives, the narrator is free to tilt the mask in such a way as to disclose its artificiality, and when he does so he need not fear that his sophisticated technique will be misconstrued. Defoe and Richardson, who like Fielding knew their audiences and who also sought to please, aimed lower and endeavoured to produce somewhat rawer if no less important satisfactions. Elizabeth Dalton, in an unpublished paper, puts the matter very well when she makes the following comparison between Richardson and Fielding.

In place of voyeurism, Fielding offers us the pleasures of inferential activity. He drops clues, gives hints, arouses our anticipations, then surprises and delights us by the exercise of an ingenuity superior to our own.... The role of the artist, then, is not to imitate the random sequences of real experience, but to create from the materials of life actions which life itself could never approximate. Thus to criticize as unlifelike the coincidences and discoveries is to miss the point. We are meant instead to quaff the peculiarly potent brew of life and art, in which single events, none of them by itself impossible, are combined in a mixture more interesting and amusing than life itself.

Everything that I have been saying so far must now be considered in the light of the first chapter of Book III of *Joseph Andrews*. The title of this chapter is 'Matter prefatory in praise of biography', and if it is taken in isolation it must qualify what I have been saying. To be sure – as the first chapter of Book I has already made apparent – Fielding does regard himself as a biographer: but, as he suggests in the preface to Book III, he is a fictional biographer in the tradition of Cervantes and Lesage. As such he stands in contrast to the *mere* biographers, and especially the autobiographers, the Colley Cibbers, as well of course as the false biographers, the Samuel Richardsons. Furthermore, a discourse on method, bound as it is to suspend the narrative proper, must lay stress on the fact of method. It must divert attention from the fictive illusion. By virtue of its very existence and in its own nature it underscores the fact that the *story* of *Joseph Andrews* is made up.

The rationale here proceeds on familiar lines. The biographer, which is the name that the narrator now dignifies himself with, is superior to the historian on the one hand, and to 'those persons of surprising genius, the authors of immense romances, or the modern novel', on the other. The reason is that historians are at best mere topographers, 'but as to the actions and characters of men, their writings are not quite so authentic'. As for novelists, they are guilty of 'forming originals from the confused heap of matter in their own brains'. Fielding names names; his examples of bad history and bad novels are cited with full adequacy. The 'biographers', of whom he approves – Cervantes, Lesage, Scarron, Marivaux – are also cited, by name or by allusion. The ground of approbation is succinctly laid down in Fielding's comparison of Cervantes with the historian Juan de Mariana:

Is not such a book as that which records the achievements of the renowned Don Quixote more worthy the name of a history than even Mariana's? for, whereas the latter is confined to a particular period of time, and to a particular nation, the former is the history of the world in general, at least that part which is polished by laws, arts, and sciences; and of that from the time it was first polished to this day; nay, and forwards so long as it shall so remain.

This appeal leads inevitably to the famous declaration: 'I describe not men, but manners; not an individual, but a species', with, as he says, satiric – that is to say, corrective – intent: 'to hold the glass to thousands in their closets, that they may contemplate their deformity, and endeavour to reduce it, and thus by suffering private mortification may avoid public shame'.

This is all so usual – Aristotle Augustanized – that it may be taken as the conventional recital of aims. And in *The Mirror and the Lamp*, Mr Abrams very usefully distinguishes between protestation and practice in eighteenth-century aesthetics.[19] But taken in its own terms there are two things to be said about this chapter: in the first place the narrator insists on fidelity to the central facts of human experience as he knows them, and as he knows them to be communicable. Second, the announced purpose of the satire – the corrective purpose – stands in contrast to what actually happens in *Joseph Andrews* in the chapters preceding and following this essay.

Surely the final chapter of Book II can have little relationship to the kind of satire which will 'hold the glass to thousands in their closets, that they may contemplate their deformity, and endeavour to reduce it, and thus by suffering private mortification may avoid public shame'. For at the end of Book II Parson Adams has been rescued from the empty promises of the 'gentleman' who had offered him accommodation, horses, and a £300 living. The rescuer is the host of the inn who gratuitously, out of respect for the clergy, gives Adams help – only to become involved in an argument with the parson as to which is superior, experience or learning. The special delight here is Adams's naïve disinterestedness in argument, an entire unawareness that he is offending the innkeeper who is being generous to him. There is no hope and there is no wish here to 'correct' Adams's astigmatism: his innocent naïveté is his special glory. Nor is there any suggestion that the innkeeper should learn to be less charitable. In short, this is a celebratory rather than a satirical tableau.

What follows Fielding's rationale is no more didactically satirical. Chapter 2 of Book III is in fact the prelude to Wilson's tale, an account of a night journey that includes Joseph arming himself against ghosts with a penknife, Fanny clinging to him in happy terror, and Parson Adams rolling down a hill. To be sure, Wilson's tale, when it comes (but it does not come until the chapter following) has as its theme vanity, and it is cautionary. But it is hardly satirical in the terms set out in the prefatory chapter to the third book. This is not to say that *Joseph Andrews* lacks satiric elements. Lady Booby, Mrs Slipslop, Peter Pounce, Mr and Mrs Tow-wouse, Tom Suckbribe, Miss Grave-airs, Mr Fickle, Colonel Courtly, Beau Didapper – these tag-names point to minor characters and thus to the extent, small though not unimportant, to which *Joseph Andrews* is satiric. The sustained satiric fable of *Gulliver's Travels*, and Fielding's own satiric series of papers which he published in *The Champion* purporting to be an account of the travels of one Job Vinegar[20] – these are far removed in spirit, in time, in meaning from *Joseph Andrews*. There is no one like Lemuel Gulliver or Job Vinegar in *Joseph Andrews*, where – if my reading is correct – satire is subordinated to celebration. A corollary is that the structure of the novel is by this reading shown to be far more designed, unified, and harmonious than if the work is regarded as a miscellany or a horse that rides off in all directions.

And *Joseph Andrews* for all its open construction is thoroughly plotted. It has a beginning, a middle, and an ending which is pointed and final. There is, in fact, an engraftment of sentimental dramatic plot upon the picaresque structure. This kind of juxtaposition was thoroughly sanctioned in Fielding's time and goes further than does the preface to *Joseph Andrews* itself to explain the coherence of the work as a whole. The general strategy is sketched out at the beginning of chapter 11 of Book I, when Fielding, having concentrated on the male-chastity theme, sends Joseph off journeying.

It is an observation sometimes made, that to indicate our idea of a simple fellow, we say, 'He is easily to be seen through': nor do I believe it a more important denotation of a simple book. Instead of applying this to any particular performance, we choose rather to remark the contrary in this history, where the scene opens itself by small degrees; and he is a sagacious reader who can see two chapters before him.

Probability and verisimilitude are, accordingly, secondary to the main design, which is that of eliciting amused pleasure at mankind in a ridiculous stance. But this remark has another job to do: it points toward the structural principle, which is that of mystifying through elaborate concealment.[21] As such it is the opposite of the picaresque method, by which the obvious is made to happen repeatedly and by implication endlessly; Lazarillo de Tormes, the eponymous hero of an anonymous tale, repeatedly seeks and fails to satisfy his hunger: at the end he has come to terms temporarily with his need to be fed, but the terms are tentative, fragile, and doomed. He is certain to be on the road soon again. The method of *Joseph Andrews* differs radically also from that of Richardson's novels. *Pamela* – at least this is true of the first two volumes; and they are what Fielding guyed – centres on the virtue of the heroine: all the action leads up to and down from that unifying fact; or, to put it another way, the book centres in the consciousness of Pamela Andrews. But *Joseph Andrews*, for all its talk of Joseph's virtue, is extensive. It would be facile to say that generically *Joseph Andrews* stands somewhere between the picaresque tale and the intensive novel of the Richardsonian type: it would be facile – and, besides that, unfair to Fielding, as though he were a compromise. But such classification does shed some light on *Joseph Andrews*.

So does the subtitle, 'Written in imitation of the manner of Cervantes, author of *Don Quixote*'. For *Don Quixote*, itself a modification of the picaresque tale, offers some parallels to *Joseph Andrews*, but more important it marks out some differences that are instructive. The omission in *Joseph Andrews* of a Sancho Panza figure is frequently discussed,[22] and thematically the two novels embody a difference in degree which amounts to a difference in kind. *Don Quixote* contrasts appearance and reality in such a way as to betray multitudinous uncertainties. *Joseph Andrews*, though it raises this question also, does so in such a way as to indicate that Fielding knows what the answers are. Parson Adams may be, on account of his innocence, opaque; but Fielding is not: Fielding knows that innkeepers are rapacious and country squires crude and widows concupiscent. This much has to be said to point to the structural contrast: *Don Quixote* is more open and less contrived than is *Joseph Andrews*; Fielding's novel is not always flawless, but it is *arranged* in a way that *Don Quixote* is not.[23] The structural difference points to a difference in meaning: Cervantes's masterpiece dramatizes an ontological uncertainty, an ontological skepticism; Fielding's first novel depicts persons of incorruptible innocence in a corrupt but knowable and 'solid' world. At the end of *Don Quixote* the hero dies because life is no longer art: Don Quixote cannot believe in the romances upon which he has based his entire career of knight errantry. When life is no longer the picture that Don Quixote himself had painted, he dies of a broken heart. But Joseph Andrews's life begins, at the end of his book.

When in the Author's Preface Fielding says that the 'Ridiculous only . . . falls within my province in the present work' he is surely implying a worldly order which his experience does not vouchsafe and which, accordingly, is not to be represented, except in art. Order is discoverable, but not the social order which a little sanative laughter will restore or purify. It is true, as Aurélien Digeon says, that in *Joseph Andrews* Fielding 'ruthlessly exposes the secret egotism which lies behind our apparently most disinterested actions',[24] but it is wrong to suppose that Fielding seeks to establish a norm of rationality in which as social beings we achieve fulfilment. What, then, is he aiming at? The answer, it seems to me, lies in the wish to make the best of things: to make do, well. There is plenty of evidence to show that Fielding was anything but satisfied with things as they were; there is also evidence, both within the novels and without, that he did not have high hopes for the perfectibility of human beings or of society.[25] The measure of his pessimism is perhaps his willingness to work with expedients, a willingness based upon his recognition of the fact, as he saw it, that man is incorrigible. 'There are', Fielding wrote in *The True Patriot*, for 12 November 1745, 'some Imperfections perhaps innate in our Constitution, and others too inveterate and established, to be eradicated; to these, wise and prudent Men will rather submit, than hazard shocking the Constitution itself by a rash Endeavour to remove them'.[26] So Fielding's 'exposure' of follies and vices was not undertaken with the aim of mending manners but of providing, sometimes desperately, a rehearsal of civilization. It is impossible to make a bad man good, and good men will very probably grow wise without much prompting. The function of art, therefore – and if this is not a tautology – is to provide a kind of ideal delight.

Vanity or hypocrisy is responsible for affectation on the individual level, and affectation is a sort of blindness that prevents charity on the social plane. This is nature, and it is not pretty – especially as there is very little which can be done about it. In fact, failure is the ultimate success of the good man, whose only armour against corruption is innocence, which can be violated but not learned. Between society and the individual, Fielding strikes a balance which would be unexpected to anyone unfamiliar with those traditions of Western civilizations calling not for despair about the human condition, not for abandonment of human hope, not for remedies which will not cure, but – paradoxically – for acceptance and rejoicing. To be sure, Fielding means what he says – there is plenty of evidence outside his novels to demonstrate his practice of what Joseph and Adams, Tom and Allworthy, Amelia and Dr Harrison preach. But by establishing a scale in which their remarks and actions are to be understood he makes *moralizing* secondary to art – and art has the wonderfully beneficent motive of idealizing morality by making the actions of men into arrangements that are amusing and sometimes even beautiful. Amiability itself is an ennobling virtue, laughter is integral to the seriousness of discourse; comedy is at once antidote and consolation, alternative and extension. When, as in *Joseph Andrews* and *Tom Jones*, it is adequately realized, it becomes not merely better than life, it becomes life itself.

In *Joseph Andrews*, it is possible to read a sermon – perhaps, as Martin Battestin argues, a latitudinarian sermon.[27] But Fielding's experience as a journalist, as a lawyer, and as a magistrate – his competence, that is to say, in the rhetoric of straightforward argument; his belief, implicit in both *Joseph Andrews* and in *Tom Jones*, that life was life and art art; above all his fatalistic view of human destiny: these make me think that realism in *Joseph Andrews* is scarcely hortatory, for the grim but at the same time consoling truth is that although 'it may not be always so easy for a serious poet to meet with the great and the admirable . . . life everywhere furnishes an accurate observer with the ridiculous'.[28] And the spectacle of mankind busily, greedily, insistently, longingly dividing itself into high and low people, this pursuit of the fashionable elicits from Fielding the following remark: 'perhaps, if the gods, according to the opinion of some, made men only to laugh at them, there is no part of our behaviour which answers the end of our creation better than this' (II, 13).

TOM JONES: LIFE AS ART

'As I am in reality,' Fielding writes at the beginning of Book II of *Tom Jones*, 'the founder of a new province of writing, so I am at liberty to make what laws I please therein.' In the corresponding chapter in *Joseph Andrews* ('Of divisions in authors' – II, 1), Fielding's relationship to his readers is magisterial, masterful. But, as he demonstrates from the very beginning of *Tom Jones*, and far more explicitly than in the earlier novel, he intends to be Master of the Revels. The title of the first chapter of the first book of *Tom Jones* is 'The introduction to the work, or bill of fare to the feast'. On the image which Fielding produces just here, the meaning of the novel depends. He says here that an author ought to regard himself in the same light as the master of an ordinary who, in order to prevent any disappointment to his customers, brings before them a bill of fare, and they,'having thence acquainted themselves with the entertainment which they may expect, may either stay and regale with what is provided for them, or may depart to some other ordinary better accommodated to their taste'. Fielding is asking us to take *Tom Jones* in this festive spirit.

The 'provision' of the feast is human nature. He is going to use the facts of life – what others are there? – to make an artifact.[29] He deals with the possible objection 'from the more delicate, that this dish is too common and vulgar', by insisting that 'true nature is as difficult to be met with in authors as the Bayonne ham, or Bologna sausage, is to be found in the shops'. Fielding knows that to be false to life is to be faithless to art. Correspondingly, when he tells the truth about life it is for the noble purpose of providing a feast. Indeed, the very structure of *Tom Jones* is put in terms of the dishes of the banquet which he is going to lay before us: 'we shall represent human nature at first to the keen appetite of our reader, in that more plain and simple manner in which it is found in the country, and shall hereafter hash and ragoo it with all the high French and Italian seasoning of affectation and vice which courts and cities afford'.[30]

My point in subtitling this book *Mask and Feast* is of course to yoke the two, I trust not by violence, together. Fielding puts on the mask of tavern keeper and serves up to his readers the varied dishes of human nature. A mask is already a disguise, and a masquerade is itself an entertainment, beguiling because false. Or is it that a masquerade offers the truth of hyperbole? At all events, it is to this other controlling image that I now wish to turn. Fielding provides it for us, spaciously and even expansively, in the first chapter of Book VII. It is called, and is, 'A comparison between the world and the stage'.

The only partly concealed premise of this chapter is that bad art results from distortion of human motive, this in turn proceeding from poor observation; by the same token, good art is founded on an accurate apprehension of the nature of man. This is all usual enough. What is unusual in this chapter is the insistence on making the reader understand *Tom Jones* within a theatrical framework: Bad art can afford to look like life because it is false; good art, on the other hand, being based upon life, must be distanced by the mechanism of art. An art founded upon life must be artificial or it will be unbearable.

For after reminding the reader that the world and the stage have often been compared, Fielding offers as an alternative reason for the comparison the Aristotelian argument that 'the theatrical stage is . . . an imitation of what really exists', and he rejects this alternative. The actors remain actors, 'whom we use as children frequently do the instruments of their amusement; and have much more pleasure in hissing and buffeting them, than in admiring their excellence'. So that Fielding is in effect drawing the line between life and art, as later did that other man of common sense, the Scotsman David Hume.

It may be possible to think that Fielding is adversely criticizing bad plays or poor audiences or both – or it would be possible to think so if he proceeded otherwise than he actually does, in his argument. He argues that the world and the stage may be compared because men themselves masquerade as what they are not; 'thus the hypocrite may be said to be a player; and indeed the Greeks called them both by one and the same name'. This is familiar Fielding territory, a favourite preoccupation because it is based upon an idea of character which lends itself to such reflection. Here, therefore, he would seem to be pointing to the artificiality with which much human motive is disguised.

Perhaps because there is nothing very original about what Fielding says here, the significance of his line of argument is not always noticed. For Fielding enters a plea the force of which is felt the more strongly if what precedes it has been taken into account. 'In all these, however, and in every other similitude of life to the theatre, the resemblance hath been always taken from the stage only. None, as I remember, have at all considered the audience at this great drama'. He thereupon proceeds to guess how *his* audience – from upper gallery to pit and boxes – will react to 'that scene which Nature was pleased to exhibit in the twelfth chapter of the preceding book, where she introduced Black George running away with the £500 from his friend and benefactor'.

Fielding in fact turns convention upside down by requiring

us to think of the Black George flight as fictional. The History of
Tom Jones is history in a very special sense. Morally it is true.
But it is true because it is a fiction. The realism of technique
designedly gives way to, indeed paves the way to, what becomes
a masquerade. This is true because to see life spectacularly is to
be generous about human motive. At a distance even Mrs Tow-
wouse and Parson Trulliber and Beau Didapper are endurable,
and there is not much good to be said about such characters.
Black George, however, belongs in a special category of which
the definition does not become complete until *Tom Jones*.

Now we, who are admitted behind the scenes of this great theatre
of Nature (and no author ought to write anything besides diction-
aries and spelling-books who hath not this privilege), can censure
the action, without conceiving any absolute detestation of the person
whom perhaps Nature may not have designed to act an ill part in all
her dramas; for in this instance life most exactly resembles the stage,
since it is often the same person who represents the villain and the
hero; and he who engages your admiration to-day will probably
attract your contempt to-morrow.

In the context of his thinking about human nature, this
remark of Fielding's is compelling. Most men, in Fielding's
view, are positively evil from birth: such a person is Blifil; or at
best wicked through indifference, selfishness, or ambition: such
a person is Black George. Black George acts the bad part but is
not evil – and Fielding dares us to be charitable to him. He goes
further, because he dares us to be uncharitable. 'The worst of
men generally have the words rogue and villain most in their
mouths, as the lowest of all wretches are the aptest to cry out low
in the pit'. This remark goes some of the distance toward a
definition of Fielding's special brand of contempt for mankind.
In a later chapter (X, 1) he makes further remarks to the
purpose. In this chapter, 'Containing instructions very
necessary to be perused by modern critics', Fielding gives a
number of cautions to the reader, the most important of which
is 'not to condemn a character as a bad one because it is not
perfectly a good one'. And for Fielding the supreme generosity
is to be charitable without the expectation of gratitude. Such is
the 'second self' he creates as master of the revels in *Tom Jones*.

A fine sample of Fielding's special domination over the novel which he constructs for our delight occurs in chapter seven of Book III, the chapter title of which is 'In which the author himself makes his appearance on the stage'. Here is a brace of paragraphs in which is contained, I think, the heart of the novel. At the beginning of the chapter Fielding explains that Mrs Blifil's open preference for Tom, at the expense of young Blifil himself, was such as to make the fair and charitable Squire Allworthy compassionate toward Blifil, and at the same time think less well of Tom than he might otherwise have done, especially as Tom's own 'wantonness, wildness, and want of caution' invited adverse judgment. Then comes the narrator's admonition

to those well-disposed youths who shall hereafter be our readers; for they may here find that goodness of heart and openness of temper, though these may give them greater comfort within, and administer to an honest pride in their own minds, will by no means, alas! do their business in the world. Prudence and circumspection are necessary even to the best of men. . . . It is not enough that your designs, nay, that your actions are intrinsically good; you must take care they shall appear so. If your inside be never so beautiful, you must preserve a fair outside also. This must be constantly looked to, or malice and envy will take care to blacken it so, that the sagacity and goodness of an Allworthy will not be able to see through it, and to discern the beauties within. Let this, my young readers, be your constant maxim, that no man can be good enough to enable him to neglect the rules of prudence; nor will Virtue herself look beautiful unless she be bedecked with the outward ornaments of decency and decorum. And this precept, my worthy disciples, if you read with due attention, you will, I hope, find sufficiently enforced by examples in the following pages.

This long admonitory passage must not be taken at face value. Again and again, Fielding as narrator stands between his novel and a didactic interpretation of the course of the narrative, not least when he is pretending to be didactic. For as a preacher he always goes too far, protests too much, and thus invites more and less than a straightforward response. For after the paragraph from which I have just quoted, follows another which must, I think, be taken as qualification of what has preceded. 'I ask pardon', Fielding writes, for this short appearance, by way of chorus, on the stage. It is in reality for my own sake that, while I am discovering the rocks on which innocence and goodness often split, I may not be misunderstood to recommend the very means to my worthy readers by which I intend to show them they will be undone. And this, as I could not prevail on any of my actors to speak, I myself was obliged to declare.

The final sentence of that paragraph – it is also the last sentence of the chapter – gives conclusively away the festive intent of *Tom Jones*. Behind the smile of the narrator lies condonation of the hero. This, which Allworthy was incapable of – at least until the end of the novel – we are invited to share and to rejoice in, from very near the beginning.

In fact, the most substantial of the preliminary chapters in *Tom Jones* – the opening chapter of Book VIII – is devoted to an attack on verisimilitude. It is called 'A wonderful long chapter concerning the marvellous; being much the longest of all our introductory chapters'. In insisting on verisimilitude he manages to enlarge the boundaries to the very limits of human credibility.[31] The chapter is a pastiche of neoclassical arguments, looking not without nostalgia to the Homeric days when it was natural to introduce heathen deities, and characteristically at what can be the subject of art nowadays: 'Man . . . is the highest subject (unless on very extraordinary occasions indeed) which presents itself to the pen of our historian, or of our poet; and, in relating his actions, great care is to be taken that we do not exceed the capacity of the agent we describe'. After a series of reflections on the consequences of this necessary focus, Fielding concludes with a dictum which, partly because of its very unoriginality, will provide him with a warrant for the events within Book VIII itself.

For though every good author will confine himself within the bounds of probability, it is by no means necessary that his characters, or his incidents, should be trite, common, or vulgar; such as happen in every street, or in every house, or which may be met with in the home articles of a newspaper. Nor must he be inhibited from showing many persons and things, which may possibly have never fallen within the knowledge of great part of his readers. If the writer strictly observes the rules above-mentioned, he hath discharged his part; and is then entitled to some faith from his reader, who is indeed guilty of critical infidelity if he disbelieves him.[32]

This is an invocation to belief made by an author who in the following pages will stretch as far as is possible his reader's capacity for maintaining faith. Book VIII is crowded with surprises, with jaunty experiments in extravagance, with meticulous arrangement of plot. There is little Benjamin, a learned barber – who reveals himself not merely as Partridge but also as the man who is assuredly not Tom's father. Surely it is fair to say that the reader recognizes the action of this book to be contrived – and yet sees within or behind the contrivance adequacy of human motivation. Such is Fielding at his most characteristic: within an entirely artificial context, made up – paradoxically – of the most natural and realistic elements, appear characters who behave with a verisimilar consistency, or inconsistency. Thus in chapter 7 of this book, Partridge's reason for attaching himself to Tom is shown to be less than fully disinterested. 'It came into his head, therefore, that if he could prevail with the young gentleman to return back to his father [as Partridge mistakenly thought Allworthy to be] he should by that means render a service to Allworthy which would obliterate all his former anger'. Nor is the manner of the telling of his story by the Man of the Hill, which also occurs in this book, to be overlooked. Like the story of Wilson in *Joseph Andrews*, the Man of the Hill's tale is repeatedly interrupted. The interrupter here is Partridge, and his intervention prevents the moralizing from making of *Tom Jones* what Fielding does not believe in, a novel with a moral.

Fielding calls one of his prefatory chapters 'Of prologues' (XVI, 1), and he gives a playful rationale for their inclusion, in order that the reader may know at how many removes to take the action. I suspect it is the flirtation with frivolity in this as in the other first chapters that irritates the readers who are unaccustomed to the comic mode of presentation. But it is a feigned frivolity that causes the narrator to offer himself congratulations 'for having first established these several initial chapters; most of which, like modern prologues, may as properly be prefixed to any other book in this history as to that which they introduce, or indeed to any other history as to this'. For among the absurdly reasonable causes Fielding gives for the inclusion of these chapters, is the reason which in various forms and under various guises he has brought forward before: the chapters are apéritifs, 'in which the critic will always be sure of meeting with something that may serve as a whetstone to his noble spirit; so that he may fall with a more hungry appetite for censure on the history itself'.

To take the role of the narrator in its most obvious and explicit sense is to regard Fielding as historian. At the beginning of Book II, he goes over some ground with which readers of *Joseph Andrews* are already familiar. The chapter, 'Showing what kind of a history this is; what it is like, and what it is not like', has its analogue in *Joseph Andrews*. Here, as in the earlier novel, Fielding distinguishes between the two kinds of history, the chronicle, wherein the writer 'seems to think himself obliged to keep even pace with time, whose amanuensis he is'; and the history in which is disclosed 'the revolutions of countries'. That is, he will fix upon what is important and deal with such areas exhaustively.

When any extraordinary scene presents itself (as we trust will often be the case), we shall spare no pains nor paper to open it at large to our reader; but if whole years should pass without producing anything worthy his notice, we shall not be afraid of a chasm in our history, but shall hasten on to matters of consequence, and leave such periods of time totally unobserved.

To apply this theory at all requires that the historian elevate himself beyond the level of time's amanuensis. He is no longer a slave but an artist. The 'pure historian' has to deal with what has actually happened, but he is by this theory given leave to let his imagination play over the events of the past until he can assess and express their significance. For it was significance that the Augustans were seeking: they were concerned with the meaning of history. As Herbert Davis points out:

Their constant preoccupation with the function of history, their study of classical and French and Italian historians, their ability to appeal to an audience who would understand their references to persons and events in classical history as parallels to guide their judgments in current political controversies – all this contributed more than is generally realized to the achievement of the great historians of the second half of the century.[33]

But Fielding, even as historian, is freer, and, while recognizing his obligation to be faithful to human nature, he makes of human probabilities a pattern of contrivance: design and distance gladden the heart.[34]

And it is as an historian that Fielding disposes of time at the beginning of the following book (III, 1), the title of the prefatory chapter being, 'Containing little or nothing'. By the rules which he laid down at the beginning of the second book, this title is perfectly correct, and the reader has been prepared for what happens here after some preliminary fanfare: what happens is that Fielding passes over a dozen years half-way through the final sentence of the chapter and blandly asserts that he is going to 'bring forth our hero, at about fourteen years of age, not questioning that many have been long impatient to be introduced to his acquaintance'.

Of course, it was no new thing in the middle of the eighteenth century to write history synthetically rather than chronically. Nor was Fielding breaking new ground in fiction when he passed over large stretches of time in order to deal with his characters emphatically. Defoe, that inveterate and incorrigible journalist, was a master of emphasis – and one of the reasons for the success of the apparently artless *Moll Flanders* is just Defoe's ability to dismiss years in a sentence or two. Thus when Moll is married to her London business friend, she is perfectly secure and therefore as a fictional character uninteresting. So Defoe compresses several years into several inches, disposes – by death – of the husband, and in effect sends Moll out again to brave the world, alone. The significance, therefore, of Fielding's little essay in criticism at the beginning of Book III lies in Fielding's sophistication rather than his simplicity, and in his assumption that his audience is possessed, as he says, of 'true sagacity', so that the highly civilized light of comedy shines upon the festive history of Tom Jones.

Before introducing Sophia – with, not incidentally, a flourish of high-flown language[35] – at the beginning of Book IV, Fielding writes a chapter in which the ornamental framework for her entrance is constructed with elaborate care. In the opening paragraph of this first chapter, Fielding as usual dissociates himself from the composers of 'those idle romances which are filled with monsters, the productions, not of nature, but of distempered brains'. He is going to be truthful, and to be truthful is, in part, to provide refreshment: 'we have taken every occasion of interspersing through the whole sundry similes, descriptions, and other kind of poetical embellishments'.

One way of interpreting this announcement is to suppose that Fielding is going to tell the truth and moreover make it palatable, to sweeten the moral pill. But the palatability is essential, not eccentric. The playful air is crucial melody. Here, at least, with almost rococo elegance and artificiality – rendered artificial when he compares himself as narrator to a manager of a playhouse, and even more elaborately to the maker of a pageant like the pageant of the Lord Mayor – who 'contracts a good deal of that reverence which attends him through the year, by the several pageants which precede his pomp': here, at least, Fielding goes far to make the entrance of Sophia operatically and thus festively satisfying. Typically, the humblest realism is put cheek-by-jowl with the most outrageous splendour. He speaks of

the custom of sending on a basket-woman, who is to precede the pomp at a coronation, and to strew the stage with flowers, before the great personages begin their procession. The ancients would certainly have invoked the goddess Flora for this purpose, and it would have been no difficulty for their priests or politicians to have persuaded the people of the real presence of the deity, though a plain mortal had personated her and performed her office. But we have no such design of imposing on our reader; and therefore those who object to the heathen theology may, if they please, change our goddess into the above-mentioned basket-woman.

As in the first chapter of Book II, Fielding in the corresponding preface to Book V insists that it is his privilege as author to make his own rules. As the head of 'all prosai-comi-epic writing', he can refuse to explain why he has written prefatory essays for each of the books of *Tom Jones*. He cavils, as do practically all of his contemporaries – it was common form in the eighteenth century and has been so ever since – at the arrogance of critics, who would prescribe the rules to artists, rather than acting as clerks. And then, after this rather intimidating series of pre-liminaries, he disarms the reader when he says that he will 'waive all the privilege above contended for, and proceed to lay before the reader the reasons which have induced us to inter-sperse these several digressive essays in the course of this work'.

The heart of the matter is what he calls the principle of con-trast, and although Fielding says that contrast 'may probably have a large share in constituting in us the idea of all beauty, as well natural as artificial', it is – I think – the artificiality of the device of the opening chapters which appeals to Fielding, and no doubt to his readers. In discussing *Joseph Andrews* I have argued that Fielding's framing and reframing of even quite horrific episodes, such as that of the robbery of Joseph, has the effect of making them morally bearable, and, when seen at some distance, amusing. The same observation applies to *Tom Jones* as well, and one of the chief (though not in fact the only) framing devices is that of the preliminary chapters – as, I think, a pair of sentences here indicates Fielding himself believed. 'Most artists', he says, 'have this secret [the principle of contrast] in practice, though some, perhaps, have not much studied the theory. The jeweller knows that the finest brilliant requires a foil; and the painter, by the contrast of his figures, often acquires great applause'. This is no doubt what Jane Austen meant when she offered some criticism of her own performance in *Pride and Prejudice*. 'The work', she wrote to her sister in a celebrated letter,

is rather too light, and bright, and sparkling; it wants shade; it wants to be stretched out here and there with a long chapter of sense, if it could be had; if not, of solemn specious nonsense, about something unconnected with the story; an essay on writing, a critique on Sir Walter Scott, or the history of Buonaparté, or anything that would form a contrast, and bring the reader with increased delight to the playfulness and epigrammatism of the general style.[36]

Fielding, in fact, taught Jane Austen something about playful-ness and something about how to write a novel.

Almost precisely half-way through *Tom Jones* Fielding takes the opportunity, in the preface to Book IX, to insist that he is to be taken seriously. And what is interesting about this chapter is the special sense in which Fielding is making his insistence. 'Of those who lawfully may, and of those who may not, write such histories as this' contains a familiar diatribe against the mendacity of the novel and romance writers, together with a considered list of qualifications which Fielding regards as desirable for 'this order of historians'. Moreover, the chapter is crucially placed, for the previous book ends with the sombre and not unchallenged conclusion of the tale of the Man of the Hill; and what follows hard upon the introductory chapter is the melodrama and farce of the Battle of Upton, including its rawly comic consequences – the most outstanding of which is Mrs Waters's successful assault, by way of mock-heroic ogling, upon Tom's all too receptive and yielding virtue. The course of the action which succeeds this introductory chapter does therefore establish the scale in which it is to be understood.

In the preface itself, Fielding sets forth three qualifications which, he says, are necessary for the kind of writing which in *Tom Jones* he has undertaken: genius, which consists of invention (and this is neither more nor less than 'a quick and sagacious penetration into the true essence of all the objects of our contemplation') and judgment; second, learning – both erudition, and the sort of learning that can only be obtained by conversation; finally, a good heart. The divergence, or perhaps I should say departure, from Horace does not appear until Fielding considers this third point, for he invites us to enlarge the boundaries of our sympathy, so as to include the ridiculous, and then to put the whole chapter into a focus that will enable us to begin to enter upon an account of the action of Book IX in a spirit of rejoicing. 'In reality', Fielding writes as his paraphrase of and gloss upon Horace,

no man can paint a distress well which he doth not feel while he is painting it; nor do I doubt but that the most pathetic and affecting scenes have been writ with tears. In the same manner it is with the ridiculous. I am convinced I never make my reader laugh heartily but where I have laughed before him; unless it should happen at any time that instead of laughing with me he should be inclined to laugh at me. Perhaps this might have been the case at some passages in this chapter, from which apprehension I will here put an end to it.

The final third of *Tom Jones* is set in London, and throughout this last act of the book is the agreeable expectation, whatever apparently frightful incidents may be taking place, that a happy ending is in prospect. Appropriately, therefore, the chapter which prefaces the first book (Book XIII) of this final section of the novel, presents Fielding in the guise of a clown. The entire chapter, which is called 'An invocation', is an apostrophe to a succession of authors' helps – Fame, Fortune, Genius, Humanity, Learning, and Experience – ranging in tone from Miltonic grandeur to the prose of common day.

> Come, bright love of fame, inspire my glowing breast:
> Not thee I call, who, over swelling tides. . . .

It is almost blank verse with which Fielding begins, and he makes the most of this elevation of tone, for his own comic purposes; after completing the invocation to fame he turns to Fortune, 'thou, much plumper dame, whom no airy forms nor phantoms of imagination clothe; whom the well-seasoned beef, and pudding richly stained with plums, delight'. This is the hearty Fielding, all right. But it is not all joint and Yorkshire: tenderness – even tenderness – breaks in. In apostrophizing Fame, he remembers his first wife: 'Foretell me that some tender maid, whose grandmother is yet unborn, hereafter, when, under the fictitious name of Sophia, she reads the real worth which once existed in my Charlotte, shall from her sympathetic breast send forth the heaving sigh'. To me this combination of heartiness and sentiment, cumbersome though it may be here, exactly defines the moral status of *Tom Jones*: a highly organized, tightly woven artistic recreation of the materials of 'Nature' – all done for a festive reason. To celebrate is to make life, and even death, endurable. Nor does Fielding underestimate the enormity of his undertaking, and at the end of his individual apostrophes he makes a collective invocation, for 'without all your assistance, [the task] will, I find, be too heavy for me to support. But if you all smile on my labours I hope still to bring them to a happy conclusion'.

The preface to the eighteenth and last book of *Tom Jones*, which Fielding calls 'A farewell to the reader', casts the reader and Fielding himself as 'fellow travellers in a stage-coach': such is the comic posture in which he would put himself and ourselves at the last. And he makes fresh use of this well-worn comparison. He says that at the end of a journey it is 'well known that all jokes and raillery are at this time laid aside; whatever characters any of the passengers have for the jest-sake personated on the road are now thrown off, and the conversation is usually plain and serious'. This preface thus warns the reader that something especially ludicrous or farcical or ridiculous is to follow; and in chapter 2, 'Containing a very tragical incident', Partridge comes in and tells Tom, 'You have been abed with your own mother'. It is the most ludicrous strand of false dénouement and as such the most superb of all demonstrations of Fielding's mastery over his novel – excepting only the brilliance with which all the resolutions are achieved in the last book of Fielding's masterwork: this is nothing less than a comic glory. But it is the achiever as much as the achievement that compels our respect and admiration. As Wayne Booth puts it, in *Tom Jones* 'the narrator becomes a rich and provocative chorus. It is his wisdom and learning and benevolence that permeate the world of the book, set its comic tone between the extremes of sentimental indulgence and scornful indignation, and in a sense redeem Tom's world of hypocrites and fools.'[37]

AMELIA: THE ART OF LIFE

In his last novel, Fielding takes off – or, as perhaps it would be more accurate to say, changes – his mask. *Amelia*, centring on marriage and the domestic life, contains an idyll smashed all too readily. Besides the grim clamour of a magistrate's busy life, in which bodily illness had begun to take its painful toll – all this making impossible the festive celebration which was achieved in *Joseph Andrews* and in *Tom Jones* – there is another threat as well, and that is exposed in *Amelia*: it is a radical inconsistency in idea. To Fielding toward the end of his life wholeness was no longer possible: the vision was blurring. To be sure there was so much that was loose, contradictory, and perhaps even untidy in his way of faith that one ought perhaps to fault Fielding as a thinker and at the same time to excuse him because he is human: to hope that his philosophical and religious inconsistencies will make no difference to the integrity of his novels. And that is just what I propose doing. In art, art comes first. I shall not need to labour here my conviction that *Joseph Andrews* and *Tom Jones* are as works of art both beautiful and true. Such ideas as these novels contain are handled with comprehensible coherence. Behind Fielding's ideas lurk difficulties and even disharmonies which can no doubt be exposed to the harsh light of philosophical inquiry and found wanting. None the less, Fielding persuades us as we read *Joseph Andrews* and *Tom Jones* that the ideas are tenable. But in *Amelia* the inconsistency is blatant.

For one thing, *Amelia* is a much more overtly philosophical novel than anything Fielding had written before. *Jonathan Wild* is neither a novel nor a philosophical work: it is an entirely simple handling of one idea – or at most two. It is a diatribe against 'greatness' and an apology for 'goodness'. *Jonathan Wild* is a tract. *Amelia* is more ambitious, and Fielding did not, perhaps could not, accommodate his genius to the challenge with which he was confronted. This is because Fielding's highest achievement lies in the realization of festive panorama rather than in the deployment of ideas within an epic structure. In *Amelia* Fielding tried to depict a hero who is philosophical to the extent that he is a believer in the doctrine of the ruling passion, philosophical also in that he wishes to talk about this belief. Against Booth's own vaporizings on the subject are put facts of life which gainsay the credo. But set against this is the Christianity which Booth all too quickly ingests at the end of the novel. The shift from religious indifferentism to a species – the Barrow species – of latitudinarian acceptance is abruptly and even carelessly handled. Throughout the novel, in fact, is an almost wilful arbitrariness in the handling of ideas, so that *Amelia* is neither novel nor treatise, but uneasy amalgam of both. From the very beginning of the novel this difficulty is apparent, and it is – in the event – insuperable.

In the dedication to his friend and patron Ralph Allen, an epistle dated not perhaps incidentally from Bow Street, Fielding begins thus: 'Sir: – The following book is sincerely designed to promote the cause of virtue, and to expose some of the most glaring evils, as well public as private, which at present infest the country' – an opening which is entirely different in tone and in content from the preface to *Joseph Andrews* with its high-spirited theory of the comic epic poem in prose; the epistle dedicatory of *Amelia* is equally to be contrasted to that prefaced to *Tom Jones*: although Fielding there says that 'to recommend goodness and innocence hath been my sincere endeavour in this history', the context in which this statement appears, together with the amiable mildness of the sentiment itself, demonstrate the fact that here as in *Joseph Andrews* doctrine is to be sub-ordinated to spectacle.

Far from insignificant, it seems to me, is the fact that – with one exception (I, 1) – none of the twelve books of *Amelia* is pre-faced by a chapter wherein the narrator ventilates his theories of art and life, and comments upon the course of the action of the novel. Prolegomenous chapters, especially when Fielding perfected them in *Tom Jones*, serve the purpose of establishing a playful relationship between narrator and reader, and thus of creating and defining the mood in which the novel is to be taken. In *Tom Jones* they have a regularity which in due course makes for inevitability. But in *Amelia*, though the narrator often comments, there is no established rostrum for Fielding's criticisms of life, art, and character. One might hope to find celerity of pace and continuity of action as compensating or surpassing excellences. In fact, there is no gain and much loss in this alteration of technique. For Fielding the narrator will speak out, and will consequently interrupt the course of the action anyway; but, having decided not to use prolegomenous chapters for this purpose, he puts his comments parenthetically within the course of the action. Of course, Fielding the narrator often makes himself felt, and he comments directly throughout *Joseph Andrews* and *Tom Jones*; but a sort of continuity is inevitably established between these remarks and those to be found in the prefatory chapters: so that *Joseph Andrews* and *Tom Jones* have as it were, dual modes of existence – as novels, and as novels about novels. In *Amelia*, however, the old certainty of touch is gone, and the perilous balance is not achieved. Fielding is no longer sure enough of himself as a narrator to be able to incorporate his remarks adequately into the fabric of his work. Furthermore – and this is a matter to which I shall have to give some attention – *Amelia* the novel is the victim of far too many entirely static discussions. All in all, *Amelia* is not a bad work – I do not wish to suggest, let alone press the view that it is bad – but it is deeply flawed because Fielding, for reasons I have sketched out, abandons the tools of his trade.

The first chapter of Book I, 'Containing the exordium &c.', promises well. The opening sentence, as Professor Sherburn declares in an excellent essay, is satisfyingly epical.[38] 'The various accidents which befell a very worthy couple after their uniting in the state of matrimony will be the subject of the following history'. How muted is this sentence, how measured, after the jaunty invitation of *Tom Jones's*: 'An author ought to consider himself, not as a gentleman who gives a private or eleemosynary treat, but rather as one who keeps a public ordinary, at which all persons are welcome for their money'. And *Joseph Andrews's*: 'It is a trite but true observation, that examples work more forcibly on the mind than precepts: and if this be just in what is odious and blameable, it is more strongly so in what is amiable and praiseworthy'. None the less, there is one epic element missing in *Amelia's* opening sentence: I mean, extensiveness. And the reader is struck by the fact that the centre of interest in Fielding's *Aeneid* will be not a vast historic drama, a delineation of the national consciousness, but a domestic representation. No epic was ever about marriage; the love of Dido and Aeneas and the subsequent betrayal of that love are strands, mere strands, of the larger fabric of Virgil's vision. But the emphasis, and thus the meaning, in *Amelia* is quite different. In *Amelia* history is taken for granted, society is grimly drawn but very much in the background compared to the marital and extra-marital drama played and played again. Even the prison scenes, which are very striking indeed, fail to dwarf the anguish of Will Booth as he succumbs to the adulterous temptation presented by the resourceful Miss Matthews. And geography in this novel is virtually non-existent. One has no more idea, after reading *Amelia*, of Gibraltar and Montpellier (let alone any of the English settings) than that they are names. The reason is that Fielding does not trouble himself with geography; his interest lies in the relationships of a handful of people.[39]

There is, naturally as it seems to me, a relationship between the domestic focus in *Amelia* and the didactic intent. Fielding has abandoned his aesthetic of the feast, not (I think) because he has lost his exuberance – there are high spirits even in this final novel – but because he can no longer give nourishment to his faith in art as civilization. Consequently, in the first chapter of *Amelia* he is as overtly and unambiguously didactic as Richardson ever was. The final sentence of *Amelia's* first chapter reads as follows:

> By examining carefully the several gradations which conduce to bring every model to perfection, we learn truly to know that science in which the model is formed: as histories of this kind, therefore, may properly be called models of HUMAN LIFE, so, by observing minutely the several incidents which tend to the catastrophe or completion of the whole, and the minute causes whence those incidents are produced, we shall best be instructed in this most useful of all arts, which I call the ART OF LIFE.[40]

Fielding's terms are the same here as in the dedicatory epistle to *Tom Jones*, but the meaning is different. *Amelia*, in the sentence I have just cited, is explicitly a history: but, just as explicitly, it is a history lesson, and the lesson to be learned is also set forth in this chapter, in a few lines of the initial paragraph. The subject is Fortune, and Fielding conveys his detestation of the habit of thought which ascribes success or failure to her.

> I question much whether we may not, by natural means, account for the success of knaves, the calamities of fools, with all the miseries in which men of sense sometimes involve themselves, by quitting the directions of Prudence, and following the blind guidance of a predominant passion; in short, for all the ordinary phenomena which

are imputed to Fortune; whom, perhaps, men accuse with no less absurdity in life, than a bad player complains of ill luck at the game of chess.

Fielding, as *Amelia* abundantly demonstrates, deplores the doctrine of the ruling passion – so notably popularized by Pope in the *Essay on Man* – and his reason is that it is used as an excuse for whatever behaviour the adherent wishes to pursue. But he has not abandoned his fatalism, with which the doctrine of the ruling passion is congruent but certainly not identical. And it seems to me that *Amelia*, to be properly understood, must be read with this fact in mind. Fielding's view that individual human nature is fixed, that character is innate, finds expression in *Amelia* to be sure; to read the first chapter of this novel without appreciating that Fielding owes nothing to Locke for his epistemology is to run the risk of supposing men to be more educable than they really are. To Fielding there is no such thing as a *tabula rasa*, and prudence is an acquisition available only to those few human beings who are born good. Amelia Harris is a good girl and seldom if ever puts a foot wrong: she is, as it were, naturally prudent. Will, whose excellence of character and generosity of spirit have landed him in prison, has no wish to play his wife false; and his misadventures, even that of adultery, are extensions of his generous and naïve spirit rather than positive evils. It is therefore fair to say that for the Fielding of *Amelia* only the good can learn to be prudent. It can equally be said that the good come to prudence without having had to learn it. So much is assuredly true of *Joseph Andrews* and of *Tom Jones* as well. When Booth becomes a convinced Christian after having read Dr Barrow's sermons, he has not become a convert: his religious apathy has been dissipated. 'Indeed,' he tells Dr Harrison, 'I never was a rash disbeliever; my chief doubt was founded on this – that, as men appeared to me to act entirely from their passions, their actions could have neither merit nor demerit' (XII, 5).[41]

And here, I think, lies a key to the fundamental weakness of the novel. Richardson, for all his prurience and no doubt unconscious motive, at least believed in the didactic utility of his enterprise. But Fielding, acting as I think from no longer controllable desperation, tried to graft a didactic intent on to a fatalistic view of man; and the result could hardly fail to lack impact. The miracle of *Amelia* is not that in these foredoomed circumstances it fails as a whole, but that here and there it succeeds with astonishing brilliance. In short, *Amelia* is the work of a Christian fatalist who was losing his faith in art; it is the flawed achievement of a great novelist who turned his back on his own fictional inventions: *Amelia*, as I have said, contains but one prolegomenous chapter; and Fielding without a mask, or Fielding with no place for a mask, is at best reduced to the expedient of embarrassed and hurtful interposition in the middle of things: for the most part, however, he is Fielding unmasked, to whom art itself has become a weary and wearying pretence: the jocularity is avuncular, the contempt of the world more pronounced, the asides sometimes random. Paradoxically, though the narrator plays a smaller role in *Amelia* than in the earlier novels, the effect is of obtrusiveness. Worst of all, Fielding who formerly was vigorous, masterful, enthusiastic and bravehearted, is now, if not a parody of these epithets, frequently merely coy.[42]

Characteristic, unfortunately, of the narrator's tone is that struck in the final chapter of Book II. Miss Matthews urges Booth to continue telling his story, and she speaks in such terms that 'to say the truth, if all which unwittingly dropped from Miss Matthews was put together, some conclusions might, it seems, be drawn from the whole, which could not convey a very agreeable idea to a constant husband'. In part, no doubt, it is the circumstance of hero and temptress which makes the jocularity offensive here. It is easy enough to excuse or rejoice in the sexual adventures of young Tom Jones: he is twenty, unmarried, and full of life; even his adventure with Lady Bellaston is mitigated by his youth and gallantry. But Booth is older, married, a father and a failure. And yet the very inexplicitness of the sentence which I have cited is itself incriminating. In *Joseph Andrews* Lady Booby is coy, but Fielding is not. In *Tom Jones*, Lady Bellaston is concupiscent, and Fielding does not mince matters. But the clause 'which could not convey a very agreeable idea to a constant husband' is an unhappy mixture of regret, outrage, and disappointed stage-management.

As for the raw disillusionment, it makes an ugly vein in this comedy of domestic life. Fielding in *Amelia* is too sour. Thus in chapter 4 of Book IV comes an outspoken remark about Colonel James, who is generous to Booth in that he helps the young officer get on his feet again after having been released from prison. Fielding says, in his own person, of James that 'generous he really was to the highest degree', but he concludes the chapter with this acid remark:

Here, reader, give me leave to stop a minute, to lament that so few are to be found of this benign disposition; that, while wantonness, vanity, avarice, and ambition are every day rioting and triumphing in the follies and weakness, the ruin and desolation of mankind, scarce one man in a thousand is capable of tasting the happiness of others. Nay, give me leave to wonder that pride, which is constantly struggling, and often imposing on itself, to gain some little pre-eminence, should so seldom hint to us the only certain as well as laudable way of setting ourselves above another man, and that is, by becoming his benefactor.

In *Joseph Andrews* it is not pretty when Joseph is stripped, beaten, and robbed – and subsequently refused even a coat to cover his nakedness, until the postilion comes to his aid; but even this incident is incorporated into the festive fabric of the novel: the facts of life are transfigured in the comic epic poem in prose. Nor, in *Tom Jones*, is it pretty when Dowling and Blifil between them conspire to have Tom charged with murder. But by the time this incident occurs, the plot direction assures us that all will be well, and this episode is from its beginning clearly meant to be a device to make Tom miserable so that when he is extricated from the trouble he will be all the happier. And my complaint about the role of the narrator in *Amelia* is that Fielding does not know what his role should be – or rather, the role which he assumes is false and unsatisfactory because strident and unbalanced.

One of the strongest appeals of Fielding the novelist lies in the uncalculating generosity of spirit which irradiates his heroes and heroines, and even some of his most minor characters, but does so only because it first and especially irradiates himself. *Joseph Andrews* and *Tom Jones* are luminous, not least because

Fielding understands the dark. But in *Amelia* the appealing generosity, the exuberance which trails clouds of glory from his characters – these are now on the wane. Even love is shackled in the irons of caution. Fielding has not ceased to believe in the desirability of generosity, the value of spontaneity, the self-justifying role of the steadfast heart: but he has stopped believing that many men and women are possessed of these qualities. So in *Amelia* appears this warning against love itself; it occurs in chapter 1 of Book VI, in which Colonel James begins to look with a too affectionate eye upon Amelia. Fielding then addresses 'my young readers':

> Flatter not yourselves that fire will not scorch as well as warm, and the longer we stay within its reach the more we shall burn. The admiration of a beautiful woman, though the wife of our dearest friend, may at first perhaps be innocent, but let us not flatter ourselves it will always remain so; desire is sure to succeed; and wishes, hopes, designs, with a long train of mischiefs, tread close at our heels.

So much might have been expected from the younger Fielding, even the not much younger Fielding of *Tom Jones*: most memorably, perhaps, the Fielding who gives us the charming portrait of Tom and Sophia before the looking glass in chapter 12 of Book XVIII. But the narrator of *Amelia* does not stop with this caution, from which a transition to the savour of rejoicing is altogether possible. No, in *Amelia* there is another long paragraph and a half before Fielding can have done with the subject; of this I cite the concluding paragraph.

> This digression may appear impertinent to some readers; we could not, however, avoid the opportunity of offering the above hints; since of all passions there is none against which we should so strongly fortify ourselves as this, which is generally called love; for no other lays before us, especially in the tumultuous days of youth, such sweet, such strong and almost irresistible temptations; none hath produced in private life such fatal and lamentable tragedies; and, what is worst of all, there is none to whose person and infatuation the best of minds are so liable. Ambition scarce ever produces any evil but when it reigns in cruel and savage bosoms; an avarice seldom flourishes at all but in the basest and poorest soil. Love, on the contrary, sprouts usually up in the richest and noblest minds; but

there, unless nicely watched, pruned, and cultivated, and carefully kept clear of those vicious weeds which are too apt to surround it, it branches forth into wildness and disorder, produces nothing desirable, but chokes up and kills whatever is good and noble in the mind where it so abounds. In short, to drop the allegory, not only tenderness and good nature, but bravery, generosity, and even virtue are often made the instruments of effecting the most atrocious purposes of this all-subduing tyrant. (VI, 1.)

It is significant, I think, that the formula calling for plain English ('in short, to drop the allegory') should be succeeded by a figure of speech no more and no less complex than the figure which precedes the phrase. Between love as a plant and love as a tyrant there is, so far as figures of speech are concerned, little or nothing to choose.

Amelia is about the perils of marriage: a domestic novel written by a man whose taste and talent are for panorama – and there, already, is the rub. Or, to put the matter another way, the thematic emphases in *Amelia* go some distance toward disclosing the intractable problem which Fielding encountered in the conception and in the writing of *Amelia*. Very much happened to Fielding in the interval between the completion of *Tom Jones* and the commencement of *Amelia*: more than the passage of fewer than three years would ordinarily indicate.[43] So far as the writing of novels is concerned, Fielding put himself, or was put by the circumstances of his life, into a position from which he was unable to write with the mastery and the accomplishment which are on every page of *Tom Jones*. Illness shrivels the spirit, pain is the agent of disillusionment; and Fielding in the last years of his life suffered bravely, but suffer he did. But more than the personal fate which was overtaking him was the experience of Bow Street, which now was beginning to impinge not simply on his day-to-day life but upon his life in art. Festivity, that excuse, justification, and rationale of his earlier work, gives way – but gives way uneasily – to a crueller sense of life and a sterner purpose of art. Consequently there is in *Amelia* a divided emphasis. On the one hand, the perils of marriage make for stern subject-matter; on the other, cheerfulness keeps breaking in, and instead of providing relief or contrast

53

or emphasis makes for subtle disharmonies that prevent *Amelia* from being, as Fielding hoped it would be, his masterpiece.

Innocence, within the framework of the subject of marriage, is the theme which Fielding treats in *Amelia* as he has in his other novels, because it is his chief idea about human nature in its benevolent aspect. Above all, Amelia is innocent – and so, in his heart, is Will Booth. They are therefore protected, as Parson Adams and Joseph and as Tom Jones are protected, against the worst that the world can do. But the enemies to innocence in *Amelia* take a somewhat less human shape than they do in the earlier novels. The succession of travellers, innkeepers, and country dwellers whom Joseph and his ghostly father meet on the road are types not of ideas but of people. Similarly in *Tom Jones* it is wicked people rather than wrong ideas who nearly succeed in bringing about Tom's ruin. But in *Amelia*, though there are fine portraits of the governor of the prison, of the Booths' gossiping neighbours in the country, and of the stoic Colonel James, none the less these figures recede before the abstract ideas at war with Innocence. Innocence, in *Amelia*, is locked in contest with Fortune, with Nature, and with the doctrine of the Ruling Passion: this is a shift of emphasis rather than a departure in a new direction; but it is a shift which makes for a difference in degree so great as to be a difference in kind. Surely this shift can be seen at a glance in the relegation of the Blifil-figure – here it is Miss Betty Harris, Amelia's elder sister – to a minor role in the novel.

As is usual in Fielding, there is little depiction of a benevolent Nature in *Amelia*. In some ways, as also in *Joseph Andrews* and *Tom Jones*, naturalness of behaviour is condoned – but only when the actor is himself fundamentally innocent. The entirely natural behaviour of Parson Trulliber, Blifil, Murphy – and, in *Amelia*, of Miss Harris, the noble lord, and Mrs Ellison – is severely condemned, and condemned as natural. Thus the title of chapter 5 of Book VI of *Amelia* is 'Containing some matters not very unnatural': the ironic double negation here underscores rather than glosses over the naturalness to be presented. The chapter contains the presentation to Amelia by Mrs Ellison of tickets to the masquerade. This is a principal feature of the noble lord's plot to seduce Amelia, and Mrs Ellison is here acting in her usual role as bawd. It is a far from pretty picture of nature. Again, and less indirectly, nature is anathematized by Dr Harrison after Amelia tells him (IX, 5) about Colonel James's design upon her. 'O Nature, Nature,' he cries, 'why art thou so dishonest as ever to send men with these false recommendations into the world?' When Amelia despairingly asserts that 'sure all mankind almost are villains in their hearts', Dr Harrison offers qualified consolation: but this is the view not of Fielding but of Dr Harrison, who – unlike Joseph Andrews but like Parson Adams and like Squire Allworthy – has a greater faith in the effectiveness of education than Fielding himself believes the facts will warrant. ' "Fie, child!" cries the doctor. "Do not make a conclusion so much to the dishonour of the great Creator. The nature of man is far from being in itself evil; it abounds with benevolence, charity, and pity, coveting praise and honour, and shunning shame and disgrace. Bad education, bad habits, and bad customs, debauch our nature, and drive it headlong as it were into vice" ' (IX, 5). Fielding's view, as one puts together the meaning of the novel as a whole, is less simple. Man is not so flexible as Dr Harrison supposes: the innocent are stauncher and the wicked less corrigible. Somewhat later, in chapter 4 of Book X, Fielding speaking in his own person – as narrator, that is, of the book which he is writing – defends his candour by remarking that 'it is our business to discharge the part of a faithful historian, and to describe human nature as it is, not as we would wish it to be'.

Fielding's novels are moral landmarks, each of them distinctively and unmistakably bearing the stamp of Fielding's outlook, and thus each resembling the others in certain fundamentals – and yet each of them delineating a stage in Fielding's development. It is an aesthetic rather than a moral development: morally, Fielding changed very little from early manhood to his death, far too early, at the age of forty-seven. The problem Fielding sought in various ways to solve was how to deal with morals in art. After turning from the drama he employed an old and popular model: he wrote satire. *Jonathan Wild*, though first published in the *Miscellanies* in 1743, may have been written in large part earlier than *Joseph Andrews* (1742).[44] It is the simplest of his four works of full stature, and it is thoroughly angry. I think it is overpraised; but it is convenient, because it sets out with entire transparency Fielding's strongly-felt – and, it must be said, though not to his discredit, not very original – moral position. But when Fielding struck out on his own, he endeavoured to find an aesthetic structure in which his exacerbated moral sense could be accommodated without dominating the whole. Moral questions to a sensitive man can be too pressing, too insistent, too painful. It is inhuman to be perpetually angry – as one must be if he does not occasionally consider the civilized outcome of good moral government.

The aesthetic answer looked to be the comic epic poem in prose. That is why *Joseph Andrews* is so radically different not only from *Jonathan Wild* but from the work of earlier writers. The juxtaposition of epic and picaresque structure, the delighted subjugation (by way of wry idealization) of moral to aesthetic purpose, the luck of having *Pamela* as a point of departure, the inspired creation of Parson Adams – these make *Joseph Andrews* a new species of writing; and it is a very great achievement indeed, surely among the grandest peaks of English fiction. But that it does not come – quite – up to the level of *Tom Jones* is generally acknowledged, and the reason surely is that moral preoccupation is even more adequately combined within the aesthetic framework of *Tom Jones* than in the earlier comic epic. Furthermore, *Tom Jones* provides a richer and more varied moral fare. It may be that comprehensiveness is reassuring to those who look to art for truth. It may also be that aesthetic control is consoling to those to whom art assuages the ironies of actuality. But Fielding was never again to achieve such perfection. *Amelia* is a failed masterpiece despite its technical achievements that in some respects go beyond those even of *Tom Jones*. Fielding's increasingly pained moral sense is constantly at war with the superb but doomed structural mastery. He loses his most ambitious battle – and like the parent of a defective child loves it with a special and touching affection. For no longer could he assert, as Lord Bathurst asserted to Swift: 'Wise men pass their time in mirth, while fools only are serious'.[45]

Chapter 2

THE COMIC STRUCTURES

'I have taken the liberty, you see, to *laugh*, upon some occasions.'
SHAFTESBURY

JOSEPH ANDREWS AS COMIC EPIC

THE traditional account of *Joseph Andrews's* genesis is that it was inspired by Fielding's distaste for *Pamela*, the first two volumes of which appeared in November of 1740. *Joseph Andrews* was being written in 1741 and was published in February of 1742. But, since the theme of male-chastity is very quickly abandoned in favour of the saga of the road the central figure of which is not Joseph but Parson Adams, it is – again traditionally – assumed that Fielding soon changed his mind about the book he was writing, turned away from the parody with which he began, and succeeded in writing a novel that has an appeal quite apart from its criticism of Richardson. Thus in his chapter on fantasy, E. M. Forster calls *Joseph Andrews* 'an aborted example' of parody, which, according to Forster, is a device of fantasy. '*Joseph Andrews* . . . is interesting to us as an example of a false start. Its author begins by playing the fool in a Richardsonian world, and ends by being serious in a world of his own – the world of Tom Jones and Amelia'.[1] To mix fact and assumption in this manner is to make a plausible case. Unfortunately, there is no external evidence which can either inflate or depress this theory. Moreover, it is not altogether satisfactory, even if true.

For, in the first place, it does not take adequate account of *Shamela*, so scurrilous and bawdy a parody that it was not acknowledged to be by Fielding until fairly recently.[2] But the evidence is indisputable, and no one now denies this work a place in the Fielding canon. The question therefore arises why Fielding should have felt it necessary to take more than one shot at *Pamela*. The answer, no doubt, is that Richardson's novel was so popular as to clamour for all the replies that could be mustered – and in fact both *Shamela* and *Joseph Andrews* do in their ways take issue with *Pamela*.[3] None the less, burlesque is a severely limited field, and Fielding went out of his way in the preface to *Joseph Andrews* to insist that the burlesque was admissible only in the diction of the book that he had written. In short, the successful attribution of *Shamela* to Fielding confirms the doubt that *Joseph Andrews's* ostensible motive is perfectly straightforward.

As for internal evidence, Aurélien Digeon goes some distance in what I think to be the right direction. Noting that after the first ten chapters of the first book there is no longer any parody of *Pamela*, Digeon writes:

> This apparent *volte-face* has surprised most critics. Their explanation is that Fielding was carried away by his story, and became so much interested in it that he forgot to parody Richardson. I mistrust an explanation which is founded on a supposed weakness of so great a writer. The truth seems to me simpler. If Fielding ceased to develop the original idea of his book, it was perhaps simply because the idea did not lend itself to further development.[4]

But this stops short: *Joseph Andrews* deserves to be looked at as its own novel from the beginning; it deserves to be looked at as the coherent expression of an experienced author's intention.

In order, however, to understand the moral status of Fielding's first novel in an adequate context, it is necessary to begin with *Pamela*. *Pamela* is a success story. The heroine rises through marriage from serving-maid to squire's lady. But the book is so thoroughly middle-class that the rise is from ultimately genteel beginnings. Pamela's father is a failed schoolmaster reduced to 'hard labour'. Very early in the book this man sets forth the great Richardsonian moral choice: 'We had rather see you', he writes Pamela, 'all cover'd with Rags, and even follow you to the Churchyard, than have it said, a Child of ours preferr'd any worldly Conveniencies to her Virtue.'[5] That is to say, virtue is for Richardson sexual integrity, and the reader must accept this as a *donnée* of Richardson's three novels; otherwise they will seem merely ludicrous. Pamela, desperate about her virtue, feels free to employ any stratagem to prevent herself from being violated. This is no doubt sensible in very many circumstances, and it would be wrong to condemn Richardson for being in favour of female-chastity. Fielding was with him there. But the difference between Richardson and Fielding, which is fundamental, radical, and irreconcilable, turns on the issue of moral passivity. For all that Pamela is strenuous in her relationship with Squire B, her effort is negative: to prevent him from possessing her person until she is his wife. But Fielding, besides disliking what he was convinced was the hypocrisy of such a position, felt that there were more important things than what he regarded as merely prudential self-protection. Furthermore, he distrusted the instructive aspect of *Pamela*: at the end of the second volume are fifteen paragraphs setting forth the lessons that can be learned from a reading of Pamela's letters. Fielding thought not only that Richardson overdid the 'bridal and maiden purity' theme, but that in addition he misused the novel when he tried to make it a vehicle of instruction. That is, Fielding deplored the doctrine and scorned the prescriptiveness of *Pamela*.[6]

It is therefore well to keep Richardson's novel in mind as one reads *Joseph Andrews*, but wrong to let *Pamela* obscure the fact that *Joseph Andrews* has an independent structure. And here I should like to take another hint from M. Digeon, who says: '*Joseph Andrews* is constructed exactly like the plays of the French classical writers, with a regular, solid, and sure plan. The four books are like four acts, of which the first contains the "exposition" and the knot of the problem, the second and third the "peripeteia" or incidents, and the fourth gives the *dénouement*'.[7] To be frank, I do not think *Joseph Andrews* will sustain this comparison, except in too general a way to signify: I admire Digeon's spirit more than the solution which he proffers; and in my view *Joseph Andrews* has a structure both generically determinable and uniquely designed.[8]

Fielding's knowledge of French drama, however – he translated *Le Médecin malgré lui* and *L'Avare* – is perhaps underestimated in reckoning the extent and quality of his preparation as a dramatist for the writing of novels he was to come to. Ordinarily, Fielding's critics, observing that the novels contain scenes in which the dialogue is witty, pointed, and telling, congratulate Fielding on having written plays, and Robert Walpole for having been the occasion for the attack that led to the Licensing Act of 1737, and thus to Fielding's forced suspension of the writing of plays. It goes without saying – at least it is a matter of common sense – that a man who has written or translated some twenty-five plays should be able to write dialogue in a novel. The transfer is entire. But to belabour this point would be to offer entirely gratuitous 'criticism'. The important fact is the central one of a useful apprenticeship.

To survey the quadripartite division of *Joseph Andrews* is to see something of the structural movement as a whole. Book I is divided into two unequal parts: of a total of eighteen chapters, nine (2-10) are devoted to Joseph in London, and nine (11-28) to Joseph on the road. The on-the-road chapters, however, are nearly twice as long as those which precede, and this statistic makes possible a comment on method. Joseph's sojourn in London, hectically centring on the repeatedly displayed affections of Lady Booby and Mrs Slipslop, belongs to drawing-room comedy and bedroom farce. But on the road the method, like the depiction of the countryside, becomes panoramic; even the Dragon Inn, under the aegis of Mr and Mrs Tow-wouse, is more capacious, if not more generous, than the London house of Lady Booby – or at least those parts of it to which a footman might have free access. Book II is about one-third longer than the first, but contains only seventeen chapters; and although the average length is the same as that of the second half of Book I, there is greater variety in that the beginning of the interpolated story of Leonora (4), twice as long as the next-longest chapter (17), is itself longer than any of the remainder. (The interpolations tend to call for more leisurely chapters; so do the dialogues, such as I, 17, which deals with Parson Adams and the bookseller on the subject of sermons, and II, 17, in which Adams and the host discourse on which is superior, experience or learning.) Book III, like Book II, contains chapters of an average length little longer than those of the second half of Book I, but III, 3 and 4, in which Wilson tells his story, are the longest, accounting indeed for not much less than half of the entire book, which contains thirteen chapters altogether. III, 4 is more than twice as long as any other chapter in the whole novel, except for the chapter devoted to Leonora, which is two-thirds as long as III, 4. Finally, Book IV, which is almost exactly the same length as the first book, contains sixteen rather than eighteen chapters; the average length of the chapters is accordingly a little more than that in the first book. Altogether the novel is fairly evenly divided among its four books. At this point a table may be helpful.[9]

	Total Number of Pages	Number of Chapters	Average Length of Chapters
Book I	59	18	3+
Book II	83	17	5 −
Book III	78	13	6
Book IV	62	16	4 −

Book I divides itself into two parts, the first devoted to Joseph in London, the second to the exit from the town, the robbery, and the adventures at the Dragon Inn. There are two structural reasons for supposing that this book was put together with some care, and some foreknowledge of the design as a whole. The first is the fact that Parson Adams's entry into the action of the story is neatly prefigured. There is mention of him in chapter 2; at the beginning of the third chapter he is described as a learned man and at the same time as a person 'as entirely ignorant of the ways of this world as an infant just entered into it could possibly be'. His connection to the Booby family, and especially his connection to Joseph, are also remarked. The chapter concludes with Mrs Slipslop's scornful treatment of him. But none of this constitutes an entry of the curate into the action of the story: this does not occur until chapter 14, when 'a grave person', whose name is later revealed to be Adams, arrives at the inn, just in time to offer strong contrast to that other parson, Barnabas, who had made his entry in the previous chapter. So much is done with fine unobtrusiveness. The other main structural reason for considering that this book was carefully made is that it ends as it began, with the subject of chastity. The concluding chapter, 'The history of Betty the chambermaid,' brings the book to a hectic and apposite anticlimax: failing in her efforts to seduce Joseph, Betty assuages her disappointment in the arms of another – and, being caught *in flagrante delicto*, is discharged. And how well the contrast is put: footman as over against chambermaid, male-chastity as over against female incontinence, Joseph as against Betty. The specificity is excellent: that Joseph's chastity should be confronted by Betty's desire to make him part with it.

The first ten chapters of the first book have a symmetry which gives the lie to the notion that Fielding constructed haphazardly; a symmetry which also has a comic appeal arising from the pleasures of repetition. Thus there is an opening chapter which in its discourse on method and its consideration of Cibber's autobiography together with a consideration of *Pamela*, makes a kind of theoretical framework. The next three chapters set the stage for the action of this half of the first book, the attempts on Joseph's virtue by Lady Booby and Mrs Slipslop in turn. The last six chapters should be ranged in three pairs: 5 and 8, in which Lady Booby tries to tempt Joseph; 7 and 9, in which Lady Booby and Mrs Slipslop discuss Joseph after Mrs Slipslop has herself tried to tempt him; 6 and 10, in which Joseph writes to his sister about the assaults on his virtue. The second half of the first book also contains a triangle, in which Joseph again figures. He is the object of the affection of Betty the chambermaid who, finding him unresponsive, goes to the arms of Mr Tow-wouse, with whom she is discovered by Mrs Tow-wouse. Thus, structurally, the first half of Book I contrasts merrily with the second: Joseph escapes the arms of Lady Booby and is dismissed her service for his resistance; Betty the chambermaid yields to the importunities of her master, and is ejected for her acquiescence.

But the main structure of chapters 11 through 18 is a paradigm of the experience of the road. There are the setting forth (Joseph leaves London and goes in the direction of Lady Booby's country seat, near which lives his Fanny Goodwill), the adventure (Joseph is robbed and beaten), the sojourn at an inn, the unexpected encounter (Parson Adams's arrival at the Dragon, chapter 14). Unity is achieved in the fact of the journey itself.

It is also achieved by the pairs of contrasts represented by Parson Adams against Barnabas, Mr against Mrs Tow-wouse, and by the discussion in chapter 17 of faith and good works. There is even an extra symmetry achieved in the setting of chapter 12 (the robbery) against chapter 16 (the escape of the thief). To end the book on the diminuendo of Betty the chambermaid's history is, as I have said, to draw the strings of the whole of the first book well together.

The central figure of Book II is Parson Adams, who appears there in all his eccentric glory. He is a splendid configuration of invincible innocence plunged into irresistible experience, of ruminative disposition cast into violence of activity. Accordingly, it is structurally appropriate that this book should alternate between scenes of utter stasis and those of the most frenetic experience. The book is well stitched, and therefore unobtrusively put together. Adams twice forgets his horse; the interpolated history of Leonora[10] is interrupted by the 'dreadful quarrel' in which Parson Adams becomes drenched in hog's blood; the interpolation is therefore brought within the compass of the main line of the action. But the principal cohesive feature of the second book is the series of discussions in which Parson Adams participates, arranged in a climactic order, so that the final dialogue, in the last chapter, is a comment on all that have gone before; coherence is achieved even more fully by the fact that after each disquisition follows action which inevitably comments on the sentiments expressed *in camera*: in chapter 3 the bewilderingly different views of a man's character which Parson Adams has been treated to are followed by the arrival of Mrs Slipslop and her ardent denigration of Lady Booby: here is confirmation, in the action of the story itself, of the all too human disposition to allow interest to cloud the vision. The second discussion, in chapter 8, is a monologue delivered by Parson Adams on the desirability of buttering up one's possible patrons; the events of the following two chapters confirm this bleak truth in the experience which Adams and Fanny have with the bird batters, whom Adams fails to ingratiate himself with: he is saved only by the accident of being recognized as a gentleman. The third discussion, in chapter 14, is the notable exchange between Adams and Trulliber on the subject of charity, this in turn followed by the want of charity exhibited by the landlady – and by the wholly satisfying rescue by 'a fellow who had been formerly a drummer in an Irish regiment'. In the last two chapters innocence is dramatized, first in the encounter with the promissory gentleman, whose protestations Adams steadfastly and entirely believes, and second in the disinterested love of truth which causes Adams to dispute warmly with the host who rescues him. Adams maintains that learning is superior to experience, the host maintains the opposite. That Adams is correct in a sense which the host cannot understand is manifest in the arrangement of Book II as a whole.

There is a change of tone in Book III, and a note of exacerbated response makes itself felt. From the very first chapter ('Matter prefatory in praise of biography'), which is a fuller discourse on method than anything to be found in the first two books, there cries the social critic, nearly persuaded that he should turn his comedy into ways less exuberantly celebratory. And throughout the book there is exacted a deeper pathos. Against the comically qualified ruin of Leonora in Book II is set in Book III the solemnly unqualified escape of Wilson from the toils of worldliness; against the nocturnal escape of Fanny from a ruffian in the earlier book is set her abduction in Book III; and against the Falstaffian Parson Trulliber can be placed the vindictive representatives of the squirearchy who cruelly hoodwink the not entirely opaque Adams.

Thematically Book III is devoted to the subject of education, and what it demonstrates is the dictum contained in the dedication of *Tom Jones*: 'It is much easier to make good men wise, than to make bad men good'. Book III divides itself into three sections: the first (chapters 2 through 4) centres on Wilson; the second (chapters 6 through 9), centres on the squirearchal attempts on Adams's gullibility and Fanny's virtue; the third (chapters 11 through 13), after the transition provided by chapter 10, contains the dénouement of the central adventure in that Fanny is rescued from the clutches of her captor, Joseph and Parson Adams are freed from their bedposts, and the party sets forth once again for Booby Hall. The final chapter contains a discussion of charity which cuts deeper than does the discussion between Adams and Trulliber in the previous book.

Of Wilson – quite apart from his tale – something must be said at once. He is here disclosed to be Joseph's father. When he has told the tale of what led him to the pleasures of retirement from the world, he says, 'But no blessings are pure in this world. Within three years of my arrival here I lost my eldest son . . . he was stolen away from my door by some wicked travelling people whom they call "gipsies" ' (III, 3). From that moment onward the reader knows that Joseph is going at last to be revealed as Wilson's son – or, at the very least, that the boy is going to be found, and that his discovery will have important bearing on the outcome of the novel; such is the force of the dramatic irony implicit in the inclusion of such an account as that of a lost child. What is important in this section of my argument devoted to structure is that here is presented incontrovertible evidence of attention to plot.[11] There is no functional reason why an interpolated story should be connected so closely to the main line of the action; the story of Leonora and later the story of Leonard and Paul have a thematic connection only, and that connection is strong enough. But Wilson's tale, longer, more detailed, and more exasperated than either of the other two, provides likewise the intimate relation of paternity.

Wilson's tale deals, like Leonora's, with the subject of vanity. Leonora was a girl, and Wilson is a man. Otherwise vanity is vanity. But the *moral* of Wilson's tale is surely that withdrawal from the town is the only way to escape the world's snares: Wilson loses but recaptures the innocence which is Parson Adams's salient characteristic. And at the end of the novel, after all has been revealed and accomplished, Joseph and Fanny as man and wife join Wilson in the same parish, where they intend to live retired lives.

Structurally this tale shares with Leonora's the device of Adams's interruptions, and for the same reasons: first, because Adams's comments say something about Adams; second, because they remove the tale from the level of the purely cautionary: they remind us that the story is a story[12]; and in the third place they help to establish the continuity between Wilson's tale and the main plot.[13] Thus when Wilson has told of debauching a girl who ended at Newgate, of adultery with another female, of joining the atheists' club and its consequences, and of the conclusion to which he came, 'that vanity is the worst of passions', Adams fumbles in his pocket for his sermon on vanity. 'I would read it,' he says – but he has been unable to find it, 'for I am confident you would admire it: indeed, I have never been a greater enemy to any passion, than that silly one of vanity' (III, 3).

Wilson's tale succeeds in persuading its auditors of the corruption of the town, and of the pleasures of country life. None the less, in chapter 4, wherein 'Mr Wilson's way of living' is described, Fielding presents the episode of the spaniel belonging to Wilson's small daughter, which is shot by the squire. This qualifies the forest-of-Arden perfection of Wilson's place of retirement. But Adams, ever ready to see things in their most favourable light, declares as they take their departure, 'that this was the manner in which the people had lived in the Golden Age'.

After this prudential tale it is curious to come upon the 'disputation on schools', which takes place in chapter 5, curious because it so severely qualifies the lessons of Wilson's tale. The usual reading of Wilson's tale is that it is autobiographical,[14] a recollection in tranquillity of the mature Fielding who at the age of thirty-four repents the follies of his youth. But to look at the story of Wilson within its context is to be brought to the realization that there is structural warrant for taking what Wilson says with considerable reservation. Preceding the story is the adventure with the robbers; within it is the account of the abduction of the Wilsons' infant son; succeeding it is the incident of the killed dog: these are surely designed discords in the otherwise harmonious depiction of the life of Wilson. And there is the further evidence of chapter 5 – itself leading to an adventure qualifying the lesson of the Wilson episode. To be brief, Wilson in middle age warns against the corrupting influence of London; chapter 5, by way of the dispute between

Parson Adams and Joseph, presents a view of human nature in which such a caution is irrelevant.

The subject being education, Parson Adams inveighs against the public school. 'I prefer', he says, 'a private school, where boys may be kept in innocence and ignorance'. Yet Fielding knows this to be simplicity. In fact, in his role as narrator he asserts of Adams here: 'If this good man had an enthusiasm, or what the vulgar call a blind side, it was this: he thought a schoolmaster the greatest character in the world, and himself the greatest of all schoolmasters'. It is or should be therefore inevitable that we take with a grain of salt whatever Adams says about education, especially as nearly everyone in the novel is ineducable; the most that can be hoped for is 'to make good men wise'.

This is a bleak and fatalistic view of human nature, far removed from the cheerful optimism sometimes imputed to Fielding.[15] But Joseph himself spells the matter out in a famous passage: 'I remember when I was in the stable', he tells Adams,

if a young horse was vicious in his nature, no correction would make him otherwise; I take it to be equally the same among men: if a boy be of a mischievous, wicked inclination, no school, though ever so private, will ever make him good; on the contrary, if he be of a righteous temper, you may trust him to London, or wherever else you please – he will be in no danger of being corrupted.

This is, as I say, a curious postscript to Wilson's tale, but it must be taken as such, when we regard *Joseph Andrews* as possessing a coherent structure. Besides, and this is conclusive proof of its value as evidence, the next section of Book III substantiates what Joseph rather than Wilson has said about human nature.

Wilson's tale, for all that it is framed by scenes of violence, for all that Joseph's remarks in chapter 5 qualify it, threatens to become sentimental. But the second act of Book III is a series of exuberant tableaus, once again rescuing *Joseph Andrews* from the tendency to become didactic. Here Parson Adams is nearly devoured by some eager hounds who mistake him for a nearby rabbit (chapter 6), and then, in 'A scene of roasting, very nicely adapted to the present taste and times' (chapter 7), he is taken to the squire's house and gulled beyond even his endurance.

The roughly celebratory tone of this section is on the whole well sustained; the festive intention of *Joseph Andrews* maintains itself, even in chapter 9 which contains nothing less than the abduction of Fanny: but in this comic context it is impossible to suppose that the worst will happen to her. The reader has the pleased certainty – from the personification of fortune, from the summoning up of Don Quixote, and above all from the superb picture of Adams and Joseph tied back to back on the bedposts – that all will soon be well. The fine artifice of construction saves the depiction from the fate of judgment in other than comic moral terms.

At the very beginning of Book III was a demonstration of charity, in that Wilson freely and almost unquestioningly entertained the strangers; in the central section was a series of adventures in which charity played no part – but should have; and in the concluding chapters Christian resignation is set over against the active principle which effects Fanny's rescue. Now, in the final chapter, is the anomaly of Adams's insistence on the active role which charity, properly defined, plays. 'Sir,' Adams says to Peter Pounce, 'my definition of charity is, a generous disposition to relieve the distressed'. Adams is inconsistent and naïve, but he is not stupid. Peter Pounce affronts him and he knows it. Typically, Adams takes an active measure: he jumps from the moving coach.

The very geography of Book IV does violence to the notion that *Joseph Andrews* is a picaresque novel, for geographically it is entirely static, taking place as it does at Booby Hall and thereabouts. What Fielding presents here is no epic of the road; it is a comedy of manners. Appropriately, the cast of characters includes Lady Booby, and Mr Booby, and Pamela herself. With the energy and confidence of the experienced dramatist, Fielding devotes himself to arriving at the happy ending by the comic routes of amazing coincidence, lucky accident, and strawberry birthmark. Marriage is the matter of Book IV. In the first chapter Adams publishes the banns of marriage between Fanny and Joseph; in the last chapter the wedding takes place and the new couple settles in the country for a lifetime of happiness. The intermediate chapters deal with the prudential and also with the evidently consanguineous reasons why the wedding should not take place, and – at last – to the removal of all lets and hindrances.

The mood is exuberant. There is in fact altogether excellent use of the materials of ordinary life for celebratory purposes. Fielding understands human motive, and he is not slow to make adverse judgments; he thus takes Lady Booby to task for her protracted absence from her country house, 'during which time all her rents had been drafted to London', with unhappy effects upon the poor of her parish. But condemnatory judgment is always subordinated to the exculpation provided by comedy. It is amusing that Lady Booby, unable to conquer her passion for Joseph, should retire to the country to which he has gone, and be all the more inflamed when she sees him. It is comic that her objection to the intended marriage should be so manifest. And it is hilarious rather than sinister that she should accuse Parson Adams of *procuring* a marriage between Joseph and Fanny, just as it is superbly fruitless that she should order him to cease and desist from the publication of the banns.

This first act of Book IV is developed by way of a satire on legal mumbo-jumbo, in which Lady Booby, having failed to make headway with Parson Adams, accepts the help of Lawyer Scout. Even here, when Fielding speaks with angry contempt of Scout, moral condemnation is secondary to comic play. 'This Scout was one of those fellows who, without any knowledge of the law, or being bred to it, take upon them, in defiance of an act of Parliament, to act as lawyers in the country, and are called so. They are the pests of society, and a scandal to a profession, to which indeed they do not belong, and which owes to such kind of rascallions the ill-will which weak persons bear towards it' (IV, 3). Of course, Fielding means what he says here, but Scout's danger to society is abated by the comic environment in which he is placed. For well-timed coincidence now begins to assert itself in lavish quantity, and Fanny and Joseph are rescued from commitment to Bridewell for 'a kind of felonious larcenous thing' (IV, 5) by the providential arrival of Squire Booby, who prevents rough country injustice from being done. The remainder of the book is devoted to the series of reflections and revelations that will enable Fanny and Joseph to proceed, in the final chapter, with their wedding.

But already in chapter 6 they are reunited. And there seems no reason not to end the book and thus the novel here – unless by comic elaboration of possibility Fielding hoped (as I believe he did) to construct the novel in such a way as to cause *Joseph Andrews* to have the doubled symmetry of form that would make it comically harmonious. Thus the greater part of chapter 6 is given over to a discussion of Joseph by Lady Booby and Mrs Slipslop; this is indelicately prurient in tone: perhaps the purpose here is to make a counterpoint to the dulcet harmonies of the reunion scene. And then in chapter 7 *Joseph Andrews* comes full circle: Pamela attempts to persuade Joseph to give Fanny up. When Joseph objects, saying that Fanny 'is your equal, at least', Pamela reveals what Fielding believes to be the fundamental hypocrisy of Richardson's moral position. ' "She was my equal," answered Pamela, "but I am no longer Pamela Andrews; I am now this gentleman's lady, and as such am above her – I hope I shall never behave with an unbecoming pride; but, at the same time, I shall always endeavour to know myself, and question not the assistance of grace to that purpose" '. The irony of this speech is deepened by the reader's knowledge, or at least suspicion, that Joseph and Pamela are not brother and sister at all.

Even an attempted rape of Fanny, culminating in a tableau of rescue, Joseph being the bloody and successful means of repulsing the vicious attacker, even in this scarifying action the reader is inhibited from severe moral censure because at the end of the scene of rescue he looks, as does Joseph, with surprise and joy upon the bare bosom of Fanny.

Again, with fine employment of the principle of contrast, philosophy is brought up against experience, directly. After Mrs Adams pleads with her husband to persuade Joseph to give up Fanny, or to refuse to publish further banns, so that the Booby interest in the Adams family can be maintained, Adams courageously refuses to accede to his wife's urgent arguments. So much is in Adams's favour. But Fielding arranges matters in such a way as to offer two comments upon the disinterested

70

innocence which he embodies. For, in the first place, Adams preaches patience to Joseph, and Christian resignation. 'Now, believe me, no Christian ought so to set his heart on any person or thing in this world, but that, whenever it shall be required or taken from him in any manner by Divine Providence, he may be able, peaceably, quietly, and contentedly, to resign it' (IV, 8). But Parson Adams preaches what he cannot practise, for when informed immediately thereafter that his son has been drowned, he is beside himself with sorrow. When the information proves false, 'the parson's joy was now as extravagant as his grief had been before'. Thus the structure of this chapter, comic in its alternations, asks for and gets a comic response. Likewise, the tale of Leonard and Paul (told by little Dick Adams who must say not Leonard but Lennard) and the celebrated night adventures are designedly comic, as are the happily resolved complexities of the parental relationships of Fanny and Joseph.[16]

TOM JONES AS EPIC COMEDY

On the structure of *Tom Jones* it is necessary to begin with Coleridge's famous encomium. 'What a master of composition Fielding was.! Upon my word, I think the Oedipus Tyrannus, The Alchemist, and Tom Jones, the three most perfect plots ever planned'.[17] Equally resplendent is Thackeray's observation. 'As a work of art', he said in 1840, *Tom Jones* is 'the most astonishing production of human ingenuity. There is not an incident ever so trifling, but advances the story, grows out of former incidents, and is connected with the whole. Such a literary *providence*, if we may use such a word, is not to be seen in any other work of fiction'.[18] And yet R. S. Crane, whose essay on the plot of *Tom Jones* is the best available – and a very good best it is – has, surprisingly, little to say about Fielding as active manager of his own narrative. Indeed, in the course of some fault-finding Professor Crane writes: 'The narrator ... though it is well that he should intrude, perhaps intrudes too much in a purely ornamental way; the introductory essays, thus, while we should not like to lose them from the canon of Fielding's writings, serve only occasionally the function of chorus, and the returns from them, even as embellishment, begin to diminish before the end'.[19] I hope that my remarks about the narrator's role in *Tom Jones* will already have demonstrated that the prolegomenous chapters serve a more central purpose. Wayne Booth puts the matter well: 'In *Tom Jones* there is a marvellous reciprocity of boast and performance.... The brilliant structure of Tom Jones's adventures, the plot in the full sense of the power which that story in its complete form has to affect us, is the chief proof of the narrator's overt claims'.[20] Or to put the matter another way: the ornamental status of the prefaces makes us take *Tom Jones* on an ornamental level. Therefore, the probably most arresting structural fact about *Tom Jones* is the series of first-chapters that exhort the reader not to constructive action but to benign amusement.

And yet that is only a beginning. It is the shape of the plot as a whole, and in its particular parts, that specially commends itself. Mr Crane is perhaps confusing when he redefines the word 'plot' in such a way as to mean what is more commonly called 'structure', but he is surely right to insist that construction, as well as the interpretation, of a plot depends on the kind of significance which the author wishes to attach to the novel as a whole. Accordingly, he is correct to claim for *Tom Jones's* plot the comic status and for the novel a comic structure.

It is generally the case that whatever tends to minimize our fear in a plot that involves threats of undeserved misfortune for the sympathetic characters tends also to minimize our pity when the misfortune occurs and likewise our indignation against the doers of the evil; and fear for Tom and Sophia as they move toward the successive climaxes of their troubles is prevented from becoming a predominant emotion in the complication of *Tom Jones* chiefly by two things. The first is our perception . . . that the persons whose actions threaten serious consequences for the hero and heroine are all persons for whom, though in varying degrees, we are bound to feel a certain contempt [but nothing stronger: even Blifil is a bungler as a villain] . . . A second ground of security lies in the nature of the probabilities for future action that are made evident progressively as the novel unfolds. . . . [We are forced to the conclusion that] since nothing irreparable has so far happened to him [Tom], nothing ever will.[21]

To have had the benefit of Mr Crane's close and pertinacious analysis is to have been carried very nearly to the centre of *Tom Jones's* structure. But he has overlooked, perhaps because it seems to him too obvious to need comment, the fundamental and overt division of the novel into eighteen books, after – as Fielding would lightly cause us to be reminded – the classical pattern. And clearly one approach to the structure of *Tom Jones* is by way of observing the movement within these eighteen books.

A preliminary observation must centre on the radical deceleration in pace as the novel proceeds. The first three books cover much ground – nineteen years in fact. Then in Book IV ('Containing the Time of a Year') and V ('Containing a Portion of Time Somewhat Longer than Half a Year'), Fielding slows down to what will be a characteristic gait. Book VI, 'Containing About Three Weeks', ushers in the dozen remaining books, none of them dealing with a period of time longer than a few days, and two (IX and X) 'Containing Twelve Hours'. The preoccupation with time does, it seems to me, do more than merely point to the fact that Fielding recognized a time scheme to be important in the contruction of his novel. It is the significance of his eighteenfold iteration of timely considerations that needs looking at. To be sure, Fielding was – like all artists – constantly at war with time, not merely as an inhibitor of simultaneity in art, but as a fact of life. This sense informs *Tom Jones* and is made bearable because amusing by the device of ostentatious control. Fielding the narrator is not merely the master of his characters, he is the master of time itself, and in art if not in life has the last laugh on it. Thus the final paragraph of the final prefatory chapter, which is called 'A farewell to the reader' (XVIII, 1), has the special importance, if not the special quality, of Feste's song of transience at the end of *Twelfth Night*. Fielding sets himself off from authors of inferior works of art. 'All these works, however', he says with hopeful, if less than perfect confidence, 'I am well convinced, will be dead long before this page shall offer itself to thy perusal; for however short the period may be of my own performances, they will most probably outlive their own infirm author, and the weakly productions of his abusive contemporaries'.

All artists, I suppose, mean to represent reality. Even non-representational art claims to depict states of feeling or imagining that seem to the artist real enough. Fielding constantly insists on his fidelity to observed fact, and when in the first chapter of Book I of *Tom Jones* he says, 'The provision which we have here made is no other than *Human Nature*', he invites our acceptance of his acuity and of his honesty and of his judgment. None the less, he does insistently, deliberately, and overtly arrange in order to control reality. This is one of the ways of representational art. But there is another way, Sterne's way – and when Sterne says that *Tristram Shandy* will be 'digressive and progressive at the same time', he is declaring war on the kind of art of which Fielding was a master. Sterne felt that the tidy straightforwardness of the usual narrative did violence to the facts of life, and so he tried what he felt was a more accurate method. In a way, therefore, *Tristram Shandy* is far nearer to being a transcript of actuality than is *Tom Jones* – and in a sense Sterne is more realistic than Fielding. I bring this point up here because of Fielding's entire and acknowledged awareness of what he was doing. 'Reader', he writes at the end of chapter 2 of Book I,

I think proper, before we proceed any farther together, to acquaint thee that I intend to digress, through this whole history, as often as I see occasion, of which I am myself a better judge than any pitiful critic whatever; and here I must desire all those critics to mind their own business, and not to intermeddle with affairs or works which no ways concern them; for till they produce the authority by which they are constituted judges, I shall not plead to their jurisdiction.

The swipe at the critics here has no doubt sometimes diverted attention from Fielding's bland announcement that he intends to digress at will. He is alluding to the interpolated stories of the Man of the Hill and of Mrs Fitzpatrick, and probably to the prefatory chapters as well. He is claiming the privilege to interrupt the narrative itself to comment, counsel, and draw playful morals. Yet the dominant effect of *Tom Jones* is, structually speaking, fineness – indeed, perfection – of arrangement.

Tom Jones begins, then, conventionally – if, as is designedly not quite possible, we forget that the novel proper begins not in the first but in the second chapter. 'In that part of the western division of this kingdom which is commonly called Somersetshire there lately lived, and perhaps lives still, a gentleman whose name was Allworthy, and who might well be called the favourite of both nature and fortune; for both of these seem to have contended which should bless and enrich him most'. After this leisurely and high-sounding beginning we are led, in the first book, from the account of Allworthy and Bridget to the arrival and settling in of the foundling, the lecture by Allworthy to Jenny Jones on chastity, and his benevolence toward her in causing her to be removed 'to a place where she might enjoy the pleasure of reputation, after having tasted the ill consequences of losing it' (I, 9), the introduction of the two Blifils, the courtship and marriage of Bridget by Captain Blifil; and, at the end of the book, yet another removal, Dr Blifil's: having acted as go-between in his brother's courtship of Bridget, he is now discarded; he goes to London, 'where he died soon after of a broken heart'.

At once, therefore, Fielding introduces us to a world of a particular kind, and invites us to take his novel in a certain way – as, that is, a comedy in which sombreness of tone, though pervasive, is very far from preventing hilarious response. About the tonality of the novel as a whole, Mr Crane has useful things to say. He writes of Tom

living in a world in which the majority of people are ill-natured and selfish, and some of them actively malicious, and in which the few good persons are easily imposed on by appearances. It is against this background of the potentially serious – more than ever prominent in the London scenes – that the story of Tom's repeated indiscretions is made to unfold, with the result that, though the pleasure remains consistently comic, its quality is never quite that of the merely amiable comedy, based likewise upon the blunders of sympathetic protagonists, of such works as *She Stoops to Conquer* or *The Rivals*. We are not disposed to feel, when we are done laughing at Tom, that all is right with the world or that we can count on Fortune always intervening, in the same gratifying way, on behalf of the good.[22]

And the death by heartbreak of the not altogether amiable Dr Blifil at the end of the first book does, it seems to me, establish this tone.

The second book also ends with death – this time the death of Captain Blifil, which is represented by the narrator as a useful joke at the expense of marital infelicity (chapter 8 is called 'A receipt to regain the lost affections of a wife, which hath never been known to fail in the most desperate cases'), and the final touch of the book is the Blifil epitaph, so entirely at odds with the facts of his character and his marriage to Bridget, which is shown to have been short and miserable.[23] But the principal structural feature of Book II is doubleness, consisting of false and true contrasts in relationships. Two unhappy marriages are dramatized, and these are ironically denominated in the title of the book as 'Scenes of Matrimonial Felicity in Different Degrees of Life'. But there is very little to choose between the unhappiness of Mr and Mrs Partridge, and that of the Blifils. The other doubleness, which henceforward will dominate the novel, takes its beginning with the birth of Blifil who at once is set over against Tom. Indeed, to the chapter in which Blifil's birth occurs, Fielding gives the title 'Religious cautions against showing too much favour to bastards'.

There is in Book III a maintenance of doubleness that is agreeable, significant, and subtle. Tom and Blifil are the first pair presented, and they exhibit a real contrast, the deeper in that they are identically educated and are for some time similarly regarded. Against this pair is presented the false contrast (so far as moral valuation goes) between Thwackum and Square. Thus in chapter 4 appears the following paragraph, which is often quoted to show how Fielding succeeds in establishing the difference between the philosopher and the divine. 'Upon the whole, it is not religion or virtue, but the want of them, which is here exposed. Had not Thwackum too much neglected virtue, and Square religion, in the composition of their several systems, and had not both utterly discarded all natural goodness of heart, they had never been represented as the objects of derision in this history'. Much later in the novel we are to learn that these two men are, though opposite in extremity of belief, by no means identical in divergence from true virtue. The Reverend Roger Thwackum is eventually shown to be irremediable in his heavy-handed, self-righteous hypocrisy; but Thomas Square at last undergoes what is not so much a change of heart as the revelation of the true nature of his own humanity, which is not so bad as his false convictions have led him to believe. But here, in chapter 4 of Book III, Fielding is not recommending the establishment of a golden mean – as though that achievement were both desirable and possible: what he is doing is ironically recommending the impossible: the plain contrast which Fielding bluffly adumbrates here, by way of spurious apology, is qualified by our recollection of the contrast which Fielding makes in his sketches of Blifil and Tom. Blifil is 'sober, discreet, and pious beyond his age; qualities which gained him the love of every one who knew him: while Tom Jones was universally disliked; and many expressed their wonder that Mr Allworthy would suffer such a lad to be educated with his nephew, lest the morals of the latter should be corrupted by his example' (III, 2). For Blifil, Fielding has told us, is 'of so different a cast from little Jones': the difference, that is to say, is one of character. So when, in the very title of Book III, Fielding has announced education to be his subject, he is referring to the bad education offered by two ill-equipped tutors to two ineducable boys.[24]

There is still another contrast: in chapter 5 Blifil is shown to be the favourite of the philosopher and of the divine; in chapter 6 Bridget's preference for Tom over Blifil is disclosed. Ironically, the two men, who are seeking Bridget's hand in marriage, are slow to realize this preference, so persuaded are they that Bridget would naturally favour her own son. But they do not appreciate, because they do not know, that Blifil is her child of hate and Tom her child of love. Nor does the reader yet know this second fact; but Fielding prepares the way, in this chapter, for the revelation of Tom's actual parenthood.

The movement of this book thereupon takes up a thread introduced in the second chapter, that of Tom's relationship to the Seagrims. In chapter 2 occurs the celebrated poaching incident, which exhibits at once Tom's high-spiritedness, and his constancy in refusing to betray Black George. This thread is taken up again in the concluding chapters of Book III, wherein it is discovered that Tom has sold his Bible, his horse, his nightgown, 'and other things', to help the Seagrims. Finally,because Blifil has carefully and thoroughly calumniated Black George, the young Tom resolves to enlist the help of one Sophia Western. Thus it is by way of the Seagrims that Tom is brought into a close relationship with Sophia: here the plot fits excellently Fielding's intention: the plot qualifies the ostensible significance of the announcement of theme made in the seventh chapter of this book, and to this chapter I must now return. The chapter itself is important as far as the plot is concerned, for it records the fact that Allworthy – racked by a sense of justice – begins to show greater favour to Blifil (because Bridget so obviously prefers Tom) and less favour to Tom. Thereupon, Fielding (the chapter is called 'In which the author himself makes his appearance on the stage') assesses the significance of what he has been presenting. Fielding asserts to 'those well-disposed youths who shall hereafter be our readers ... [that] they may here find that goodness of heart and openness of temper, though those may give them great comfort within, and administer to an honest pride in their own minds, will by no means, alas! do their business in the world. Prudence and circumspection are necessary even to the best of men'. This passage must surely be qualified, as I have already argued,[25] by its surroundings.

Book IV, 'Containing the Time of a Year', begins and ends with Sophia, but centres on Molly Seagrim. Again, therefore, Fielding uses contrasting characters to establish a fact which, observed comically, is both beautiful and true. The focus shifts from Tom to Molly, and then to Sophia. Sophia likes, and is prepared to love, Tom, for to her his gallantry in rescuing her when she is thrown by her horse gilds over the involvement with Molly Seagrim. The book therefore ends on a happy note: Sophia's knowledge that Tom finds her attractive and the reader's knowledge that Sophia is attracted to him.

After the ostentatiously depicted antitheses in the course of the narrative, the reader is hardly surprised to find in the chapter prefatory to Book V an argument in favour of the principle of contrast. Especially does Fielding's argument about two sorts of female establish a connection with what has been already depicted in Book IV. For in the first chapter of Book V the narrator alludes as follows to the contrast between Molly and Sophia: 'But to avoid too serious an air: can it be doubted but that the finest woman in the world would lose all benefit of her charms in the eye of a man who had never seen one of another cast?' The pretence of light-heartedness stems from the reason for his argument, which is to justify – by the principle of contrast – the prolegomenous chapters. But the reader, fresh from the experience of Molly and Sophia, observes retrospectively the structural relevance of narrative as well as of prefatory contrast.

Book V contains two narrative lines, one of which is the resolution of Tom's dilemma in his relationship to Molly; the other is the illness of Squire Allworthy followed by his recovery and a Bacchic celebration by Tom that leads to a scene in which Molly makes a brief reappearance, and is the cause of the battle royal which occurs at the end of the book. The two narrative lines may thus be said to meet in the concluding pages.

In fact, the main difficulty about Molly is resolved. The moral dilemma, which deeply troubles Tom (and thus shows him to be a good sort, impulsive but not incapable of reflection), disappears by the indirect route of the pious lessons to which, broken-armed and temporarily immobile, he is subjected in the second chapter; the subsequent heart-searchings in which Tom, in love with Sophia, nevertheless feels he must abide by Molly; thus far the moral direction of the book is straightforward. Then, in chapter 4, is related the story of Sophia's muff: this 'little chapter, in which is contained a little incident', is part sentiment (the muff itself is dear to Sophia because Tom once put his hands in it), part Juliet's Nurse (Mrs Honour delightedly postpones telling Tom about the muff, for she will whet his appetite as long as possible), and part eccentric extravagance (Squire Western flings the muff into the fire, and Sophia pulls it out again). The chapter is above all designed to establish a comic focus for the moral dilemma of Tom, and to prepare the way for the farcical discovery of Square behind the arras in Molly's bedroom; and also for the consoling discovery by Tom of Molly's promiscuity, including the near certainty that Molly is pregnant not by Tom but by a certain Will Barnes.

But the fresh difficulty into which Tom plunges is going to have grave consequences. He lays the groundwork for his eventual expulsion when, to celebrate the news of Allworthy's recovery, he gets drunk and subsequently – while under the influence of drink – retires with Molly to 'the thickest part of the grove', Tom not being 'at this time perfect master of that wonderful power of reason, which so well enables grave and wise men to subdue their unruly passions'. I cite this phrase, which Fielding writes in extenuation of Tom's behaviour, to show how far from Squire Allworthy's simple reasonableness lies the central meaning of *Tom Jones*: and how far, moreover, from the purposes set forth in the Dedication is the real significance of the novel. For Tom's retirement with Molly provides the impulse for the mock-heroic opening of chapter 11, and the comic exuberance of the bloody fray in which Tom, nearly overwhelmed by Thwackum and Blifil, is rescued by Squire Western, and in turn revives the swooning Sophia. In addition it provides the festive note on which the book all but closes ('this tragical scene was now converted into a sudden scene of joy'). Yet, in a passage seldom remarked (or at least seldom remarked on), Fielding puts his comedy on a somewhat sombre plane as he expresses, *in propria persona*, the wish that battles could always be fought with fists, rather than with firearms. 'I would avoid', he says, 'if possible, treating this matter ludicrously, lest grave men and politicians, whom I know to be offended at a jest, may cry pish at it; but, in reality, might not a battle be as well decided by the greater number of broken heads, bloody noses, and black eyes, as by the greater heaps of mangled and murdered human bodies?' (V, 12). After reading such a passage, it is difficult not to take seriously the comedy of *Tom Jones*. It is true that Fielding constantly subordinates such pleas and such matters, but this is because, as I have attempted to show, Fielding believes the function of art to be that of providing a rehearsal of civilization. This is the more affecting when we are made to realize that for Fielding civilization is made of alternatives to what is often too clamorous to ignore, resist, and subdue.

The central subject of Book VI is marriage, the principal

events are those dealing with the courtship of Sophia by Blifil and by Tom, and the central moral issue is whether a girl may have the freedom to refuse a man whom she does not wish to marry. The book provides a double contrast – one between Tom and Blifil as suitors to Sophia, the other between Western and Allworthy on the subject of arranged marriages. But this pair of contrasts is framed by another element, which helps to put them in an illuminating focus: Mrs Western's town-based morality comes in conflict with the purely rustic morality of her brother, who says to her, 'I had rather be anything than a courtier, and a Presbyterian, and a Hanoverian, too, as some people, I believe, are'; (VI, 2), and in the final chapter of the book, it is the antipathy between brother and sister, a difference of opinion as to strategy rather than as to choice for Sophia's hand, which is behind her insistence that the girl be released from captivity. And this book records not merely the end of a phase, but the end of an era. Tom, though this is not the principal matter of Book VI, is expelled by Squire Allworthy (who, in conformance with his credulous nature, has believed the calumniations by Thwackum and Blifil), and henceforward – until he finds his way to London – he is to be wandering.

But the action of Book VII does not shift at once and entirely to the road. Structurally the transition from geographical stasis to journeying movement is provided in this book by a twin focus – half on Sophia, who remains at home, and half on Tom, who for the course of this book only is the lonely wanderer: his pedantic barber of a Sancho Panza will not make his appearance until the following book. Tom, that is, in this seventh book is a picaresque hero out of an old tale: 'Jones, no more than Adam, had any man to whom he might resort for comfort or assistance' (VII, 2). Typically not only friendless, he is also uncertain of his way, and even when he makes up his mind to go to sea and heads, as he thinks, for Bristol, he is misdirected. As for Sophia, she prepares herself for a season of wandering; against this development is set the irregular journey of Tom, who ends not at Bristol but at an inland ale-house. Then, in the concluding chapters of the book, the focus and intent achieve fully comic outcomes. It is fair to say, therefore, that this book meanders toward the festival with which it concludes.

And yet it is a special kind of festival, after the Fielding manner, and of the Fielding type. We do know, of course, that Tom and Sophia will eventually be happily and permanently reunited, and one of the special pleasures of the novel is observing the difficulties of the young girl and her lover in the light of this certainty. Life, the readers of *Tom Jones* have never needed to be reminded, is less happily forseeable. But Fielding constructs his novel in such a way as to sustain the confidence by extra measures of prescient and amusing events. Thus Tom's first sustained conversation after his departure from Allworthy's house is with a Quaker whose discourse echoes Squire Western's efforts to arrange a marriage for his daughter. Tom is explicitly maddened by this echo. Henceforward the mood of the book is notably boisterous. In chapter 11 a group of soldiers who 'were marching against the rebels, and expected to be commanded by the glorious Duke of Cumberland' appear at the inn, and Tom goes off with them as a volunteer. And the same chapter provides a festive incident with distinctive Fielding hallmarks. There is the bittersweetness of the near-sixty-year-old lieutenant with the classical education; a French officer, 'who had been long enough out of France to forget his own language, but not long enough in England to learn ours, so that he really spoke no language at all'; and there is the redoubtable Ensign Northerton, who flings a bottle at Tom and knocks him out, when Tom takes exception to his insults of Sophia. I say this is markedly Fielding because moral sordidness is made bearable by admixture of comedy, some high and sophisticated (the elderly lieutenant's learned disquisitions), some low and rambunctious (the flinging of the bottle).

The moral fireworks produced by this knockout are, characteristically, irradiated by the laughable. In the concluding chapters of Book VII, the force of the evidently fatal blow suffered by Tom is dissipated by the surgeon's high-flown jargon, through the thickets of which is discernible the fact that Tom's injury is not so bad as was first feared; and the venality of the landlady, who allowed herself to be bribed by Northerton so that he might escape – this is comically qualified by the abject terror which the blood-stained Tom inspires in the sentinel ('his hair began to lift his grenadier cap; and in the same instant his knees fell to blows with each other' [VII, 14]). And the book concludes on a note of forgiveness: in the last chapter the elderly lieutenant, on Tom's petition, decides to forgive the sentinel. This, too, has its comic aspect, for the lieutenant says in the final paragraph of this chapter, 'But hark, the general beats. My dear boy, give me another buss'.

Two characters, both professing learning, dominate Book VIII. The introduction of the pedantic little Benjamin in the early part of the book helps to establish an atmosphere within which the tale of the Man of the Hill, which occupies the concluding chapters, can have the deliberately muted impact that accords with the design of the novel as a whole. For little Benjamin is not what he seems. He is really Partridge the schoolmaster. But Partridge is not what he has seemed to Tom (and others): he is, as is revealed here, not Tom's father. Nor does he accompany Tom for quite the disinterested motive that he alleges: he pretends to go for love, but the narrator tells us of another motive: 'It came into his head . . . that if he could prevail with the young gentleman to return back to his father, he should by that means render a service to Allworthy, which would obliterate all his former anger' (VIII, 7).

Of importance in this book is the careful interlocking of the plot which makes harmonious the appearance of both Partridge and the Man of the Hill here, and which also connects both of these characters to the rest of the novel. At the beginning of the book Tom is ill, suffering from the head injury inflicted upon him by Ensign Northerton; and the ignorant and gibberish-speaking physician, who made his first appearance in the previous book, now abandons Tom. The gap is filled by Partridge masquerading as Benjamin. His involvement therefore is justified by the plot; and his revelation, in chapter 6, that he is not Tom's father is well timed: it is one of the most important of the series of revelations culminating in the discovery, at the end of the novel, of Tom's actual parenthood. But the centre of the book, that is to say, the central meaning which it exhibits, comes halfway through. Tom

believed that Partridge had no other inducements but love to him and zeal for the cause; a blamable want of caution and diffidence in the veracity of others, in which he was highly worthy of censure. To say the truth, there are but two ways by which men become possessed of this excellent quality. The one is from long experience, and the other is from nature; which last, I presume, is often meant by genius, or great natural parts; and it is infinitely the better of the two, not only as we are masters of it much earlier in life, but as it is more infallible and conclusive; *for a man who hath been imposed on by ever so many, may still hope to find others more honest; whereas he who receives certain necessary admonitions from within, that this is impossible, must have very little understanding indeed, if he ever renders himself liable to be once deceived.* (VIII, 7)

Behind the ironies of the passage which I have italicized lies – surely – a defence not of imprudence but of that generosity of spirit which lets prudence go hang. The paragraph continues as follows: 'As Jones had not this gift [of 'caution and diffidence in the veracity of others'] from nature, he was too young to have gained it by experience; for at the diffident wisdom which is to be acquired this way, we seldom arrive till very late in life'. This is plain enough so far, but lest the reader be tempted to wish that Tom be hurried toward that advanced stage of maturity in which at last prudence is achieved, Fielding concludes the paragraph as follows, in a clause attached to the sentence which I have just cited: '. . . which is perhaps the reason why some old men are apt to despise the understandings of all those who are a little younger than themselves'. If the Man of the Hill's is a cautionary tale, the paragraph I have just cited – which appears in the same book and forms as it were a prologue to the entrance upon the scene of the Man of the Hill – is a cautionary caution.

En route to the encounter with the Man of the Hill, Tom and Partridge travel in such a way as to make possible the commentary by Fielding on the '45 (as he had already done at the end of the previous book) and other matters of topical interest, and at the same time to knit, now with excellent unobtrusiveness, the plot. So the master of the inn at Gloucester is 'brother to the great preacher Whitefield; but is absolutely untainted with the pernicious principles of Methodism' (VIII, 8). And at this inn Dowling, that important lawyer from Salisbury, makes one of his several brief appearances. Also, there is depicted the irony of the political persuasion of Partridge, himself a Jacobite, who assumes, entirely incorrectly, that Tom is *en route* to join the rebels. Partridge's instant abandonment of his adherence to the Pretender is ultimate proof of his devotion to what is practical: he continues with Tom in the hope that a reconciliation, profitable to Partridge himself, will soon take place between Tom and Allworthy.

The remainder of Book VIII is devoted to the encouter with and the tale of the Man of the Hill; and, tempting though it sometimes is to consider this to be a retelling of Wilson's story in *Joseph Andrews*, the two recitals have in fact far less in common than is sometimes supposed. To be sure, they are both cautionary tales, and each is told by a man who has in youth led a dissipated life in London, and then turned his back on urban temptations and retired to the tranquillity of the country. Other resemblances can also be found: Jones saves the Man of the Hill from robbers, and this, like the frame of sheep-stealers and dog killing around Wilson's tale, helps to qualify the straightforwardly didactic intent of the narrators of the tales themselves, or perhaps I should say (for the narrators are aware of the dangers from which Joseph and Tom save them) helps to qualify the ideas of perfection contained in the country setting.[26] Fielding also uses here the integrative, digressive, and, as I think, festive device of interruptions in the course of the narrative: Partridge's interruptions are no less credulous than those of Parson Adams in the earlier novel.

But in *Tom Jones*, which is a more tightly-knit work than *Joseph Andrews*, the tale of the Man of the Hill is – very significantly, as it seems to me – a grotesque version of Wilson's tale. Wilson is Joseph's father and a civilized man whose adventures in London were, though highly culpable, faults of exuberance, high spirits, ignorance, and selfishness. They were not crimes. The Man of the Hill is a vague, dark character of Gothic stature – unattached, lonely, and deeply misanthropic.[27] His housekeeper says of him: 'He keeps no company with anybody, and seldom walks out but by night, for he doth not care to be seen; and all the country people are as much afraid of meeting him; for his dress is enough to frighten those who are not used to it. They call him the Man of the Hill'. In fact, his very surname is concealed from the reader, as it is from Tom and Partridge. He allows his first name, no doubt only a soubriquet, to be revealed. He is merely 'Jack'.

But the atmosphere in which this tale is set, and the harshness of the events in the story itself, are no more, and no less, than mock-Gothic. The comic spirit is a constant threat to any Gothic structure – *The Mysteries of Udolpho*, for all the rationality which differentiates it from *The Castle of Otranto*, fails – nowadays anyway – to sustain the horrific intention: in truth, the Gothic is a humourless style when, as happened in the eighteenth century, the shadows, the liturgies, the gargoyles, and the cloisters, are trundled forward to produce vicarious thrills rather than spiritual satisfactions. The setting of the Man of the Hill's tale does in fact anticipate the Gothic novel in certain respects, though the tale itself belongs to the cautionary tradition so fully alive in the century that saw hundreds of tales hung upon Oriental or European or (as in *Rasselas*) African pegs, in order to point a moral without having to keep to the rules of versimilitude inevitably more stringent in stories laid in England. The tale of the Man of the Hill *is* laid mainly in England, and the juxtaposition of realism and extravagance are what make Fielding's contribution here both comic and pleasing.

When he meets but of course does not recognize the man who is his own father in the place which is to be his future home, Joseph Andrews is on his way to a joyful union with his beloved Fanny Goodwill. Between Joseph and Fanny lies nothing but the calling of the banns. Or so Joseph thinks. When Tom, accompanied by Partridge, comes upon the Man of the Hill, he has been turned out of his home by the man whom he loves as a father; becomes separated – as he thinks for ever – from the girl he adores; and, making his way to Bristol in order to go to sea, has got lost, and then quite casually become involved with some soldiers *en route* to crush the rebellion. That is to say, Tom is ready to be melancholy, ready to put a black construction on the encounter with the Man of the Hill in the sense that he is willing to meet melancholy with sadness. Having been given – by the housekeeper – a preview of the old man, having then prevented two ruffians from putting him to death; having, that is, been fully prepared for something extraordinary, the reader, like Partridge, is struck by the grotesquerie of the presentment.

To say the truth, it was an appearance which might have affected a more constant mind than that of Mr Partridge. This person was of the tallest size, with a long beard as white as snow. His body was clothed with the skin of an ass, made something into the form of a coat. He wore likewise boots on his legs, and a cap on his head, both composed of the skin of some other animals. (VIII, 10)

It is certain from what has preceded his arrival that he never would entertain strangers ('I have', says the housekeeper, 'lived with him above these thirty years, and in all that time he hath hardly spoke to six living people') for any reason short of the life-saving which Tom has just performed.

Accordingly, the Man of the Hill strikes a responsive note in Tom himself. It is touching but it is also amusing that the hero should be melancholy: after all, comic heroes by definition have to extricate themselves from various difficulties before they can expect to begin living happily ever after. When, therefore, Tom asserts to the grateful old man that 'nothing is so contemptible in my eyes as life', he elicits from the Man of the Hill a remark upon Tom's unhappiness. ' "Perhaps" ' – he continues – ' "you have had a friend, or a mistress?" ... – "How could you", cries Jones, "mention two words sufficient to drive me to distraction?" ' (VIII, 10). This is, for the reader, not sad: because of the extravagant language, too heavy for the weight of the discourse, and because of the comic expectation that all eventually will be well. But comedy is given special emphasis here as elsewhere by the presence of Partridge, that rare and delightful blend of the credulous and the worldly, the practical and the absurd, the direct and the opaque: all these combinations are exhibited in the course of his interruptions of the tale itself. When the Man of the Hill speaks of his own mother as a Xanthippe, Partridge identifies the historical Xanthippe's husband; when the Man of the Hill speaks of his mother's over-

indulgence of his elder brother, Partridge cries out, 'Yes, yes . . .
I have seen such mothers; I have been abused myself by them,
and very unjustly'; when the Man of the Hill hesitates to relate
a particularly shameful incident in his life, Partridge cannot
help exclaiming, 'Oh, pray, sir, let us hear this; I had rather
hear this than all the rest; as I hope to be saved, I will never
mention a word of it'; and – after a further interruption by
Partridge to ask for corroboration of a detail of which the old
barber is uncertain – when, in the course of the Man of the
Hill's narration Partridge is chaffed by Tom about the fear of
ghosts, he interrupts for some little time, in order to tell a ghost
story (VIII, 11). It is, literally, gallows-humour – the poor
fellow whose testimony had caused a horse thief to be hanged
was haunted and beaten by the decedent's ghost in a lane where,
on the following morning, is found a dead calf with a white face.
That is to say, the solemnity of the Man of the Hill's tale is constantly leavened by the interruptions of Partridge, who is a far
more extravagantly drawn caricature than is Parson Adams.

And even within the tale itself are ludicrous extravagances,
and at least one classic parallel, or rather backward analogue.
Part of the Man of the Hill's tale is *Oedipus Rex* in reverse.
Oedipus searches for his father; the Man of the Hill's father was
seeking his son; Oedipus kills a man who turns out to be his
father; the Man of the Hill saves the life of a man who turns out
to be his father. The alterations are such as to reduce the father-
son relationship from the vast and universal to the domestic
level. None the less, the adventures of the Man of the Hill have
been very far from pretty. His robbery of a friend at Oxford, his
cruel and selfish and improvident life as a gambler in London,
his experience of persons who were cold-hearted, selfish, vain,
foolish, and discontented – these experiences, together with a
self-administered education in the classics and in the reading of
the Bible, have made him a misanthrope of Rasselas-like
dimension.

The lesson, which the Man of the Hill sketches out in the concluding chapter of Book VIII, is that 'human nature is everywhere the same, everywhere the object of detestation and scorn'.
Consequent upon this discovery is the entire withdrawal from

human society, to the remote part of the country in which Tom and Partridge find themselves. The extremity of the Man of the Hill's position is self-qualifyingly extravagant. Tom himself, for all his recent ill-usage by Allworthy, by Blifil, and most recently by Northerton, reacts against the unqualified judgment that man is 'so vile an animal'. Tom says:

'I believe, as well as hope, that the abhorrence which you express for mankind . . . is much too general. Indeed, you here fall into an error, which in my experience, I have observed to be a very common one, by taking the character of mankind from the worst and basest among them; whereas, indeed, as an excellent writer observes, nothing should be esteemed as characteristical of a species, but what is to be found among the best and most perfect individuals of that species. This error, I believe, is generally committed by those who from want of proper caution in the choice of their friends and acquaintance, have suffered injuries from bad and worthless men; two or three instances of which are very unjustly charged on all human nature'.

This important speech helps put the Man of the Hill's tale in *Tom Jones's* moral focus.

At the end of Book VIII the tale of the Man of the Hill concludes gravely and bitterly, but Tom, though polite and respectful, is candid enough to disagree with the totally misanthropic view which his host has expressed. And high spiritedness quickly takes over, in the subsequent prefatory chapter, 'Of those who lawfully may, and of those who may not, write such histories as this'. Fortunately, Fielding cannot resist the playfulness of this opening sentence of chapter 2 of Book IX: 'Aurora now first opened her casement, *Anglicè* the day began to break'. Thereupon Tom rescues a screaming and half-naked woman from violent attack – and this incident, except for Tom's redoubtable behaviour, would seem to bear out the observations on humanity to which the Man of the Hill has given voice. But the centre of this book is Upton, and as that drama is delineated in the following pages the mood becomes hilarious.

It seems to me extremely significant that the centrally located books of *Tom Jones* – Books IX and X – occur at Upton. Here Fielding's spirits are at their highest; here Tom gets into the characteristic scrape of an impetuous and masculine nature, by packing himself off to bed with Mrs Waters; here Sophia, escaping the fate of a marriage to Blifil, arrives, and departs without having seen Tom. The Upton mood is rowdy, high-pitched, fast-moving, farcical, and attractive.

The action at the Upton inn commences with what Fielding calls in the title to chapter 3 of Book IX the Battle of Upton. The reason for this battle is the suspicion, by the landlady, that Mrs Waters is a whore. The battlefield itself consequently contains soldiers of both sexes; the weapons include the tongue and the broomstick, the cudgel and fists; there are addresses to the reader; and there is an abundance of mock-heroic diction: 'Now the dogs of war being let loose, began to lick their bloody lips; now Victory, with golden wings, hung hovering in the air; now Fortune, taking her scales from her shelf, began to weigh the fates of Tom Jones, his female companion, and Partridge, against the landlord, his wife, and maid...' and so forth (IX, 3).

Over against this preliminary skirmish is set another kind of battle, 'a battle', as the chapter title indicates, 'of the amorous kind'. As is customary in comedy, the woman performs the seduction: Tom, who was in this sense the victim of Molly Seagrim just as he is subsequently to be the victim of Lady Bellaston, here succumbs to a massively mock-heroic barrage. And here Fielding puts the account within inverted commas, as if he were writing out the words of an epic poet. ' "First, from two lovely blue eyes, whose bright orbs flashed lightning at their discharge, flew forth two pointed ogles; but, happily for our hero, hit only a vast piece of beef which he was then conveying into his plate, and harmless spent their force. The fair warrior perceived their miscarriage, and immediately from her fair bosom drew forth a deadly sigh" '. That Mrs Waters wins her battle is, considering the quality of her performance in the field, hardly surprising.

Upton remains the focus of incident in Book X – which, like Book IX – contains twelve hours. So the titles of the books themselves tell us. Inevitable in farce is embarrassing discovery – and so Tom is caught by one Fitzpatrick in Mrs Waters's bedroom and a fight ensues because the Irishman mistakenly supposes Mrs Waters to be his own errant wife. The climax of this chapter is Mrs Waters's crying of rape, so as to avoid being thought what she is, a whore after all.

The other narrative line in this book centres on the arrival of Sophia, who has run away from home, her discovery (by way of Partridge's indiscretion) that Tom is in bed with a wench, and her resolution to forget him. This last is important in that she does not make her resolution lightly, nor does she undertake it because of Tom's sexual generosity, but because she thinks Tom has traduced *her* good name. She hears from Susan the chambermaid a garbled version of the already garbled tale told by Partridge in the kitchen, and it is this which makes her determine to forget him: 'I can', says Sophia, 'forgive all rather than his exposing my name in so barbarous a manner' (X, 5). In fact, Tom has not exposed her name at Upton in any manner whatever. Finally, there is the arrival of Squire Western at the inn, only two hours after Sophia has departed. This is the end of the Upton adventure, but it is not the end of the book: in chapters 8 and 9 'the history', as the title of chapter 8 indicates, 'goes backward', to tell of Sophia's adventures from the time of the determination by her father to marry her at once to Blifil until he pursues her to Upton. This serves the structural purpose of permitting the simultaneity and surprise of the earlier chapters of this book, and equally of giving the reader adequate background for the three days of action in Book XI.

Book XI contains a journey which has a beginning and an end: it starts at Upton and ends in London. But this is by no means the sole unifying principle of the book, which is in fact a paradigm of the structural perfection of *Tom Jones* altogether. The journey to London is mainly that of Sophia and Harriet Fitzpatrick – the one fleeing a prudential match, the other the victim of her own impulsiveness. In the course of the journey each tells her tale, and both are quasi-cautionary. Both, moreover, omit a salient feature: any account of the presently beloved man. Harriet manages her story without any mention of the Irish peer, and Sophia omits any account of Tom Jones. Finally – for *Tom Jones* has as its subject not merely the adventures of its principal persons but English society – there is the incursion of politics, and the scaling even of the '45 to manageable dimensions, in the mistaking of Sophia for Jenny Cameron of the Jacobite cause.

The actual arrangement of these harmonies is likewise delightful. Sophia's encounter with Harriet Fitzpatrick has been prepared for. Harriet arrived at Upton – almost un-noticed, in chapter 3 of Book IX – but the two girls do not actually meet until now. Thereupon, in chapter 3 – 'A very short chapter, in which, however, is a sun, a moon, a star, and an angel' – individual and social fate coincide, even though mistakenly. *Tom Jones* becomes topical and politics become endurable. At the inn where she and Harriet spend the night, Sophia enchants the landlady and effects a conversion.

Such charms were there in the voice, in the manner, and in the affable deportment of Sophia, that she ravished the landlady to the highest degree; and that good woman, concluding that she had attended Jenny Cameron, became in a moment a stanch Jacobite, and wished heartily well to the young Pretender's cause, from the great sweetness and affability with which she had been treated by his supposed mistress.

Readers of Fielding's journals, *The True Patriot* (5 November 1745-17 June 1746) and *The Jacobite's Journal* (5 December 1747-5 November 1748), will recollect the embattled anti-Jacobite position which as a political man Fielding took; but as an artist he had no political axe to grind. In a novel he could make partisan politics into the stuff of comedy. And so chapter 3, which ends on a note of agreement between the two girls that each will tell her story, makes brilliant the tonal ambience of these stories.

Thus Mrs Fitzpatrick's tale is only comically cautionary. And the comic dimension is deepened by the fact that it is a parody of sentimental romance. Harriet, 'fetching a deep sigh', begins her story with Richardsonian unctuousness: 'It is natural to the unhappy to feel a secret concern in recollecting those periods of their lives which have been most delightful to them. The remembrance of past pleasures affects us with a kind of tender grief, like what we suffer for departed friends; and the ideas of both may be said to haunt our imaginations' (XI, 4). Then, instead of proceeding by way of these muted and dulcet strains to melancholy and perhaps horrible disclosures, Harriet tells a tale which is boisterous, quarrel-filled, extravagant of statement – and centred in Ireland. Then, when desperation begins to become too poignant – when, that is, Harriet tells of becoming 'a mother by the man I scorned, hated, and detested' (XI, 5) – Fielding interrupts the tale to write a comic scene (chapter 6) wherein the landlord makes some circumlocutory remarks to Sophia, thinking her to be a political figure, and comic irony is produced because Sophia supposes this obliqueness to refer not to her Jacobitism but to the fact that she is being pursued by her father. Thereupon, Mrs Fitzpatrick concludes her history which by this time includes even that indispensable sentimental ingredient, the confidante. And the level of seriousness at which the reader is meant to take this recital is summed up in Sophia's response: 'Indeed, Harriet, I pity you from my soul! – But what could you expect? Why, why, would you marry an Irishman?' (XI, 7).

Comic construction must be undertaken with two sometimes contradictory aims in view: the artist must try to make his edifice cleverly enough to draw attention to his own cleverness – and in this effort deception and speed are essential. The comic pace is breathless. Nevertheless, it is equally important that an impromptu air be achieved, not for the purpose of realism, but because a story is better if it seems to be invented on the spot. Furthermore, the feigned meandering of a good comic plot can have the happy effect of adjusting the moral temperature to the comic purpose. Book XII, I think, well exemplifies these several generalizations: and it is itself contributory to the meaning of *Tom Jones* as a whole.

For Book XII contains Squire Western's furious but interrupted pursuit of his daughter from Upton – but, because it is a fine day for hunting and because there is opportunity to join a hunt, he abandons the chase of his daughter for the chase of the fox. This famous incident works two ways: most obviously it prevents us from becoming excessively solemn about Sophia's flight from her father and it gives Fielding opportunity to characterize and to forgive Squire Western. It also serves the structural purpose of explaining why Squire Western gives up the pursuit of Sophia altogether: he is, without great difficulty, dissuaded from continuing the chase, and persuaded to return home, 'expressing great joy that the frost was broken (which might perhaps be no small motive in his hastening home)' (XII, 2).

Structurally, chapters 2 and 3 are related in that in each the principal departs from Upton and neither arrives at a destination which he intends: Squire Western is diverted by the hunt in chapter 2, and in chapter 3 Tom fails to find the paths of glory which he now despairingly seeks after the rejection indicated by the muff on his bed. The exigencies of the plot now call for something to happen that will deflect Tom from his journey into valour, and that is provided, by the lucky encounter with a beggar. Characteristically, it is Partridge, that preacher of Christianity, who resists being charitable to the poor man; equally characteristically it is Tom who, having helped the beggar from the generosity of a warm heart, is rewarded by obtaining from the illiterate beggar Sophia's pocket-book, containing £100.

But the chase does not move straight forward. Of course, Tom and Partridge frequently get lost or misled or tired. So the sound of a drum heralds not a rebellion but a puppet show; and here is contained a merry caution against didacticism. The Master has jettisoned comedy and instead presents 'the fine and serious part of the "Provoked Husband" ' (XII, 5) – so solemn and satisfying that the Master is inspired to make a speech afterwards against frivolity, with which Tom disagrees. That is to say, Fielding's distaste for didacticism is reflected in the sententiousness of the Master – as well as in the more extreme sentiments of the landlady of the alehouse, who remembers – 'when puppet-shows were made of good scripture stories, as Jephtha's Rash Vow, and such good things, and when wicked people were carried away by the devil' (XII, 6). And this distaste is given exuberant dramatization also, because Grace the maid is discovered to be cavorting improperly with the Merry Andrew of the puppet show, whose own morals are thus shown to be uninhibited by the ostensible purpose of the play he has helped put on.

Again, an adventure in primitivism provides, like the adventure with the puppets, opportunity for comic exposure of moral clichés. In chapter 12 Fielding has good fun with his gypsy king's dialect, with Partridge's adventure in making advances to a gypsy woman. But just when the reader, accustomed to the thinly veiled satire and moral intent of such encounters (at least literary encounters), begins to suspect that the gypsy band bears witness to a simplicity grandly simple and greatly to be desired, Fielding punctures that balloon by sketching out the dangers of one-man rule: 'In this case it will be much wiser to submit to a few inconveniences arising from the dispassionate deafness of laws, than to remedy them by applying to the passionate open ears of a tyrant'.

As the book ends Partridge and Tom arrive in London. This therefore is the end of an act. The new one begins in Book XIII, the first chapter of which – with its orotund invocation to Fame, Fortune, Genius, Humanity, Learning, and Experience – specifically points 'to a happy conclusion'. London is the setting and Fielding can thus delineate against the background of the town the *mores hominum multorum* as he has already done in the country and on the road. In the remaining books of *Tom Jones* two principal plot strands must be fully unwound, so that the conclusion will be happy: first, Tom must be reconciled to Squire Allworthy; and, second, Sophia must be reconciled to Tom. The reader knows that these reconciliations are going to take place, not simply because this is a comedy but because there have already been hints, in Sophia's forgiving nature, in Squire Western's mercurial and generous temper, in Partridge's revelation that he is not Tom's father, in Dowling's well-italicized reference to Allworthy as Tom's uncle – there have, in fact, been enough hints to point to the direction of the routes to happiness that the Ariadne's thread of the plot may lead. It will, therefore, be the task of each of the books henceforward to propel Tom a certain distance in the direction of the happiness which he deserves by the grace of having been born good, lucky, and handsome.

Inevitably the London scenes will satirize the town, but there is no baseless excursion into high life: every incident is made to contribute to the final dénouement. Tom's purpose in being in London is to find Sophia – and the scheme, hatched by Mrs Fitzpatrick and elaborated by Lady Bellaston of keeping Tom from Sophia actually makes possible their meeting, which takes place at the end of the book. Tom has thus far been presented as a country lad whose ignorance of the town is something to his credit. Arriving in Holborn, he is unaware that the rich inhabit Hanover and Grosvenor Squares; he is unfamiliar with the custom of bribing footmen; he does not know how to take part in 'brilliant' conversation: 'Jones had natural, but not artificial, good breeding' (XIII, 4). All this is conventional enough, but it involves the risk that the reader will be diverted by the social criticism from the main purpose, which is Tom's progress toward the double reconciliation that will bring about his fulfilment. But the introduction of Nightingale, in chapter 5, removes this risk by concentrating in this new young man the collection of townly extravagances that both contrast with and complement Tom's. Nightingale is not, essentially, unlike Tom; he represents and is 'much good sense, though a little too much tainted with town foppery'. Like Tom, he is naturally good, and he is 'a modern fine gentleman' not by inheritance but 'by imitation, and meant by nature for a much better character' (XIII, 5).

It is within this context (and not in isolation) that the moral importance of Tom's liaison with Lady Bellaston must be considered. Tom is propelled toward his meeting with Sophia by the indirect route of a masquerade, the favours and financial support of this noblewoman, and by the latter's own importunities. Structurally, it is important that Tom should have money, that he should be indebted to Lady Bellaston, and that he should emerge unscathed, quite unscathed, from even this encounter. Whether he is successful in escaping the reader's censure must depend partly on the predispositions which the reader himself brings to this affair. Many readers have complained about this episode in the career of Tom Jones.[28] And that Fielding is aware of the dangers involved is indicated in his effort to take the curse off Tom's acceptance of the money: in the first place, there is the tale of Mrs Miller's cousin indigently married to one Anderson (who, it will soon be revealed, was the amateur highwayman). Tom offers all of the fifty pounds he has from Lady Bellaston to relieve the distress of this man and his wife and their children. Furthermore, Tom's gesture as it is compared with Nightingale's faint offer of a guinea, which in the event he does not produce, provides Fielding with the opportunity to discourse on the two kinds of charity. Also, Tom is, if not totally exculpated, at least whitewashed by Fielding's insistence that Tom is honour-bound to give the woman satisfaction for her patronage of him. Tom 'felt his obligations . . . nor did he less plainly discern the ardent passion whence those obligations proceeded, the extreme violence of which if he failed to equal, he well knew the lady would think him ungrateful; and, what is worse, he would have thought himself so' (XIII, 9).

But the tale of Anderson's indigence has still other reasons for being placed here. It is a cautionary tale, the lesson of which Tom cannot fail to absorb, and when, in chapter 11, he and Sophia meet, it is very much on his mind that it would be folly for Sophia to marry him in his present circumstances. The other reason for the structural importance of this story is that it enables Tom to behave with such large generosity as to convince Mrs Miller of his goodness of heart, so that she will defend him, very persistently, to Allworthy.

By the end of Book XIII Lady Bellaston's machinations have been such as to provide a meeting alone between Sophia and Tom. This is a useful irony, and here begins the series of explanations and revelations which will lead to the permanent union of the heroine and the hero. From the viewpoint of construction the first necessary step is that Sophia should begin to modify her view of Tom, and it is to this end that, in chapter 11, the youth begins to speak – thinking, mistakenly, that she cannot forgive him for the Upton adventure. But Sophia disabuses him of this mistaken notion. What still troubles Sophia is her misapprehension, owing to Partridge's excessively loose tongue, that Tom has traduced her name 'in public; in inns, among the meanest vulgar'. This blame is quickly placed where it belongs. The book then concludes with the comedy ensuing upon Lady Bellaston's finding Sophia and Tom together, and the elaborate pretences of ignorance which none of them believes. These scenes are elegantly Farquharesque: their festive notes serving to establish a tone in which joyful revelations, happy scenes of forgiveness, and blissful reunions can take place.

Appropriately, therefore, farce tempers and modifies moral indignation in the following book, XIV, the action of which begins classically, in the triangular embarrassment suffered by Tom as he is called upon by Lady Bellaston and Mrs Honour in turn. And as this first section of Book XIV praws to a close a third consequence of Tom's gallantry causes modulation to a more sombre key. Mrs Miller, fearful for the reputation of her house, rates Tom – kindly – for his entertainment at night of Lady Bellaston there; and the conclusion of their talk is a decision by Tom to lodge elsewhere.

For the other concern of this book – lightened though it is by the farcical prelude – centres on the relationship of Nancy Miller and Jack Nightingale. Of the many marital arrangements in *Tom Jones* this of Nightingale, whose father has quite another match in mind, is a parallel to the arrangement made by Squire Western for Sophia to marry Blifil, when she loves Tom. But in reversing the sexes in this example, Fielding makes all the more absurd the case for merely prudential marriages – the dictatorial father being more outrageous when a son's choice than when a daughter's choice is being reprehended.

There is a wry – even bleak – employment of the principle of contrast in the depiction of Nightingale Senior and his brother. Nightingale Senior is quite clear-cut. He is a 'man of the world' – that is to say, 'he had indeed conversed so entirely with money, that it may be almost doubted whether he imagined there was any other thing really existing in the world' (XIV, 8). He is therefore adamant against even the most ardent arguments of Tom – or of his evidently more liberal-minded brother; for, as Fielding observes (and not without bitterness), 'Neither history nor fable have ever yet ventured to record an instance of any one who, by force of argument and reason, hath triumphed over habitual avarice'. The brother is hardly more admirable, though they are described as 'almost the opposites to each other' (XIV, 8). As long as he thinks Jack Nightingale is already married to Nancy, all is well; but when, enfeebled by drink, Jack discloses that the marriage has not yet taken place but was said to have been celebrated as a stratagem to induce his father to relent – at this point, the uncle advises Jack to detach himself from Nancy. 'Let your reason have fair play, Jack, and you will see this match in so foolish and preposterous a light that there will be no need of any dissuasive arguments, (XIV, 9). On this sombre note the book draws to a conclusion, leaving the Jack and Nancy relationship unsettled and unresolved; and Tom is told 'dreadful news concerning his Sophia' – which, however, the narrator reserves for the following pages and, as Book XIV ends, another structural principle, a principle of contrast that, in setting the farce of the opening pages against the sentiment of the second half of the book, makes lights and shades which preserve the perfection of scale that is *Tom Jones*.

Extravagance, exuberance, farce, and celebration are the moods of Book XV, during the two days' time of which, though Tom does not gain his objects of reconciliation to Allworthy and Sophia, the shape of events begins to point toward that outcome. The first five chapters centre on Lady Bellaston's design of removing Sophia from Tom Jones's purview by the expedient of marrying her to Lord Fellamar. These chapters are prevented from being solemn or sentimental in tone by the excessive and thus self-defeating solemnity and sentimentality with which they are set forth, by the flourishes of melodrama which Fielding provides, and above all by the drunken and violent rescue of Sophia performed by her father.

Everything about Lady Bellaston's elaborately-laid plot is redolent of comic disaster. With consistent indelicacy, she misunderstands the nature of love and imputes Sophia's attitudes about love to rusticity. To Fellamar Lady Bellaston says, 'Alas! my lord ... consider the country – the bane of all young women is the country. There they learn a set of romantic notions of love, and I know not what folly, which this town and good company can scarce eradicate in a whole winter' (XV, 2). She persuades one of her hangers-on, a certain Tom Edwards, to report in Sophia's presence that Tom Jones has been killed in a duel, so as to convince Lord Fellamar of her attachment to the young man. Finally – and most extravagant of all – she persuades Fellamar to pay assiduous, unremitting, and if need be, violent addresses to Sophia. 'Are you frightened', the noble lady asks the noble lord, 'of the word rape?' (XV, 4).

After such a prelude comedy must ensue, especially when it is set in the mock-tragic frame of chapter 5, which begins as follows: 'The clock had now struck seven, and poor Sophia, alone and melancholy, sat reading a tragedy'. This is matched by the stereotypical extravagance of Lord Fellamar's declaratory speech: 'I doat on you to the highest degree of distraction. O most adorable, most divine creature! what language can express the sentiments of my heart?' (XV, 5). This is interrupted by the celebrated high comedy of Squire Western's rescue, and by a number of other comic anti-climaxes, all of which have an important impact: a propulsive force toward the happy ending. A minor event, in chapter 11, has cumulative importance: Tom refuses the proposal of marriage tendered by one Arabella Hunt – and so the shadow of the kept man begins to fade from Tom.[29]

Book XVI has a well-defined frame, for it begins with the confinement of Sophia and ends with the imprisonment of Tom. Between these two halves of the book is a centrally-placed entr'acte which offers the most antipodal contrast: chapter 5 itself, 'In which Jones receives a letter from Sophia, and goes to a play with Mrs Miller and Partridge', contains the contrast that lights and shadows the whole of this book. The two centres of interest in chapter 5 are Sophia's letter to Tom saying she will never 'act in defiance of' her father, and that their correspondence must close; this is to be set up against the free world of play at the play, the delightful episode of Partridge and Mrs Miller and her young daughter and Tom at Garrick's *Hamlet*.

There is a neatness of design, and a harmony of arrangement in this book which is itself delightful. Gaiety irradiates the book and makes laughable even the violences of Squire Western and the treachery of Lord Fellamar and – above (or below) all – the arrival by Jones at the nadir of his fortunes. Indeed, it would be very difficult after a prolegomenous chapter in which Fielding rationalizes the inclusion of prologues by such reasons as 'the prologue serves the critic for an opportunity to try his faculty of hissing' – it would, I say, be difficult to regard too bleakly even the most violent and evidently fatal accidents which ensue. Besides, the balanced arrangement of the book is itself a source of delight: chapters 2, 3, and 4 deal with Sophia's confinement and her release from it. Chapter 5's twin focus on Sophia's letter and on the playhouse have already been remarked. And the remaining chapters deal with Tom's progress toward and arrival at despair-laden confinement in the Gatehouse.

The central chapter – 5 – is charming. Sophia's letter to Tom, though in it she promises never to disobey her father, contains several loopholes through which hope enters: 'A promise is with me a very sacred thing . . . and this consideration may perhaps, on reflection, afford you some comfort'. She speaks of what 'fortune hath (perhaps) made impossible'. She says in her postscript, 'I charge you, write to me no more – at present at least'. Tom can therefore be comfortable when he goes to the playhouse to observe and rejoice in Partridge's reaction to *Hamlet*. Most notable here is the preference by Partridge for the actor who plays Claudius: 'he speaks all his words distinctly, half as loud again as the other. – Anybody may see he is an actor'. What contributes most obviously to the reader's happiness of response here is Partridge's contempt for Garrick's verisimilitude: 'I am sure, if I had seen a ghost, I should have looked in the very same manner, and done just as he did'. Equally delightful is the detachment from the whole spectacle: a reader watches a number of fictional characters reacting to a play performed upon the stage.

Thematically the principle of contrast makes the stronger Allworthy's distress at Sophia's evident distaste for Blifil, and his determination that she should have the freedom to refuse. 'I will never give my consent to any absolute force being put on her inclinations, nor shall you ever have her unless she can be brought freely to compliance' (XVI, 6). Henceforward the movement, by way of Lady Bellaston's scheme of revenge, and the duel with Fitzpatrick, toward Tom's imprisonment and despair (despair added to despair when Sophia, having been shown his letter of proposal to Lady Bellaston, casts him off) – these occur within a comic framework, beautifully intricate, which guarantees a happy outcome.

Book XVII belongs to Mrs Miller, whose extremely ardent defences of Tom are necessary in order to begin to reverse the current of disfavour which has been running against him. She defends him to Allworthy, even in the face of Blifil's allegations; she defends Tom to Sophia – and then again to Allworthy. And although both Allworthy and Sophia try to resist her persuasion, they are unsuccessful. Mrs Miller is not the whole structural force of Book XVII – not by any means. The structure here is extremely intricate, and the book (like the novel as a whole) repays re-reading because of this fact. I instance here only the efforts made by the pertinacious Nightingale to discover what he can about the fight between Fitzgerald and Tom. He returns to the Gatehouse with the news that he has talked to two sailors, witnesses to the fight, who have sworn that Tom struck the first blow. There is another person present at the interview, un-known to Nightingale, who is given such scant mention that he can easily be overlooked. Nightingale asks the sailors whether they are certain Tom struck the first blow.

'I repeated the question to them several times, and so did another gentleman who was present, who, I believe, is a seafaring man, and who really acted a very friendly part by you; for he begged them often to consider that there was the life of a man in the case; and asked them over and over, if they were certain; to which they both answered, that they were, and would abide by their evidence upon oath'. (XVII, 9.)

This man, as it will turn out, is Dowling, the suborning lawyer who, we discover in the course of this book, has been preferred through Bilfil's influence to the place of Allworthy's steward.

But Mrs Miller, as I say, dominates this book, and it has not, I think, been sufficiently noticed that she belongs to Fielding's gallery of lucky innocents. And although she is even more simple than Parson Adams she resembles him not merely in depth of naïveté but in the possession of the grace of the innocent. The narrator comments on the ease with which Mrs

Western can impose upon her. Fielding then says: 'This poor creature might, indeed, be called simplicity itself. She was one of that order of mortals who are apt to believe everything which is said to them; to whom nature hath neither indulged the offensive weapons of deceit, and who are consequently liable to be imposed upon by anyone who will only be at the expense of a little falsehood for that purpose' (XVII, 8).

The principle of contrast exhibited in this book is that between the hectic and passionate activities for good and ill undertaken by Mrs Miller, Nightingale, Partridge, Blifil, Fella-mar, Mrs Western and Squire Western – all this against the comparatively passive roles of Sophia and Tom. Sophia, it is true, must resist steadfastly the proposals of Lord Fellamar, and she is quite equal to the task. But her role here is negative, just as is her attitude to Tom – although her acceptance from Mrs Miller of the letter from Tom points the way to the ultimate change, or rather revelation, of heart. Tom, in the Gatehouse, has little choice but to be passive, and there is every reason to suppose that his case is a hopeless one – every reason, that is, for him thus to suppose: the reader, because he is reading a comic epic poem in prose and is repeatedly reminded of this fact, knows better.

And the structural challenge presented by this penultimate book is how to progress while seeming to remain stationary. Tom remains in prison throughout. Fellamar continues to pay his addresses to Sophia. Squire Western continues to insist, even in the face of Allworthy's opposition, that Sophia shall marry Blifil. This is all – apparently – the mixture as before. And yet, the book moves the characters further toward the happy ending which Fielding has preached the difficulties of achieving. The most significant advance – and I do not overlook such plot manœuvres as those by which Dowling has a role in the drama – is the idea, so eloquently put into words by Allworthy, that a woman is free to refuse a man she dislikes. He is altogether plain to Blifil and Western: 'Now to force a woman into a marriage contrary to her consent or approbation is an act of such injustice and oppression that I wish the laws of our country could restrain it' (XVII, 3). Here the passionate belief in freedom, to which a world of play opens itself, gives hope that in this novel if not in this life freedom will have the day.

By the end of Book XVII it is clear that Tom is soon to enjoy the rewards of his good nature. The last book of *Tom Jones*, therefore, will not surprise us by saving Tom from the gallows, but delight us with a fine show of ingenuity. Structurally it is wonderfully mock-epical, the wheel of fortune commencing with Tom at the position of woe – an Oedipus of the golden age, for no one reading the novel will think that Tom has, as Partridge 'discovers', really 'been a-bed with your own mother'; and of course the end of the book carries Tom to the splendid weal of the double reconciliation which has all along been the aim and the direction of the novel's movement. As usual the principle of contrast is at work in the meeting between the generous Allworthy and the greedy father of Nightingale – a further contrast being offered between old Nightingale and his brother; again, in the two letters, one from Square, now on his deathbed converted to Christianity and exculpatory of Tom, the other from the vehemently parsonical Thwackum, eagerly but disagreeably seeking preferment for himself; again, between Blifil and Tom: as the depth of Blifil's villainy comes to light, so the goodness of Tom's character becomes all the more radiant; finally, there is the contrast between the two country squires. And so, as revelation follows upon revelation, the novel draws to a conclusion in which Tom, now the acknowledged nephew of Allworthy, gains his Sophia and the novel itself gains immortal glory.

The spectacle which is laid before the reader, so lifelike and so unlike life, so versimilar in detail and so operatic on the whole, so elaborately and delightfully composed – this is not an imitation of nature but a splendid rearrangement, a wonderful divagation from the stringencies, the bleakness, the undifferentiated dullness and beastliness of much ordinary life. This mixture, Professor McKillop quietly reminds us, 'of hidden and overt action, hidden and overt motives, does after all solicit attention as a mechanism'.[30]

And I think it is fair to say that the more often one reads *Tom Jones* the more often its graceful structure delights. It is a novel not perhaps to live by, but with.

AMELIA AS DOMESTIC EPIC

For all its Virgilian integrity the structure of *Amelia* is anything but satisfactory. Of course, Fielding never claimed in the Author's Preface to *Joseph Andrews* or anywhere else that the comic epic poem in prose is in fact an epic on the Greek or Roman model: it is, explicitly, an adaptation of the ancient model to modern requirements. But *Amelia* is a deeply flawed conflation of satire and the novel. Fielding says that he bestowed great pains on the composition of *Amelia*, and there is no reason to disbelieve this assertion.[31] In fact, however, the result is less harmonious and successful than Fielding hoped it was: it is necessary, in art as perhaps not always in life, to judge by achievement rather than by expectation, hope, and intention. As a literary form, the novel is both loose and generous, but it cannot successfully resist every importunity.

The radical defect can be illustrated by an incident in which Amelia tells her son a bitter fact of life, an incident that cannot be accommodated within the framework of the comic epic poem in prose. Booth has been released from prison but the acid of remorse has burned away all joy he might have felt if he had not committed adultery. Furthermore, he has been taken to task by Dr Harrison for setting up an equipage. In short, he is distracted with misery – 'like a man in the most raging fit of the gout, he was scarce capable of any additional torture'. In this circumstance, young Booth asks his mother,

'Why will anybody hurt poor papa? hath he done any harm to anybody?' 'No, my dear child,' said the mother; 'he is the best man in the world, and therefore they hate him'. Upon which the boy, who was extremely sensible at his years, answered, 'Nay, mamma, how can that be? Have you not often told me that if I was good everybody would love me?' 'All good people will,' answered she. 'Why don't they love papa, then?' replied the child, 'for I am sure he is very good'. 'So they do, my dear,' said the mother, 'but there are more bad people in the world, and they will hate you for your goodness'. (IV, 3.)

This exchange, with its Shakespearean echo,[32] a remarkably raw exhibition of hatred for the greater part of the human race, is Amelia's own utterance. Nor does she stop there. She gives her son, as he pursues the matter, a taste of the bleak Christianity which is her cold comfort. Young Booth attempts to assess the significance of his mother's evidently despairing remark:

'Why, then, bad people,' cries the child, 'are loved by more than the good'. 'No matter for that, my dear,' said she; 'the love of one good person is more worth having than that of a thousand wicked ones; nay, if there was no such person in the world, still you must be a good boy; for there is one in heaven who will love you, and His love is better for you than that of all mankind'.

In *Amelia* moral outrage has collapsed the distance between event and reader.[33]

A signal of structural failure in *Amelia* is the number and quality of static and detached discussions of topics whose relationship to the main course of the action is tenuous at best. Although such discussions find a place from time to time in *Joseph Andrews* and *Tom Jones*, they are always subordinated and incorporated satisfactorily. In *Amelia*, whether because of fatigue or illness or exasperation or irrepressible bitterness or a combination of these, most of the discussions obtrude. There are some twelve such interruptions in Fielding's last novel, ranging in subject-matter from the law's delay to duelling, adultery, and preferment; and as the number increases sharply in the latter half of the novel, the impression given is of a glut of talk.[34] Likewise, the interpolated tales – those of Miss Matthews (Book I), Booth (Books II and III), Molly Bennet (Book VII), and Trent (Book XI) – are handled with less than the adequacy that the Fielding of *Joseph Andrews* and *Tom Jones* so happily displayed.

Most important among the failures of a domestic novel which intends to teach the art of life is the sorry parade of marriages, each more sourly exemplary than the last. The relationship between the Booths is loving but for various reasons imperfect, and the conclusion one draws is that Amelia is bravely and affectionately loyal, though sorely tried, while Will is, in view of his extra-marital adventures, treated by his wife better than he deserves. Nor are any of the other marriages in *Amelia* better:

all are blemished, and more deeply blemished, than that of the
Booths. The shortlived love between Robert James and Miss
Betsy Bath becomes a grotesque echo rather than a memory
which can nourish their marriage; Mrs James, by way of com-
pensation, becomes a fine town lady and thus a ridiculous figure
whose falsity Amelia cannot understand for some time. Molly
Bennet's first marriage, to a clergyman, was rent by the
difficulties of preferment and by her terrible indiscretion: and
brought, in the event, prematurely to an end by Bennet's early
death. Her second marriage, to Serjeant Atkinson, is better and
no doubt the best in the entire novel. But even this has its
imperfect aspect in the superiority of Mrs Atkinson's learning to
that of her husband: comically disproportionate to be sure, but
the source of friction. Deeper, however, than the difficulty about
erudition is the truth, revealed only when the serjeant thinks
himself to be on his deathbed, that toward Amelia he has an
ancient, inextinguishable, and surpassing tenderness. As for the
marriage between George Trent and his wife, that is a cynical
picture indeed: the man makes his wife into a bawd, and is himself her pimp. Surely there are few more disagreeable vignettes
of marriage delineated in fiction.

Amelia's beginning in the middle of things is a plunge into the
worst of marital matters short of death: an adultery on the part
of the heroine's husband; and surely among the most important
of the relationships in the book is that between Booth and Miss
Matthews. The outcome of Fielding's depiction here is, it seems
to me, that of moral unease. The reader hardly knows how far
to condemn Booth for his willingness to respond to Miss
Matthews's lures, and, on the other hand – or, on the contrary –
how far to condone an adventure whose consequences, except
for minor tremors of conscience and minor inconveniences of
deception (mostly self-deception), are amusing. This is the
central ambiguity of the novel. So far as wives are concerned,
entire fidelity is not only expected but necessary – Amelia is
the heroine both of the novel and of her marriage, in part
because she forcefully resists the importunities which threaten
throughout. But husbands, evidently, are allowed to stray –
perhaps, and perhaps not. Fielding is generous about Will

Booth, too generous it may be, but it is an oversimplification to argue that Booth is a married Tom Jones.[35]

The celebratory gleam, which occasionally shows itself through the lineaments of the moral fable that is *Amelia*: this is what confuses the intent of the novel. Biographically it is comprehensible, but artistically indefensible. The structure of the opening books of the novel is itself flawed by this antithetic division of interest. Exposure of prison conditions and pious recital of tales with a moral – Miss Matthews's account of her ruin by Cornet Hebbers, and Booth's account of the improvidence which has brought him to prison: these are overlaid with the flirtation which begins at once, and ends in seduction.

The first chapter of Book I explicitly points the way to a novel which will contain instruction suitable for individuals who will, because they are human beings, need to know how to conduct themselves. But the first book fails to fulfil this promise, for on the one hand it goes behind and beyond the art of life to an indictment of the judicial and police systems, in which England's very constitution is mentioned with scorn: that is to say, the first book finds rotten the very fabric upon which the art of life ought to be stitched. And on the other hand, in the relating of Miss Matthews's tale, the counsels of prudence – of which Fielding makes much in the Exordium – fade before the chivalrous behaviour of Will Booth, a mode of behaviour that has brought him to prison, and the ardent response of Miss Matthews, who has – so far as the reader of *Amelia* is concerned – not by any means culpably stabbed the man who ruined her. Finally, there is something discomforting and infelicitous in the jocular dramatic irony involved in the temptation of Booth by Miss Matthews.

After the prefatory chapter Fielding plunges uncomfortably not, indeed, into the middle of a domestic crisis, but into an exposition of urban injustice. At once a disadvantage of abandoning the prolegomenous chapters is apparent. To be sure, Book I uniquely among the twelve that comprise *Amelia* contains a prologue. But Fielding has jettisoned the whole strategy of the prefatory chapters in *Amelia*, and so has made the status of this novel as a work of art uneasy, uncertain, and even ambiguous. For in *Joseph Andrews* and *Tom Jones* the prologues serve to make those novels self-consciously and even ostentatiously works of art. Here, in *Amelia*, the impatient and heavy-handed interposition in a chapter that is meant to be devoted to action, has the effect of flawing the course of the novel. Thus in chapter 2 of Book I the narrator arraigns the constitution and the laws for producing and then tolerating a trading justice of the ignorance and of the stripe of Mr Thrasher. He is wholly venal. But, as the narrator scornfully puts it, 'the magistrate had too great an honour for Truth to suspect that she ever appeared in sordid apparel: nor did he ever sully his sublime notions of that virtue by uniting them with the mean ideas of poverty and distress'.

At the time he was writing *Amelia* Fielding was experiencing at first hand the frustrations and the horrors of being a magistrate, and he was actively involved in the making of reforms in which such depictions as those contained in the early chapters of this novel were intended to be instrumental. But for a novel – a novel, anyway, according to Fielding's recipe – these are interruptions. And the difficulty is aggravated by what must be called the philosophical themes which interpose themselves here. Booth is a proponent of the theory of the ruling passion, Robinson the gambler an exponent of fatalism – and, for good measure, there is the Methodist pickpocket, whose view is that 'perhaps the worse a man is by nature, the more room there is for grace'. The difficulty is not that these characters talk about and exemplify certain ideas – Parson Adams notoriously does just this in *Joseph Andrews* – but that nothing these three men exemplify points to the most important of all the characters of Book I, Miss Fanny Matthews.

Fanny Matthews's tale is cautionary – against the imprudence of giving way to the importunities of a scoundrel, however handsome; but as she tells her story she manages to include a great many remarks by which she hopes to arouse the amiable Will Booth. Furthermore, she is an extraordinarily strange example of womanhood: vindictive toward her sister who can play the harpsichord better than she, indifferent to the loss of her virtue except as it means she must sit in the gallery of the

theatre; 'O heavens! When I have seen my equals glittering in a
side-box, how have the thoughts of my lost honour torn my
soul!' (I, 9). Indeed, Miss Matthews is a kind of waif: a Defoe
character in a Fielding world. Most important of all, it seems to
me, is the fact, quite unobtrusively disclosed, that art is no
longer trustworthy: what endears Cornet Hebbers to Fanny
Matthews's father 'was his skill in music, of which you know
that dear man was the most violent lover' (I, 7). What leads to
Fanny's ruin is a dance held to celebrate the wedding of her
sister 'to a young man as musical as herself' (I, 8). And, in the
final chapter, which contains a discussion of the law and legal
proceedings, the intent is practical: it is to satirize.

Booth's story, as he relates it in Book II, is neither domestic
nor realistic: it is operatic and sentimental. As one reads it, one
is struck by its sometimes wild departure from the promise held
out at the beginning of *Amelia*, that this novel is to be domestic-
ally centred. More than that, one wonders why Booth's tale
must be told to Miss Matthews rather than to the reader. To be
sure, the various interruptions *en route* keep reminding the
reader of Miss Matthews's amorous hopes and seductive intent,
and thus they throw light on the perhaps excessively obliging or
overgallant aspect of Booth's character. But is this necessary?
Finally, the tale is anything but cautionary in the sense promised in the first chapter of Book I: Booth's story celebrates not
the virtues of prudence but the claims of affection, loyalty, and
honour. In fact the structural principle of the first three books
of *Amelia* – of, that is to say, the first quarter of the novel – is
founded upon the seduction intended, planned, and executed
by Miss Matthews.

In this light, the cautionary flavour of Miss Matthews's tale
assumes a curiously ironical aspect, for as she tells it in the first
book, she reveals that she is not a reformed sinner preaching
virtue but a temptress spreading her net, so that there is an
irony already in full operation in Book I; and this is doubled in
Book II, for Booth's also is the tale of an elopement, leading,
however, not to the ruin of either of the principals, but to
connubial bliss. And yet, as he relates the history of his courtship of Amelia, of their escape, and of their marriage, Booth

betrays an incautiousness and a credulity, as well as a warmth of heart, that demonstrate to the reader the inevitability of his soon falling into the toils of the resourceful Miss Matthews.

From Booth's story, the art of life would seem to consist in being a naturally good man acting spontaneously. If there is a lesson here it is that the prudent founder sooner and fare worse than the spontaneous and the generous of heart. Indeed, there is not much in the courtship of Amelia and its consequence that sounds prudential, for Amelia and Booth are in love, and she will marry him regardless of his poverty and 'the poor provision of an ensign's commission' (II, 3). Mrs Harris's concealment in the closet, her raving denunciation of an honourable man who hopes to marry her daughter, her sly effort to marry Amelia off to a man with a coach and six – all these are so extravagant as to make Lady Capulet's behaviour seem soft and yielding by comparison. Furthermore, Fielding himself declares war on probability when he causes Booth to be carried off to a sentimental death-bed scene – that of his beloved sister Nancy – just at the moment when the consent has finally been obtained, owing to the intervention of the good and influential Dr Harrison. In the midst of this tale, the comedy of the hamper, in which Booth is hidden and then discovered (II, 5) jars uncomfortably, especially as it is followed by the excessively sentimental incident of the elopement (complete with despairing line from Congreve – II, 6), and the flight to the cottage of Mrs Atkinson. Fielding does not know what notes he can strike in Book II of *Amelia*, and the result is not quite discordant, but it is dissonant.

In the course of Book III Booth concludes the telling of his tale and brings therefore the two time schemes of *Amelia* together at the beginning of Book IV. Until then Booth and Miss Matthews in the prison relate stories about themselves which are entirely in the past. Thenceforward the present time of *Amelia* will embrace their relationship as well as the story of each of them separately. I think Fielding's handling of the matter of Books I, II, and III to be somewhat cumbersome; and I wish that the novel had begun somewhat more briskly. As the structure stands, Fielding is trying to make the most of the advantages of what is now called the flashback, and at the same time of what can be called straight narrative. The difficulty is not so much aesthetic as it is one of challenging the reader's willingness to attend.

Book IV begins with Booth's adultery and ends with the opening moves in the plot of the noble lord to possess Amelia. That is, two interlocking triangular relationships dominate, though they do not comprise the whole of, the book. Besides the two liaisons, one consummated and the other envisioned, there are subordinate interests dramatized in the relationship of Booth to Colonel James, of Amelia to Mrs James, and of Serjeant Atkinson's reappearance, which proves to be a benediction to both Booth and Amelia. So regarded, the structure of Book IV would seem to be quite acceptable, especially as adequate attachment is provided to the foregoing book, and adequate provision for attachment to that succeeding. Yet there are two major flaws, which are best regarded as structural. The first is that there is very little depiction of the domestic bliss which is for ever threatened in *Amelia*. To be sure there are brief descriptions of the Wiltshire idyll of Book III, but these occupy the space of less than a chapter and are the perhaps understandably abbreviated account of a man who has been driven to the edge of ruin by his own vanity. But in Book IV, it is Fielding rather than Booth who is telling the story, and he conveys very little idea of how the Booth family comported itself privately. Though we are repeatedly assured by the narrator that Amelia is an exemplary wife and mother, and though we are told that Booth is an affectionate man with a conscience, we are forced to accept these claims rather than to weigh the evidence for ourselves. That is to say, Fielding's failure to illustrate the domestic life of the Booths weakens very considerably the force of this book.

Book V is structurally far more successful than any of its predecessors, not because of a superior framework but because within a quite passable framework Fielding, much more than formerly in *Amelia*, establishes a viable relationship between narrator and story. The centre of interest in this book is the putting into execution of the noble lord's plot to ensnare Amelia.

In order for this design to have some hope of success, Booth himself must be necessitous and thus have to be obliged to the noble lord for relieving his distress: indeed, that condition Booth has already fulfilled in Book IV. But, more than that, Booth must be credulous and yet not so naïve as never to entertain any suspicion of the noble lord's intentions. These conditions Booth fulfils neatly. By contrast, and indeed by way of comic amplification, there occur here the excellent dramas of the irascible Colonel Bath's duel with Booth, because Bath has – like Colonel James – believed Miss Matthews's cruel calumniations of the young lieutenant; and, as a matter of broad comedy, the warm attachment which Mrs Ellison conceives for Atkinson, who himself – though neither we nor Booth and Amelia discover the fact in the course of this book – loves and wishes to marry Mrs Bennet. Beside these principal movements, the courtship by Atkinson of Mrs Bennet, and Mrs Bath's short-lived distress at the news of her husband's having been in a duel – these are secondary but apposite: Atkinson's fidelity and Mrs Bath's indifference both helping to define the central relationship, of Booth and Amelia.

Excellence of construction, including excellence in the mounting of individual scene, characterizes Book VI as well. The main course of the action focuses on the noble lord's intention to possess Amelia; subsidiary to this but also closely connected to it is the financial difficulty from which Booth does not extricate himself but which, requiring his attention (and, if possible, the peer's assistance), prevents the making of a break with a man who is already a benefactor to the Booth children, and who promises to be a patron to Booth himself. But the construction of this book goes beyond these two main concerns to two others: an affection which Colonel James conceives for Amelia, and a mistake made by Dr Harrison that will lead some time later to the catastrophe which Booth suffers just before his conversion to a more vigorous Christianity than he has been capable of owning until that time.

But Booth is unaware of the desire which has been born in Colonel James's breast. This is because Booth does not know him as we do: no narrator tells Booth, as Fielding tells us, that the principal reason why James wishes to spend the day with Booth is 'the desire of passing it with his friend's wife' (V, 1). Fielding, indeed, insists in the paragraphs which conclude chapter 1 that fire will burn. Behind this openly didactic insistence lies a view of Colonel James's character that is not apparent until Fielding's portrait of him is complete: James's egotism is so deep as to make him dangerously selfish. But Fielding never suggests that self-centredness may be susceptible of amendment. Fielding desired a better society, but his portrait of James demonstrates that the art of life may not be so easy for a faulty man to learn. Hence the sophistication, as it seems to me, of what follows. 'His mind, however, no sooner suggested a certain secret to him than it suggested some degree of prudence to him at the same time; and the knowlege that he had thoughts to conceal, and the care of concealing them, had birth at one and the same instant' (VI, 2). Prudence, it will be remembered, is what Fielding announces he will teach in the course of *Amelia* – and I think it is fair to charge him with desperate disingenuousness rather than with forgetfulness here. *Amelia* is the work of a man for whom the function of art as he saw it was coming to seem frivolous. So he tries to write a novel that teaches a lesson: but he cannot help revealing his distrust of prudence as a virtue, his faith also that education does not educate. For Amelia remains purblind – 'so much more quick-sighted, as we have somewhere else hinted, is guilt than innocence' – even when Booth directly tells Amelia that he is suspicious of the noble lord's intentions.

Fielding does his best to make credible Amelia's becoming caught in the noble lord's toils. Booth's financial distresses cause him to swallow his suspicions and remain kindly enough disposed toward the lord as to allow Amelia to go to Ranelagh. And the comic show of scholarship by Mrs Bennet – indeed the development of her character generally in the final chapters of this book – diverts attention from the fact that Amelia is on the verge of making a serious mistake.

Except for an introductory and concluding chapter, Book VII is devoted entirely to Mrs Bennet's history of herself. From oratorio to Ranelagh the noble lord's plot is identical with that which now puts the virtue of Amelia in jeopardy; the cautionary purpose of this tale is thus patent, but there is much besides, and this must engage our attention also. Notably, Mrs Bennet's tale is a melodrama – 'O Mrs Booth!' says Mrs Bennet in the first paragraph of chapter 1, 'You would not wonder at my emotion if you knew you had an adulteress and a murderer now standing before you'. This is the old Fielding, the man who will trans-figure the materials of life and make them into the stuff of art, and it is welcome after the unease which he betrays from time to time in the course of *Amelia*.

As is traditional in the cautionary tale, Mrs Bennet begins *ab ovo*; her story is replete with horrific or merely hideous adventures, from a mother drowned in the well, to cruel step-mother, and eccentric paternal aunt. They in fact begin to overshadow or at least rival the merely melodramatic interest of the tale – and contempt of the world breaks in, rather too often. Thus on the stepmother and her father:

'But though his wife was so entirely mistress of my father's will that she could make him use me ill, she could not so perfectly subdue his understanding as to prevent him from being conscious of such ill-usage; and from this consciousness he began inveterately to hate me. Of this hatred he gave me numberless instances, and I protest to you I know not any other reason for it than what I have assigned; and the cause, as experience hath convinced me, is adequate to the effect'. (VII, 3.)

For Molly is cut off, when her father dies, with £100, and her aunt turns so far against her as to advise her to go to service. The sentimental value of the story Mrs Bennet never allows the reader to lose sight of.

The experience of the Bennets is to be contrasted to that of the Booths in that it is Mrs Bennet who is unfaithful to her husband, owing to her having taken an evidently drugged drink (like Clarissa before her), after the masquerade at Ranelagh. But there is a fundamental difference in character between Mrs Bennet and Amelia. Mrs Bennet is not entirely indisposed to think of dalliance. Amelia is pleased with the noble lord, but only as far as 'any virtuous woman can possibly be with any man, besides her own husband'. But Molly Bennet says in this book: 'I will – I will own the truth; I was delighted with perceiving a passion in him, which I was not unwilling to think he had had from the beginning'. And as the book draws to an end, the full story of Mrs Bennet has been all related, except for one important development: the maid inadvertently lets Amelia in on the final secret, that Mrs Bennet is now Mrs Atkinson. This is not only a usefully neat way for Mrs Bennet's tale to be brought to a conclusion, but can provide a transition to the subsequent book: for at the end, Atkinson comes in and reveals that Booth has been arrested, at the suit of Dr Harrison. This is sufficiently distressing to make Amelia despair, and sufficiently mystifying to make the reader turn the page.

Thus, the reader is anxious to know why Booth has been arrested – and, unless I am mistaken, the mystery will not be dissipated at once, by reflection on the stranger who came to call upon the Booths and was much struck, horror-struck, by the valuable trinkets which he observed to be in the room. But, besides that mystery, there is the fine construction of Book VIII in itself, with its contrasting chapters set in the sponging house and at Mrs Atkinson's, the excellent framework of the first and last chapters: the first dealing with Booth's arrest and incarceration, the last with his release and liberty: affected by the same man who was responsible for his having been arrested: by, that is, the Dr Harrison about whom the mystery remains for the duration of the book unsolved. More than a century before the celebrated Zola was making pioneer efforts in the technique of naturalism, Fielding was providing detail of much the same sort – and in fact for something like the same purpose: he wished to *épater le bourgeois*, so as to bring about reforms in the lower courts, to disclose the inequities of arrest for debt, to lay bare the discomforts of the sponging houses together with the disagreeableness of their keepers, and to achieve some reforms in police method. Fielding the novelist and Fielding the social reformer, too often at odds in *Amelia*, meet usefully in Book VIII.

Book IX begins with a flashback which explains Dr Harrison's decision to cause Booth to be arrested. As is customary in *Amelia*, there is a cluster of misapprehension founded on evil will. Thus

Booth and Amelia were both calumniated to the credulous Dr
Harrison. For instance,

on his return to his parish, [the doctor] found all the accusations
which had been transmitted to him confirmed by many witnesses, of
which the curate's wife, who had been formerly a friend to Amelia,
and still preserved the outward appearance of friendship, was the
strongest. She introduced all with 'I am sorry to say it, and it is
friendship which bids me speak; and it is for their good it should be
told you.' After which beginnings she never concluded a single
speech without some horrid slander and bitter invective. (IX, 1.)

There is a structural problem which has to be dealt with in Book
IX. Booth has been released from confinement and will be
reunited with Amelia and his children. Therefore, a fresh
dilemma must be produced, and Fielding is equal to the
challenge. He is foresighted enough to produce the dilemma out
of the two problems which mere freedom does not answer: the
first is a livelihood, and the second the designs of Colonel James
upon Amelia. These are joined in the false friend's plot to get at
Amelia by getting Booth out of the way – that is, by helping him
to a commission in the West Indies. In order to make this
dilemma effective, Booth welcomes and Amelia resists the con-
ferment of this favour. Of course, the 'rights of the story'[36]
demand that Booth eventually discover what his wife labours so
assiduously to conceal; and Fielding makes the discovery occur
in circumstances wildly and indeed hilariously improbable: the
fact that *Amelia* is technically a comedy licenses him to behave
with the freedom which he successfully took upon himself in
writing not a domestic comedy but a comic epic poem in prose.

The fresh difficulty introduced is in the person of the lustful
Colonel James, whose real intentions are known to all the
principals except to Dr Harrison and to Booth himself. His first
sinister move is to invite the Booths and Dr Harrison to dine
with him. The actual problem is put succinctly by the narrator:
'To avoid giving any umbrage to her husband, Amelia was
forced to act in a manner which she was conscious must give
encouragement to the colonel; a situation which perhaps
requires as great prudence and delicacy as any in which the
heroic part of the female character can be exerted' (IX, 2). The

chief interest in the book and thus the central structural principle stems from this dilemma. Ultimately there is no way out of the difficulty in which Amelia finds herself. Some radical alteration has to be made – and it is only to tell Dr Harrison, who here comports himself with a good sense which his co-religionist Parson Adams does not possess. Dr Harrison realizes the importance of handling the situation carefully. But Booth must be apprised of the actual design of Colonel James – in stages gradual enough, however, so as not to be inflamed with rage against him. The first step is by way of Atkinson's night-mare about Colonel James's designs on Amelia, and the consequence, the near strangling of his wife, the spilled cherry brandy, the blurting out of the dream in Booth's hearing.

A sad relic of the old festive Fielding occurs in the well-known ninth chapter, in which the Booths, Dr Harrison, the young deacon and his father, and the Booth children go to Vauxhall. For it is a sour experience, after all; but instead of being a mere satire of high life, it begins as though festivity will have the central meaning. The seven members of the party go to Vaux-hall by way of St James's Church, for the purpose of worship. So far all is well done. And Vauxhall itself is delightfully sketched. But the happiness of the day is effaced by the insults to Amelia by the two rakes; the day is also clouded by the cowardice of the young deacon ('If I had had them in another place, I would have taught them a little more respect to the Church' – IX, 9). The feast, for Fielding, no longer works. In the final chapter – given over in the main to another discussion, this time of what sins a clergyman should specially avoid – disquiet is deepened: for the young deacon's father proves to be as despic-able as his son: both regard Dr Harrison contemptuously because he is, in their eyes, a failure.

In the final chapter of Book IX, Amelia urgently summons Dr Harrison to come and see her and advise her: the suspense, which has the look of having been established rather impromptu is however adequate to carry the reader forward to Book X, where at once the subject of her anxiety, and indeed the central focus of the book, are disclosed. 'The fact is, that my husband hath been presented by Colonel James with two tickets for a masquerade' (X, 1). This is indeed cause for alarm: it is also matter for Fielding's skilful manipulation of plot. Inharmoniously an atmosphere of gaiety pervades this book – in part because of the several mocking discussions which Dr Harrison has on the subject of learning in women, in part because the stratagem of Mrs Atkinson employed to foil any attempt on Amelia's virtue is foreshadowed at once in the exclamation, 'Fear nothing, my dear Amelia; two women will surely be too hard for one man' (X, 1).

Chapter 2 is called 'What happened at the masquerade': but Fielding's revelation here is by no means entire. Indeed, he conceals throughout the important fact that it is Mrs Atkinson who impersonates Amelia at the masquerade; equally, he conceals the sense of the conversation between the noble lord and the pretended Amelia, the upshot of which will be a lieutenant's commission for Serjeant Atkinson. Upon these concealments hang the lines of development and revelation of Book X. Even more subtle is the way in which Fielding arranges matters so that Booth discovers the full intent of the false-friend Colonel James. It must be done little by little, so that Booth will at last be able to believe in James's dastardy and at the same time will be able to school his outrage far enough as to be able to prevent himself from demanding satisfaction of the man. Finally, since this dilemma, set forth in Book IX, is now entirely cleared up, there must be another difficulty to propel the reader forward to the following book. This difficulty is brought about through the agency of that Captain George Trent, whose oblique but unmistakable proposals to Booth about how to employ Amelia to elicit favours from the peer, prove to be disquieting and then sinister.

In accordance with the requirement of comedy that the darkest hour precede the dawn and because of its darkness make the dawn seem the more radiant, the eleventh, and penultimate, book of *Amelia* takes both of the Booths to what seems like final ruin, Booth himself to the most evidently hopeless imprisonment, and Amelia to despair about her marriage. But Fielding has perhaps too much on his mind to be able to construct with the mastery which he displayed in *Joseph*

Andrews and, more especially, in *Tom Jones*. There is thus, in chapter 7 of this book, a diversion, and an unwelcome one from the viewpoint of the book's structure, when Booth pursues the maid who has stolen and sold some of Amelia's clothes; for here the bringing of the girl before the magistrate is made the occasion for the exhibition of a curious inequity in the law: the maid cannot be indicted for felony because she has been entrusted with her mistress's clothes, and because their value is under forty shillings.

If the concluding book of *Amelia* fails to satisfy, the reason must be sought of course in what has preceded. Accordingly, I hope that what I have said about the structure of the novel up to this point has shown up the weaknesses which are bound to become glaring in Book XII. As I consider the impression that this final book makes, I am struck by the fact that the character of Amelia emerges strong, clear, individual, and attractive – despite the general structural weakness. Amelia, the heroine, is a triumph over her creator's plot. It is not simply that the plot is artificial, contrived, unrealistic; so, designedly, are the plots of *Joseph Andrews* and *Tom Jones*. Nor do I complain that there is in *Amelia* a mixture of realistic treatment of detail and anti-verisimilar working out of structure. What makes the novel unsatisfactory is that Fielding abandons the comic epic poem in prose, a unique form which he brought to perfection in *Tom Jones*: Fielding abandons the form but does not alter his technique, so that there is in *Amelia* a disquieting failure to blend aim and art. Fielding means to write a novel about the trials of a fine woman in her domestic role. Instead, he succeeds in writing an episodic adventure story on which domesticity and latitudinarian piety are imposed: but I find the happy ending too huddled, too little prepared for, to be convincing. The luck and happiness which crown the disasters of Booth and the loyalty of Amelia – these joys, however they may compensate for the unhappiness and ill luck and imprudence of the action of *Amelia* itself, hardly seem to exhibit what Fielding meant to demonstrate in the course of this novel. Indeed, the outcome of the novel looks to embody a lesson exactly the reverse of that originally intended. When in the final chapter of the concluding book of *Amelia* we read, 'As to Booth and Amelia, Fortune seems to have made them large amends for the tricks she had played them in their youth' – we realize that despite his explicit intention, despite his creation in *Amelia* of an adequate heroine, despite great individual scenes, despite that generous humour which pervades the whole of *Amelia*, Fielding has in his last novel constructed what is, structurally and therefore ultimately, a failure.

Chapter 3

TABLEAU

'My picture is my stage, and men and women my players.'
HOGARTH

'H E who should call the ingenious Hogarth a burlesque painter', Fielding writes in the preface to *Joseph Andrews*, 'would in my opinion do him very little honour; for sure it is much easier, much less the subject of admiration, to paint a man with a nose, or any other feature, of a preposterous size, or to expose him in some absurd or monstrous attitude, than to expose the affections of men on canvas'. It has, I think, been sufficiently remarked that Fielding aimed to achieve in his novels what his friend Hogarth succeeded in depicting in the pictorial art.[1] And observation of Fielding's achievement discloses a juxtaposition of the pictorial and the dramatic, in such a way as to produce relatively static scenes that are in fact neither purely pictorial nor purely dramatic. Fielding's admiration for Hogarth, his experience as a playwright, his knowledge of stagecraft, his use of the device of the genial and chatty narrator – all these made possible the making of something new in fiction: novels which are a series of speaking pictures, but always so evidently composed, arranged, fabricated, that they establish and maintain, or help to maintain, the air of artifice which makes for a festive atmosphere.

In the chapter called 'The Festive Stance', I suggested that what *Joseph Andrews* exhibits is not truth to life but truth to art: that what Fielding achieves is not the representation of reality but that of a harmony which is ostentatiously designed.[2] The question which arose then (and which was not answered) was – what harmony? And it seems to me that the answer may emerge from a consideration of the series of dramatic and melodramatic tableaux. On the stage, Fielding was able to present scenes in which much happened. He liked nothing better than to hide one of the characters in a cupboard, while one or more of those in view discussed the absentee. The discovery of Square in Molly Seagrim's closet, and Lady Bellaston in Tom's closet – these devices are to be found in Fielding's own plays, as well as in comic drama tradition generally.[3] But on the stage Fielding never tried to represent anything so scenically complex as Joseph's encounter with the highway robbers, or the fight at the Dragon Inn, or the incident of Adams's near demise at the jaws of the dogs who mistake his wig for a rabbit, or even the night adventures in which Parson Adams and Beau Didapper crawl into the wrong beds. They are more than mere scenes: not perhaps more complicated in action than the techniques of stagecraft could allow, but more distant, and therefore morally different from anything which could be represented on the stage.

The first great tableau in *Joseph Andrews* is the melodrama of Joseph's robbery and the consequence (I, 12). Thematically it is not a pretty story, and under the festive superstructure the disagreeableness of the usual human response is never lost sight of – here or elsewhere in Fielding's work. Yet whenever the presentation looks as if it may be on the verge of becoming a criticism of life, the philanthropy of the narrator transfigures grim fact to tolerable art.[4]

The framing of the scenes of this chapter commences with a brace of paragraphs in the plain style. These describe Joseph's journey on foot at night toward Booby Hall and his encounter with the robbers, this central fact announced with the understatement of a subordinate clause at the end of a sentence – 'when he was met by two fellows in a narrow lane, and ordered to stand and deliver'.

Characteristically Fielding describes and thus by summary telescopes all of this scene except for some snatches of conversation that make the intended impact. For Fielding wants to get to the encounter between the naked Joseph in the ditch and the travellers in the stage-coach.

What is remarkable to me about this chapter is that, despite the brutality of the beating which Joseph suffers at the hands of the ruffians, there is no shock. It is not a pretty sight, Joseph being cudgelled, but neither is it specially horrifying. The reason, I think, lies in the choice of the words which Fielding will render in dialogue: 'You are cold, are you, you rascal!' one of the robbers says to Joseph after the latter has been stripped naked, 'I'll warm you with a vengeance'. If that expostulation were presented in a scene composed mainly of dialogue, it might succeed in having a shocking effect. But as it appears together with two even briefer remarks in a paragraph mainly consisting of the most ordinary tonality of straightforward exposition, its horrific force is lost – deliberately, I should think: it is framed and so becomes detached.

There follows a more dramatic scene, ironic because of the contrast between the pressing need of Joseph's nakedness and the leisurely, talkative selfishness of all the occupants of the coach. It would be possible after the coachman and the witty old gentleman and the lawyer and the lady's footman all refuse to assist Joseph – it would be possible to read this scene as simply condemnatory of human beings who refuse to be charitable. The fact that the postilion, 'a lad who hath been since trans-ported for robbing a hen-roost', helps Joseph, is the distinctive twist of the ironic knife. Thus may the scene be understood. And yet such an understanding would, I think, be incomplete, for it would reckon without the high-spirited exuberance of presenta-tion which certainly does not offer a condonation of violence and selfishness, but which does transfigure them. Thus the brutal indifference of the coachman is mitigated by what he actually says: 'Go on, sirrah,' he says to the postilion, 'we are confounded late, and have no time to look after dead men'. It is easy to believe that the coachman might feel thus, but difficult if not impossible to believe that he would reveal his feelings with such economical lack of disguise. Or, if by some special talent it might be possible for this man to utter his unacceptable sentiment straightforwardly, the presentation of it by Fielding to an audience which he knew would find such a sentiment dis-agreeable, is such as to render the scene hyperbolical.

That, at least, is the atmosphere of the scene as it seems to me; and the impression is reinforced by what the inhabitants of the coach say and do – or do not say. They all refuse to help, but the opprobrium attached to their refusal is qualified by the legalistic mumbo-jumbo uttered by the lawyer as this recital is placed over against Joseph's approach to the coach stark-naked. It is further qualified by what happens when Joseph is actually taken into the coach, for then the lawyer and the elderly gentleman make jests that are in fact amusing, particularly the lawyer's allusion to Joseph's nakedness vis-à-vis the lady in the coach. 'If Joseph and the lady were alone, he would be more capable of making a *conveyance* to her, as his *affairs* were not *fettered* with any *incumbrance*; he'd warrant he soon suffered a *recovery* by a writ of *entry*, which was the proper way to create *heirs in tail*'. And so forth.

This conversation occurs after the occupants of the coach have themselves been robbed, and it is almost as though the account of their robbery were put in here – it is passed over in a short paragraph – for the principal reason that it enables the lady to be revealed as a liar in her denial that she carried spirits with her. Surely the elevation of the Nantes *versus* Hungary Water incident to the level of the robbery is to re-scale the latter in such a way as to relieve the reader of the necessity of moral condemnation.

And the complications of what happens to Joseph at the Dragon Inn fix the temper of the robbery-and-rescue. To be sure, the surgeon is reluctant, Mrs Tow-wouse is shrewishly selfish – and Joseph may be dying. But lest we find this melodrama too moving or too coarse and thus intolerable, Fielding introduces a mock-heroic paragraph describing the dawn – 'Aurora now began to show her blooming cheeks over the hills, whilst ten millions of feathered songsters . . .': this is put up against the anything but heroic dialogue between Mr and Mrs Tow-wouse on the subject of shirts, charity, and Joseph's probably imminent death.

Another great scene in *Joseph Andrews* is the 'dreadful quarrel' which temporarily arrests the history of Leonora; the quarrel occupies a chapter by itself, chapter 5 of Book II. This interruption of an interpolation serves the dual purpose of connecting the young woman's history to the main plot and of reminding the reader of the festive nature of the recital. Absorption, and boredom, are forestalled by this break. And it is a long break, extending from the arrival of the travelling party at an inn to a departure some time later. During the sojourn at the inn there is, besides the battle itself, the massage of Joseph's leg by the landlady, the bilingual boastfulness of a man who has been to Italy, a legal discussion, a quarrel about gentility maintained between Mrs Slipslop and Miss Grave-airs, and (after Miss Grave-airs' departure) a discussion of Miss Grave-airs led by Mrs Slipslop. But it is the tableau of the actual battle that is especially memorable.

The altercation comes about because Joseph, having fallen beneath Adams's kneeling horse, has a bruised leg which the innkeeper makes light of. Adams is angered and speaks angrily. Hence the quarrel, which comes rapidly to the boil. In fact, Adams's innocence and naïveté are matched by a peppery temper and an effective fist. He lays out the innkeeper with a blow. Then Fielding begins to make the tableau, the greater part of it rendered in vividly visual terms. When the inn-keeper's wife flings the hog's blood at Adams, it 'trickled . . . in so large a current down to his beard, and all over his garments, that a more horrible spectacle was hardly to be seen, or even imagined'. It is a spectacle indeed, and it must be visualized on a canvas which is already interestingly full, containing as it does Joseph injured, the landlord laid out, the landlady frenzied – and Adams himself surprised into stillness. There is a static moment. This instantly becomes frenzy as Mrs Slipslop enters and flies at the landlady. Finally the scene is composed again, and the picture is drawn in its ultimate manifestation.

Poor Joseph could hardly rise from his chair; the parson was employed in wiping the blood from his eyes, which had entirely blinded him; and the landlord was but just beginning to stir; whilst Mrs Slipslop, holding down the landlady's face with her left hand, made so dexterous a use of her right, that the poor woman began to roar, in a key which alarmed all the company in the inn.

That is a crowded scene. But Fielding could paint a portrait as well, and again he insists that the reader *look*; in this respect he is the reverse of Jane Austen, who is chary of describing the appearance of her settings, her characters, her scenes – no doubt because talk, the subtle variation in tonality of speech, is the characterizing tool.[5] Fielding's employment of this device is skilful but far less subtle and, I think, far less important to him than the spectacular scenes depending upon physical description. Madam Slipslop's solecisms are notorious and inenarrable. Jane Austen never tried anything so broad.[6] Nor does she ever come so near sheer caricature as does Fielding in delineating the appearance of Adams who strides at a great pace along a country road, loses his way ('he had a wonderful capacity at these kinds of bare possibilities'), sits down to read his Aeschylus, and is approached by a gentleman who has shot a partridge.

Adams stood up and presented a figure to the gentleman which would have moved laughter in many; for his cassock had just again fallen down below his greatcoat, that is to say, it reached his knees, whereas the skirts of his greatcoat descended no lower than half-way down his thighs; but the gentleman's mirth gave way to his surprise at beholding such a personage in such a place. (II, 7.)

In another famous scene there is the combination of movement, interruption, stasis, and stylized description which renders wonderfully Fielding's mainly festive intent. This occurs in chapter 9 of Book II, the opening pages of which are devoted to a round encomium on bravery delivered with intolerant straightforwardness by the gentleman who at the first sign of danger takes flight. The matter is grim enough: a woman (later revealed to be Fanny Goodwill) is being cruelly assaulted, and Adams goes to her rescue. But Fielding contrives to make the scene morally tolerable. Adams 'levelled a blow at that part of the ravisher's head where, according to the opinion of the ancients, the brains of some persons are deposited', and so forth. It is the summoning up of classical authority that puts the requisite distance between event and reader. But morally this scene is such strong stuff that Fielding increases the distance by the repeated use of parenthesis: '. . . and which [the brains] he had undoubtedly let forth, had not Nature (who, as wise men have observed, equips all creatures with what is most expedient for them) taken a provident care (as she always doth with those she intends for encounters) to make this part of the head three times as thick as those of ordinary men'. Our attention is further diverted from the scene itself to its spectacular aspect by the mock-heroic simile introducing the following paragraph: 'As a game cock, when engaged in amorous toying . . .' – this to announce the fact that Fanny's would-be ravisher springs to his feet to do battle with Adams. In short, this whole scene is so carefully framed and re-framed, focused and re-focused, adjusted and re-adjusted that the reader must attend as carefully to the contriver as he does to what the contriver has contrived.

In another tableau, Adams is nearly devoured by some eager hounds who mistake him for a nearby rabbit (III, 6). As usual the preliminaries are important. The chapter is entitled 'Moral reflections by Joseph Andrews; with the hunting adventure, and Parson Adams's miraculous escape'. For several pages, Joseph gives a lecture on charity. It is well organized, thoughtful, and abstract; the style is formal and elevated but not orotund: the following sentence, with its generalizing diction, its balances, and its antitheses is characteristic: 'Indeed, it is strange that all men should consent in commending goodness, and no man endeavour to deserve that commendation; whilst, on the contrary, all rail at wickedness, and all are as eager to be what they abuse'. Stylistically, this opening section of the chapter belongs to the genre of Menippean satire – one of the four forms of prose fiction differentiated by Northrop Frye.[7] But, as if fearful that the speech will be taken on any but the comic level, the narrator intervenes toward the end of Joseph's lecture to reveal that Adams is asleep 'and had so been from the beginning of the preceding narrative'.

When this fact is discovered, dalliance succeeds oration as Joseph grasps Fanny's hand. Thus the overt moralism of the sermon is amiably qualified by sleep and caress. So much precedes the main business of this chapter, which is a panorama of hunting climaxed by the attack of a number of hounds upon the cassock and wig of the napping Parson Adams. The description is anything but straightforward; the narrator repeatedly nudges the reader into accepting the incident on the playful level. Thus, 'had not the motion of his [Adams's] body had more effect on him than seemed to be wrought by the noise, they [the dogs] must certainly have tasted his flesh, which delicious flavour might have been fatal to him'. To remind the reader of Adams's forgetfulness even at this moment – indeed, especially at this moment – is to ask for an amused rather than horrified reaction. Furthermore, and to make the incident even more pleasing, the narrator uses the device of classical justification to exonerate Adams from the possible charge of timidity in running away from the aroused dogs. Outrageous behaviour is thus matched with outrageous, though not outraged, rhetoric, and extravagance of action meets extravagance of utterance – an encounter which produces that restorative of sanity, laughter. So when the master of the pack determines to make Adams his quarry, 'swearing it was the largest jack-hare he ever saw', there ensues an apostrophe to the muse of biography: 'thou who, without the assistance of the least spice of literature, and even against his inclination, hast, in some pages of his book, forced Colley Cibber to write English; do thou assist me in what I find myself unequal to'.

Nor does Fielding proceed even after this invocation, the whole of which makes up a medium-sized paragraph, to a description of Joseph's valiant battle with the dogs. Instead, there is an even lengthier description and appreciation of Joseph's cudgel (right out of the *Iliad*, XVIII) followed by an apology by the narrator for his inability to produce a simile adequate to indicate Joseph's handsome figure and redoubtable behaviour. While the battle between Joseph and the dogs is under way, Fielding even addresses one of the hounds: 'O Ringwood! Ringwood . . .' Finally, the dogs having been vanquished, the squire and his companions draw together and face the valiant parson and Joseph in a fixed defiant portrait: 'both he and Adams brandished their wooden weapons, and put themselves into such a posture, that the squire and his company thought proper to preponderate before they offered to revenge the cause of their four-footed allies'. To complete the picture, Fanny approaches and unwittingly signalizes the next course of action, for the squire and his company, having regarded her 'in silent amaze', decide that she must be lured to the squire's house. But already – such is the comic confidence – we know she will escape the clutches of the wily men, and she will be unscathed. Thus does the representation of reality give way to the ideal rearrangement of festive comedy.

But in the game which is played at Parson Adams's expense at the Squire's house in the following chapter (III, 7) there is a failure of play. For it seems to me important as one of the scenes of the novel in which festivity threatens to give way to criticism: Adams's rage at his ill treatment is naked and sore. And yet it is only a ducking, the more likely to be acceptable (to the reader) in that it dramatizes once again the entire credulousness of Parson Adams in believing the extraordinary tale of Socrates and the King and Queen, as well as his vanity in eagerly taking Socrates' place in the 'game' of wisdom made up on the spot by the doctor. Moreover, there is sweet revenge in that Adams manages to dunk his host, who thereupon 'caught a cold by the accident, which threw him into a fever that had like to have cost him his life'. Such sentiment outside of the context of the chapter might seem fairly brutal, but its roughness is mitigated by the roughness with which Adams has been treated. Realism in detail is used to support operatic structure, and thus the chapter as a whole must be understood by the artificial light of Fielding's artificial design.

Finally, there is chapter 14 of Book IV, 'Containing several curious night-adventures, in which Mr Adams fell into many hair-breadth 'scapes, partly owing to his goodness, and partly to his inadvertency'.[8] This is superb farce, amusing because of a series of repeated and compounded mistakes. The essence of farce is a single situation happily ramified, doubled, and untwisted. The night adventures, accordingly (and in accordance with ancestral tradition) centre on the getting into several beds. It begins, quite ordinarily, with Beau Didapper's eagerness to ravish Fanny leading him by mistake into the bedroom of Mrs Slipslop, the discovery of the mistake, and Mrs Slipslop's crying rape. This is amusing enough. But when Parson Adams, responding to Mrs Slipslop's cries for help, rushes into the room and mistakes Didapper's soft skin for that of the lady (and thus releases him), and Slipslop's rough chin for that of the ravisher (and thereupon belabours her) – when this happens, the scene achieves comic splendour. Since all this takes place in the dark, there is little sense of scene as viewed here; there is, instead, a sense of black confusion. It is not until Lady Booby comes in with a candle that the incident becomes envisageable, and very laughably so.

At last, when everything seems to be mended, Adams returns, as he thinks, to his own room and gets quietly into bed – but he is in bed with Fanny. And so the comedy of discovery repeats itself. This is amusing enough as a repetition, and is in fact a much diminished version of the climactic incident in Mrs Slipslop's chamber. And the scene is most delightfully rounded off with Parson Adams's irremediable skepticism about what actually happened. He cannot quite persuade himself that in doing battle with Mrs Slipslop he was not engaged against a witch, and 'whilst he was dressing himself, he often asserted he believed in the power of witchcraft . . . and did not see how a Christian could deny it'.[9]

It is hard to believe that Fielding's handling of the scene could be improved on. Doubtless the maturity and experience – in literature as in life – which he brought to bear on the writing of *Joseph Andrews*, accounts for the skill, flexibility, and accomplishment of his scenic technique. And I should say that the scenes which I have just been discussing are of their kind almost unsurpassed in prose fiction. But *Joseph Andrews* is not quite so fine a novel as *Tom Jones* because the former has not the perfection of structure, the shape which can frame and expose those scenes with flawless balance. None the less, *Joseph Andrews* is very well put together and to damn it with the faint praise that as one of the first English novels it is remarkably good, is to make the mistake Dr Johnson did in the Preface to Shakespeare, in allowing Shakespeare to be good despite the disadvantage of having lived in a barbarous era, when drama was in its infancy.

Hogarth, to whom Fielding not once but repeatedly refers with approbation,[10] is an artist who puts two things before verisimilitude: exuberance, and art itself. The first of these is apparent in even the most satiric of his works. The art of Hogarth is ornate, even at times rococo, and, as the *Analysis of Beauty* demonstrates, founded on a belief in gracefulness. And it is in this light that I should like to examine several celebrated and structurally central scenes in *Tom Jones*, for an analysis in pictorial terms yields, it seems to me, a more accurate account of the matter than does an analysis in other terms. The examples I have chosen do not exhaust all possibilities in *Tom Jones* but they do suggest the range of Fielding's pictorial power.

Chapter 4 of Book II is entitled 'Containing one of the most bloody battles, or rather duels, that were ever recorded in domestic history'. The duel is the one-sided and indeed bloody altercation between Mr and Mrs Partridge. Already, in the foregoing chapter, Hogarth has been summoned up in order to help in the depiction of Mrs Partridge: 'Whether she sat to my friend Hogarth, or no, I will not determine; but she exactly resembled the young woman who is pouring out her mistress's tea in the third picture of the Harlot's Progress'. The central feature of chapter 4 is the battle itself, described as though it were a painting, and in its impact mainly static. Time stops and even motion, despite the frenzy, is arrested.

Her tongue, teeth, and hands fell all upon him at once. His wig was in an instant torn from his head, his shirt from his back, and from his face descended five streams of blood, denoting the number of claws with which nature had unhappily armed the enemy.

Mr Partridge acted for some time on the defensive only; indeed he attempted only to guard his face with his hands; but as he found that his antagonist abated nothing of her rage, he thought he might, at least, endeavour to disarm her, or rather to confine her arms; in doing which her cap fell off in the struggle, and her hair being too short to reach her shoulders, erected itself on her head; her stays, likewise, which were laced through one single hole at the bottom, burst open; and her breasts, which were much more redundant than her hair, hung down below her middle; her face was likewise marked with the blood of her husband; her teeth gnashed with rage; and fire, such as sparkles from a smith's forge, darted from her eyes. So that, altogether, this Amazonian heroine might have been an object of terror to a much bolder man than Mr Partridge.

Inevitably, an artist is at war with his medium – and so perhaps Hogarth and Fielding, fighting different, indeed opposite, campaigns, won victories the consequences of which are as nearly identical as in the circumstances they could be.

Hogarth's paintings and prints – both individually and in such series as *The Rake's Progress* and *The Harlot's Progress* and *Marriage à la Mode* – suggest movement. Fielding's scenes, though time-bound in a sense that no painting can ever be, suggest simultaneity. In the brace of paragraphs which I have just cited there is the sense not of the passage of time, not of developing action, but of gradual revelation of a depicted scene – it is as though one were looking carefully at a picture until the whole fell into shape. The reasons for this effect are, I think, that narrative matter is all but excluded, that pictorial detail is emphasized (and presented in the order, so to speak, of seeing: the hair, the breasts, the bloody face), and, finally, that this described scene occurs within a very thoroughly contrived framework. To this last matter it is now necessary to give some attention.

No chapter in a novel can stand by itself: if it can there is something wrong with it. To be sure, there are detachable episodes – the tale of the Man of the Hill, for instance – but these yield up their full meaning only as they inhabit a context. And one of the dangers of criticism is that of separating the inseparable, of talking about an intermediate chapter as though it had no environment. Every intermediate chapter must be bonded to what precedes and also to what follows it. Accordingly, therefore, Fielding employs syntactic and thematic glue here. The first two paragraphs of the Partridge battle chapter do perform this job with a certain deliberateness of narrative movement. I cite only the opening sentence.

For the reasons mentioned in the preceding chapter, and from some other matrimonial concessions, well known to most husbands, and which, like the secrets of freemasonry, should be divulged to none who are not members of that honorable fraternity, Mrs Partridge was pretty well satisfied that she had condemned her husband without cause, and endeavoured by acts of kindness to make him amends for her false suspicion. (II, 4.)

Here, as usual, the narrator calls attention to himself and by insisting that he is a jocular story-teller, reminds the reader that what he is telling is a story, that what is being presented is not fact but fiction.

Such is the outer rim of the frame of this chapter. There

follows a mock-pompous generalization ('Perfect calms at sea are always suspected by the experienced mariner to be the fore-runners of a storm') – made as though this were a fresh insight into the nature of things, together with a classical allusion (to Nemesis), and the affectation of humility: 'for it is our province to relate facts, and we shall leave causes to persons of much higher genius'. Then Fielding begins all over again with the same formula: 'Mankind have always taken great delight in knowing and descanting on the actions of others' – this to introduce, by way again of classical allusion, an anti-climax followed by another anti-climax: rapidly moving from the sentence I have just cited, by way of a barber's shop (for men) to a chandler's shop (for women). Surely all this preliminary is rococo framing, wonderfully effective in making the scantily reported scene that follows even more anticlimactic. And yet this too – giving Mrs Partridge fresh reason to suspect her husband of infidelity – is at the edge of the picture which Field-ing here intends to paint; and it is more or less absorbed in the paragraph following (as Mrs Partridge sorts out her suspicions). This in turn is followed by a mock-heroic simile, describing Mrs Partridge's feline fury before the battle.

Such, I submit, is the Fielding method; and consideration of the almost labyrinthine construction betrays the festive aim, as well as the pictorial effect. After the battle has taken place, the concluding paragraphs of the chapter serve the purpose of examining the consequences and anticipating what will take place in subsequent chapters.

The method makes for irony. Thus in chapter 5 of Book IV Sophia expects Tom to declare himself to her, when in fact his conversational preliminaries lead not to that but to a proposed intervention on behalf of Black George. Here the metaphor of tableau is insufficient. It is the subtlety and complexity of the handling of scene that I wish to look at. The chapter is called 'Containing matter accommodated to every taste', suggesting but not defining the variety of matter included. What 'happens' in this chapter is that Tom speaks to Sophia on behalf of Black George, she promises to intervene, does so, and is successful in her application to her father. Contrapuntally, and (as I say) ironically, runs the theme of love which this series of actions exhibits.

But the chapter is more complicatedly constructed than this course of action would seem to warrant. The dialogue between Tom and Sophia does not take place until more than half way through the chapter. In the preliminary section Fielding, besides establishing the connection of this to the foregoing chapter, enters into the book as narrator, jovially drawing the sting of the reader's possible involvement with the characters. For, after beginning with a Latin tag that can be made to apply to the relationship between Sophia and Tom, Fielding relates the history of her attachment to him and her corresponding dislike of Blifil. But, in the course of this recital occurs the generalizing, philosophizing intervention of the narrator, not, I think, to give these characters universal stature, but to objectify the action in such a way as to make it accord with the novel's economy of delight. The paragraph displays, it seems to me, fine narrative control, moral firmness, and objectifying skill. Fielding means to contrast Tom and Blifil. And the paragraph is, besides these things that I have mentioned, a statement of regret.

These two characters are not always received in the world with the different regard which seems severally due to either, and which one would imagine mankind, from self-interest, should show towards them. But perhaps there may be a political reason for it: in finding one of a truly benevolent disposition, men may very reasonably suppose they have found a treasure, and be desirous of keeping it, like all other good things, to themselves. Hence they may imagine that to trumpet forth the praises of such a person would, in the vulgar phrase, be crying Roast-meat, and calling in partakers of what they intend to apply solely to their own use. If this reason does not satisfy the reader, I know no other means of accounting for the little respect which I have commonly seen paid to a character which really does great honour to human nature, and is productive of the highest good to society. But it was otherwise with Sophia. She honoured Tom Jones, and scorned Master Blifil, almost as soon as she knew the meaning of those two words.

Such an elaborately worked comment helps to frame the small stretch of dialogue which is at the heart of the chapter.

But it is not the only piece of framework. There follows a recapitulated conversation between Honour and Sophia in which the girl's aversion to Blifil and affection for Tom are revealed; a narrative account of the young man's manly gallantry; Sophia's responsiveness; and then – still by way of preliminary – an account in the third person of the conversation in which Tom solicits 'her interest on behalf of the game-keeper'. The conversation which follows is quite brief – confirming, as it were, what the narrator has prepared us for. The ensuing scene, even briefer, is of Sophia persuading her father to withdraw charges against Black George and to give him help. Finally Fielding puts the scene in its place by moving away from it person by person, recording the reactions in turn of Blifil, Thwackum, Square, Allworthy – and finally Fortune herself.

In this light it is useful to examine the celebrated chapter 10 of Book V, whose long and quasi-exemplary title sinks when set against the brisk lightness – and brevity – of the chapter itself. The chapter is called: 'Showing the truth of many observations of Ovid, and of other more grave writers, who have proved beyond contradiction, that wine is often the forerunner of incontinency'. The centre of the chapter is Tom's retirement with Molly Seagrim and of his being 'found sitting' by Blifil and Thwackum. But neither Tom's comportment in the grove nor the consequence of being found sitting (this latter is taken up in the subsequent chapter) is described or dramatized here.

The chapter begins with a scant minimum of narration, Tom's going out to get some air after the refreshment he has treated himself to in celebration of Squire Allworthy's recovery from an apparently fatal illness. There follows a comment which serves as the tantalizing outer framework of the action which is to be the matter of the chapter: 'an accident happened, which with sorrow we relate, and with sorrow doubtless will it be read; however, that historic truth to which we profess so inviolable an attachment, obliges us to communicate it to posterity'. This is the sort of irony with which Fielding regularly announces the onset of a salty scene.

The frame is continued by a series of panels delightful because of the versatility which Fielding displays. There is a romantic setting 'in a most delicious grove . . . the gentle breezes fanning the leaves' – and so on, for the space of a paragraph; there is a heavily romantic soliloquy, in which Tom says, 'My Sophia, if cruel fortune separates us for ever, my soul shall dote on thee alone'; there is the intention of imitating Orlando in *As You Like It* and carving Sophia's name 'on every tree' – and thus, when Molly Seagrim appears, 'in a shift that was somewhat of the coarsest, and none of the cleanest, bedewed likewise with some odoriferous effluvia, the produce of the day's labour, with a pitchfork in her hand', the anti-climax is splendid, especially as the central incident is buried in a mocking reticence, in the shortest possible paragraph. 'Here ensued a parley, which, as I do not think myself obliged to relate it, I shall omit. It is sufficient that it lasted a full quarter of an hour, at the conclusion of which they retired into the thickest part of the grove'. Thereupon is a narrator's disquisition on 'that wonderful power of reason' and a pedantic treatment of drunkenness together with a reference to Fortune – this followed by the intervention of Blifil and Thwackum.

Of all the single and – as a matter of fact – highly individualized scenes in *Tom Jones*, surely the Battle of Upton is among the most compelling and memorable. A look at chapter 3 of Book IX (the full title is 'The arrival of Mr Jones with his lady at the inn; with a very full description of the battle of Upton') discloses a fine variety of tricks, at which Fielding shows himself to be a practised hand. There is a central tableau, that of the battle itself, and it is treated with some differences from certain of the other tableaux in *Tom Jones*.

What happens in the establishment of the framework for this tableau requires a different critical metaphor from that which I have used so far: 'overture' is, I think, the right word for what precedes the tableau itself, and 'heroic coda' is sufficiently pompous for what follows. Fielding delights in pressing forward with the narrative, and then breaking off for a slow, meandering passage that has its analogue in the music of Handel.

To say that Fielding is less than straightforward is to understate the truth. At the end of the chapter preceding the one with which I now wish to concern myself, Tom and the half-naked woman whom he has rescued have just arrived in Upton, the order of their travel being 'in the same manner as Orpheus and Eurydice marched heretofore. . . . However, he had better fortune than what attended poor Orpheus'. Surely the woman (not yet revealed as Mrs Waters, let alone Jenny Jones) is going to show her gratitude to the young man who has come to her help. Therefore, with a sure sense of construction, Fielding moves slowly toward that outcome, partly to whet our appetite and partly to evoke in us a response that is delighted because of the very paraphernalia which he can deploy with high skill.

Thus the chapter begins not with a narration of incident but with that frequently employed trick, an address to the reader. 'Though the reader, we doubt not, is very eager to know who this lady was, and how she fell into the hands of Mr Northerton, we must beg him to suspend his curiosity for a short time, as we are obliged, for some very good reasons which hereafter perhaps he may guess, to delay his satisfaction a little longer'. The allusion is multiple here – to Mrs Waters's relationship with Captain Waters (in that she is not really Mrs Waters at all), but more importantly to her relationship to Northerton, and – remotely – to the revealing and for a time alarming fact that she is Jenny Jones. Of course, the reader hardly stops to work this out here – and on a first reading he cannot: but it is one of the pleasures of a renewed acquaintance with *Tom Jones* that such *obiter dicta* are revealed to be germane to the main structure.

There follow two paragraphs of narration which set Tom and his 'dishevelled fair' down at the inn. Then comes the elaborate prologue to what will become by a process of accretion the battle itself. The narrator, with mock-solemn leisureliness, delineates the quality of the inn. 'Our travellers had happened to take up their residence at a house of exceeding good repute, whither Irish ladies of strict virtue, and many northern lasses of the same predicament, were accustomed to resort in their way to Bath'. The word 'predicament' has a fine cutting edge here, and turns the phrase 'Irish ladies of strict virtue' into an oxymoron that points the way toward the outcome of the relationship between Tom and the lady as well as to the hypocrisy implicit in the landlady's insistence upon virtue. Here the narrator soars into classical allusion.

> Not that I would intimate that such strict chastity as was preserved in the temple of Vesta can possibly be maintained at a public inn. . . . But to exclude all vulgar concubinage, and to drive all whores from within the walls, is within the power of every one. This my landlady very strictly adhered to, and this her virtuous guests, who did not travel in rags, would very reasonably have expected of her.

Here is Fielding at his best, and at his best because intention and outcome so happily coincide: social criticism, unsparingly straightforward, is contained within an aesthetic framework that curbs outrage.

By this time it is clear that a contest is in the making, but Fielding does anything rather than hurry toward the catastrophe. After an oblique and delightful meditative sentence on the subject of Tom's intention,[11] Fielding gives a roundabout account of the landlady's equipment – a broomstick – for preventing the intention from being fulfilled. Then, after Fielding records Tom's demands for clothing to cover the lady, there ensues a generalization (with appropriate reference to *Othello*) about the provocation caused by 'solicitations of extraordinary offices of kindness on behalf of those very persons with whom we are highly incensed'.

Nor is the battle to be joined yet. The landlady's formidable tongue is the theme of the two succeeding paragraphs; only when the landlord takes sides against Tom does the conflict become physical. The tableau itself, when it comes, is drawn with simplicity, so that the basic structure is established when there are but four antagonists. The action – though furious – is for a moment arrested, in such a way as to fix the picture.

> My landlord . . . fell to with his fist, and the good wife, uplifting her broom and aiming at the head of Jones, had probably put an immediate end to the fray, and to Jones likewise, had not the descent of this broom been prevented – [Note that Fielding deliberately arrests the action in order to draw the picture] – not by the miraculous intervention of any heathen deity, but by a very natural though fortunate accident, viz., by the arrival of Partridge, who entered the house at that instant (for fear had caused him to run every step from

the hill), and who, seeing the danger which threatened his master or companion (which you choose to call him), prevented so sad a catastrophe, by catching hold of the landlady's arm as it was brandished aloft in the air.

The interrupted movement of the final sentence of this paragraph makes deliberately static the battle-scene tableau.

The basic picture having been established, new recruits now join in the fight – not merely Partridge, but also Mrs Waters herself, and Susan the Amazonian chambermaid. But the movement is all non-progressive. And Fielding will keep it from becoming anything else: he contains the scene within epic description. 'Now the dogs of war being let loose, began to lick their bloody lips; now Victory, with golden wings, hung hovering in the air'. and so forth: all this precedes the account of the outcome, which is the cessation of battle on the arrival of a coach and four.

Finally, there is chapter 7 of Book XV. Fielding constructs it with such guile that he who reads on the run may suppose it simply to be taken over from the drama of the third-person-in-concealment scene. It begins, after a four-line opening paragraph of narration, with Mrs Honour's hectic and disorganized recital to Tom. As in *Romeo and Juliet* the dignity of servants must be ministered to; and as in *Romeo and Juliet* the necessary facts are contained, though in disorder, within the discourse. After some time, the narrator, not Tom, takes the floor. 'Whether Jones gave strict attention to all the foregoing harrangue, or whether it was for want of any vacancy in the discourse, I cannot determine; but he never once attempted to answer, nor did she stop, till Partridge came running into the room, and informed him that the great lady was upon the stairs'.

Narrative ensues, partly no doubt for the purpose of compression, and Fielding is able to do here what no playwright is capable of. He is able to backtrack, and take the reader into Tom's mind. Lady Bellaston being about to enter the room, Mrs Honour is thrust behind Tom's bed. 'The hurry in which Jones had been all day engaged on account of his poor landlady and her family, the terrors occasioned by Mrs Honour, and the confusion into which he was thrown by the sudden arrival of

Lady Bellaston, had altogether driven former thoughts out of his head'.

And during the opening conversation between Lady Bellaston and Tom, Fielding again interrupts, once more partly to compress but, and equally as it seems to me, to incorporate the dialogue and the scene within the novelistic framework. When Lady Bellaston tells Tom, 'You might at this instant sit for the picture of Adonis', Fielding interposes as chatty and generalizing commentator: 'There are certain words of provocation which men of honour hold can properly be answered only by a blow': this is the sort of remark which, so to speak, takes the characters off the stage and puts them in the novel.

The remainder of this chapter includes Nightingale's arrival drunk, in which state he frightens Lady Bellaston into scurrying behind the curtain where Mrs Honour is hidden. Inevitably there is highly spiced and highly amusing recriminatory exchange between the two women, ending on a note of quiet promise: Mrs Honour's mouth is to be sealed by her becoming the object of Lady Bellaston's benefaction. But dialogue and summary narration are followed by narrator's comment, with which the chapter is framed and concluded.

Thus ended this unfortunate adventure to the satisfaction only of Mrs Honour; for a secret (as some of my readers will perhaps acknowledge from experience) is often a very valuable possession; and that not only to those who faithfully keep it, but sometimes to such as whisper it about till it comes to the ears of everyone except the ignorant person who pays for the supposed concealment of what is publicly known.

The best scenes in *Amelia* occur at the beginning of the novel, when Booth is in prison. The double-narrative device (Miss Matthews relating her story to Booth, and vice versa) within the larger framework of commencement *in medias res* followed by flashback – these are instruments well within Fielding's range of competence: so well within his range that we are liable to forget how easy it would be for the machinery to lumber. But there is something wrong, not with the mechanism itself of the opening sections of *Amelia*, but with the aim of the novel as a whole: it is a divided aim. Fielding is trying to criticize and celebrate at the same time. The prisons are bad, Miss Matthews is a temptress, Booth is in desperate straits: but depiction in critical terms gives way to the exuberance of the flirtation which Miss Matthews successfully begins with Booth; and, at the beginning of Book IV, the seduction by Miss Matthews of Booth has an ambiguous moral ring. In short, the first three books of *Amelia* taken by themselves are brilliant comedy, but, as I have already pointed out, they are not adequately developed and resolved. Fielding has abandoned his aesthetic of the feast, begun to introduce his exacerbated social criticism into the comic epic romance: and the elements will not mix. *Amelia* is a failure not in detail but in whole conception.

And yet it would be unfair to *Amelia* to dismiss it thus, and I now want to look very briefly at several of the tableaux contained in the novel, to show that Fielding remained master of this important technique, but employed it in impossible circumstances. I should like to show also how these efforts at static spatial composition fit into the larger schemes provided in their contexts.

In the second book of *Amelia* Booth relates to Miss Matthews the tale of his courtship of Amelia and of his elopement with her. In the course of his suit to the young lady he contrives to be conveyed to the house in a hamper.[12] The tone established, therefore, is agreeably and indeed hilariously comic. When this contrivance, like Falstaff's, has ended disastrously, sheer elopement is the course chosen, taken, and successfully taken, until, in chapter 7, Mrs Harris catches up with the fleeing couple. When the news is brought that Mrs Harris is at the door, Fielding draws an excellent picture, Hogarthian in its sense of movement within the fixture of pose and stance. He even invites the reader, in an adjectival phrase ('with the countenance in which ghosts are painted') to think of tableau:

'Amelia turned pale as death . . . indeed, I feared she would have fainted, if I could be said to fear, who had scarce any of my senses left, and was in a condition little better than my angel's.

'While we were both in this dreadful situation, Amelia fallen back in her chair with the countenance in which ghosts are painted, myself at her feet with a complexion of no very different colour, and nurse screaming out and throwing water in Amelia's face, Mrs Harris entered the room. At the sight of this scene she threw herself likewise into a chair, and called immediately for a glass of water.'

This excellent and economical piece of painting has the effect of completing one aspect of the action. Thereafter, Booth and Amelia 'proceeded directly to church'. But it is the inclusion of the tableau within the narrative of the elopement which defines its meaning as festive.

Perhaps more conventional – because of the Virgilian parallel – but no less important for the meaning of the novel as a whole is the tableau of the storm at sea contained in 'A sea piece' (III, 4). Booth is *en route* to Gibraltar and he very much misses his wife. For the classically educated reader there is surely nothing out of the way in having a storm at sea, but there is, it seems to me, a certain exuberance in relation, by Booth to Miss Matthews:

'A violent storm arose at north-east, which soon raised the waves to the height of mountains. The horror of this is not to be adequately described to those who have never seen the like. The storm began in the evening, and, as the clouds brought on the night apace, it was soon entirely dark; nor had we, during many hours, any other light than what was caused by the jarring elements, which frequently sent forth flashes, or rather streams, of fire; and whilst these presented the most dreadful objects to our eyes, the roaring of the winds, the dashing of the waves against the ship and each other, formed a sound altogether as horrible for our ears; while our ship, sometimes lifted up, as it were, to the skies, and sometimes swept away at once as into the lowest abyss, seemed to be the sport of the winds and seas. The captain himself almost gave up all for lost, and expressed his apprehension of being inevitably cast on the rocks of Scilly, and beat to pieces.'

This is not, I think, an especially distinguished or original piece of description; but it is gratuitous only if we forget that the relation by Booth of his tale to Miss Matthews is, in part, an unconscious flirtation by Booth, and Miss Matthews's posture as auditor is that of concealed coquette. The horrific is precluded from being sentimental because of the playful context in which it appears.

Atkinson's nightmare (IX, 6), which is extremely important in the intricate plotting of *Amelia*, is a device used by Fielding to make possible the serjeant's revelation of his suspicions about Colonel James's intentions vis-à-vis Amelia. The touch of tableau provided in the narration of this event gives emphasis to the improbability of the whole incident. Atkinson has

a most horrid dream, in which he imagined that he saw the colonel by the bedside of Amelia, with a naked sword in his hand, and threatening to stab her instantly unless she complied with his desires. Upon this the serjeant started up in his bed, and, catching his wife by the throat, cried out, '—n you, put up your sword this instant, and leave the room, or by heaven I'll drive mine to your heart's blood!'

This scene is perhaps better visualized as happening on the stage than on a canvas; but I have wanted to include it here because of its fantastic quality, and if it is not quite a tableau within the framework of my definition, it has something of the effect of tableau, especially in its consequence, which is Atkinson's snatching up, in order to revive his wife, a bottle not of water but of cherry brandy. And then the comically distressful scene is fully available for pictorial representation.

The serjeant had no sooner taken the candle than he ran with it to the bedside. Here he beheld a sight which almost deprived him of his senses. The bed appeared to be all over blood, and his wife weltering in the midst of it. Upon this the serjeant, almost in frenzy, cried out, 'O Heavens! I have killed my wife! I have stabbed her! I have stabbed her!'

Among the English novelists the pictorial talent repeatedly shows itself, and it is a subject not enough examined. Even Egdon Heath is taken for granted: admired, wondered at, and accepted. But while assent is readily given to the notion that, except perhaps in Scott, the depiction subserves or creates the larger purposes of the novel in which it appears, the set pieces of pictorial work have generally been seen only as set: why they are set, and in a certain way, has been a question at best taken for granted. To be sure, the scenes which I have been looking at in this chapter are among the most famous in Fielding, and I do not want to suggest that no one has looked at them before and found them festive: I only want to articulate what no doubt many a common reader observes, but does not phrase – and perhaps does not connect with the central purposes of Fielding's fiction.

Chapter 4

CHARACTER AS BAS RELIEF

'I am seldom the same Man for a whole Day together.'
JOB VINEGAR

ADAMS AND THE ANATOMY OF PRIESTHOOD

IN the important 'Essay on the Knowledge of the Characters of Men', Fielding writes of 'that very early and strong inclination to good or evil, which distinguishes different dispositions in children, in their first infancy . . . so manifest and extreme a difference of inclination or character, that almost obliges us, I think, to acknowledge some unacquired, original distinction, in the nature or soul of one man, from that of another' (Henley ed., XIV, 281, 282). To denominate such a view predestination or fatalism is doubtless useful deployment of metaphor. But it is no more than that, and it may confuse the issue by suggesting that Fielding is more consistent and therefore likely to be more doctrinaire than the evidence of his life and work will permit us to suppose. Fielding, like everyone else, thought differently on various subjects at different times, and contradictorily about some matters at the same time. He was a communicant of the Church of England who would and did argue ardently in favour of free will. He also believed in 'unacquired, original distinction'. This is a more accurate though more diffuse view of Fielding than is the assertion that he is fatalistic. And enough, I hope, has now been said to begin to make sense of his methods of characterization.

When in *Joseph Andrews* Fielding writes, 'I describe not men, but manners; not an individual, but a species' (III, 1), he is at once denying that in his fiction are to be found representations of living persons, and at the same time claiming that his characters are 'taken from Life' in that they are universal types. On this subject Ian Watt's comparison of Fielding and Richardson is illuminating.

146

The scope of the word 'manners' has dwindled so drastically in the last few centuries – no doubt as a result of the way individualism has reduced the areas in which identity of thought and action is generally expected – that the phrase 'characters of manners' no longer means very much. It can perhaps be best explained in terms of the contrast with Richardson's 'characters of nature'. Richardson's literary objective . . . is not so much character – the stable elements in the individual's mental and moral constitution – as personality: he does not analyse Clarissa, but presents a complete and detailed behavioural report on her whole being: she is defined by the fullness of our participation in her life. Fielding's purpose, on the other hand, is analytic: he is not interested in the exact configuration of motives in any particular person's mind at any particular time but only in those features of the individual which are necessary to assign him to his moral and social species. He therefore studies each character in the light of his general knowledge of human behaviour, of 'manners', and anything purely individual is of no taxonomic value. Nor is there any need to look inside: if, as Johnson said, Fielding gives us the husk, it is because the surface alone is usually quite sufficient to identify the specimen – the expert does not need to assay the kernel.[1]

Writing with superb erudition of the nude as a form rather than as a subject of art, Sir Kenneth Clark reminds us of Aristotle's dictum, 'Art completes what Nature cannot bring to a finish. The artist gives us knowledge of Nature's unrealized ends'.[2] This idealizing tendency thrusts itself, Sir Kenneth rightly reminds us, from many assumptions. Indeed the dictum can be used as the outcome of different premises, even contradictory ones. I am struck by the quotation because I think it can without strain point the way to certain assumptions behind Fielding's practice. Possessing a fairly simple and not wholly consistent idea of character, and convinced at the same time of the prevalence of the selfish motive (vanity and hypocrisy are all but universal), Fielding decided – or so his practice would seem to indicate – to project mankind as a stylized and therefore morally tolerable artifact. If this be idealism, no doubt the most will be made of it. But I cannot find much preaching of idealism in Fielding. He thought too ill of mankind to be able to idealize, except as a desperate antidote to the facts of life – that is to say, he idealizes only in his art as art.

In *Joseph Andrews*, and in the other novels as well, Fielding enlarges the boundaries of fiction. In his dramas he had fallen in with stage tradition. Apart from the characters who normally inhabit drawing-rooms in drawing-room comedies – samplings of high-life people and a footman or two, as in *The Modern Husband* – there is the sprinkling of bawds and rakes in the farces, as in that most famous of all Fielding plays, *Tom Thumb*. Besides, there is a thrust at politicians, as in *Pasquin*, the satire that helped to bring about the Licensing Act. But there is not the sense, at least in *reading* Fielding's plays, of the panorama of society that is central to all the novels.

The new departure which Fielding took, and he proclaims his originality in the Preface to *Joseph Andrews* is 'the introduction of persons of inferior rank'. Needless to say, inferior persons had been presented before, most notably by Defoe – not to mention the inferior Pamela Andrews. But Defoe could not write about the higher ranks, and Richardson's efforts in this direction produced uneven results. Fielding was by birth and education an aristocrat, he was by temperament gregarious and by experience widely acquainted with men and women of many ranks. And he is the first writer in English, excepting only Chaucer and Shakespeare, to communicate the sense of the whole sweep of English society.

To look at this range in *Joseph Andrews* is to observe that Fielding despised the ordinary representatives of the higher ranks (the two gentlemen who swear and bet about a dog at the Dragon Inn (I, 16); the French-English Bellarmine; and Beau Didapper), detested the rougher sort of representatives of the lowest ranks (the thieves, the concupiscents, the mercenary constables and innkeepers); but he reserved his special scorn for the *arrivistes*, the persons eagerly on the make, or those who on the other hand are desperately holding on to a greater share of gentility than their situation warrants.

The 'dissertation concerning high people and low people' in *Joseph Andrews* makes this point. He singles out 'those bordering nearly on each other, to wit, the lowest of the high, and the highest of the low, [who] often change their parties according to place and time'. Then, constructing a ladder from postilion to sovereign, he concludes that 'to a philosopher the question might only seem, whether you would choose to be a great man at six in the morning, or at two in the afternoon' (II, 13).[3] This most interesting chapter points not to any egalitarian tendency in Fielding, but rather to a quite pointed distaste for much of humanity. In any event, there is sufficient evidence that Fielding finds the structure of society acceptable.[4] The passage recording Parson Trulliber's astonishment is a case in point.

Suppose a stranger, who entered the chambers of a lawyer, being imagined a client, when the lawyer was preparing his palm for the fee, should pull out a writ against him. Suppose an apothecary, at the door of a chariot containing some great doctor of eminent skill, should, instead of directions to a patient, present him with a potion for himself. Suppose a minister should, instead of a good round sum, treat my Lord –, or Sir –, or Esq. –, with a good broomstick. Suppose a civil companion, or a led captain, should, instead of virtue, and honour, and beauty, and parts, and admiration thunder vice and infamy, and ugliness, and folly, and contempt, in his patron's ears. Suppose when a tradesman first carries in his bill, the man of fashion should pay it; or suppose, if he did so, the tradesman should abate what he had overcharged, on the supposition of waiting. In short – suppose what you will, you never can nor will suppose anything equal to the astonishment which seized on Trulliber, as soon as Adams had ended his speech [revealing that he is a parson rather than a pig-dealer]. (II, 14.)

Relish and disdain are two of the spices which make the flavour of this passage. But there is no revolutionary fervour, little even to suggest that society is remediable within the 'given' framework, let alone fundamentally alterable. Joseph, it will be remembered, expresses himself as content with his lot; reading has not made him ambitious for a higher rank in life; and Parson Adams applauds the boy's acquiescence (I, 3). Ambition leads to the vanity or the hypocrisy of a Pamela, or to the *arrivisme* of the father of Mrs Graveairs, who has risen from postilion to steward and is the worse for having thus risen (II, 5). Finally, the not altogether logical corollary to Fielding's assertion that 'the highest life is much the dullest' is the fact that the lowest is much the most charitable. It is the postilion who lends Joseph a coat after the robbery, when no one else will help.

In possession of certain convictions about the nature of human nature, ambitious to tell the truth about all kinds of men, confronted with the challenge which the comic epic romance both makes and offers, Fielding chooses – or invents – what can be called the technique of bas relief. I have to use this rather than E. M. Forster's metaphors, because Fielding's characters are in some senses 'flat' and in others 'round'.[5] Fielding's is the method of scant detail – an economical number of strokes serving to bring the characters not to life but to liveliness. Verisimilitude is scamped and indeed scorned. In *Joseph Andrews* the most nearly rounded portrait of them all, that of Parson Adams, is made of a handful of details – pipe, crabstick, snapping fingers, and Aeschylus.

Assuredly Fielding owes much here to his training in the theatre; he was not only a playwright but also a manager. Furthermore, he had his greatest successes when he was at his most outrageous: his farces and burlesques are far superior to his domestic comedies and his political satires. Thus when he comes to writing novels he applies his chisel boldly. He works with the address of a portraitist who is adept at suggesting movement where little or none exists and of suggesting stasis even in scenes of frenzy. Nor is he afraid to exaggerate: Mrs Slipslop

was not at this time remarkably handsome; being very short, and rather too corpulent in body, and somewhat red, with the addition of pimples in the face. Her nose was likewise rather too large, and her eyes too little; nor did she resemble a cow so much in her breath, as in two brown globes which she carried before her; one of her legs was also a little shorter than the other, which occasioned her to limp as she walked. (I, 6.)

This is broad: indeed it is very broad – and it is also typical of Fielding's method, so richly exploitable in fiction. For the playwright is seldom permitted the luxury of selective description on the scale that the novelist can take for granted, nor can the playwright often find actors who perfectly exemplify what he intends in the way of characterization. And Fielding often pauses to bring a character before our eyes. Leaving Parson

Adams out of consideration for the moment, Fielding's notable word portraits include Joseph (I, 9), Mrs Tow-wouse (I, 15), Betty the chambermaid (I, 18), Lindamira (II, 6), Fanny (II, 13), Parson Trulliber (II, 14), and Beau Didapper (IV, 9). It is possible, in fact it is desirable, to visualize these characters, to see them as physical creatures, and yet so designedly extravagant are the descriptions that we tend to see them as Hogarthian figures. For there is a relationship, repeatedly insisted on by Fielding, between appearance and reality.[6]

Fielding's genius permits him to choose telling and memorable details: Parson Trulliber

was liable to many jokes, his own size being, with much ale, rendered little inferior to that of the beasts he sold. He was indeed one of the largest men you should see, and could have acted the part of Sir John Falstaff without stuffing. Add to this, that the rotundity of his belly was considerably increased by the shortness of his stature, his shadow ascending very near as far in height, when he lay on his back, as when he stood on his legs. . . . He had a stateliness in his gait, when he walked, not unlike that of a goose, only he stalked slower. (II, 14.)

This fine cartoon is Fielding at his best. Morally also it is exemplary of Fielding's stance. Trulliber is an evil man, or would be in almost any but Fielding's hands. But it is impossible to condemn too solemnly a man who stalks slower than a goose and looks like Falstaff.

Beau Didapper is treated with more open scorn. He 'was a young gentleman of about four foot five inches in height. He wore his own hair, though the scarcity of it might have given him sufficient excuse for a periwig. His face was thin and pale; the shape of his body and legs none of the best, for he had very narrow shoulders and no calf; and his gait might more properly be called hopping than walking' (IV, 9). As always, moral stature stands in a direct relationship to physical appearance; and what is true of Didapper is equally applicable to the others among Fielding's characters, namely that physical shortcoming signifies moral inadequacy.[7]

But what sets the limit on my metaphor of bas relief is the auditory sense which Fielding brings to his characterization. Adams's fingers audibly snap; Mrs Slipslop's volubility overwhelms; Parson Trulliber's 'voice was loud and hoarse, and his accents extremely broad' (II, 14); Beau Didapper 'could talk a little French, and sing two or three Italian songs' (IV, 9).

It is not surprising that Fielding as the author of several plays with music – in the style of *The Beggar's Opera* – should pay attention to the ears. Nor is it surprising that harmoniousness should indicate a quality of the soul. But to consider this fact together with the significance of the physical descriptions of the characters is to understand that Fielding's practice here is deliberately stylized. Hence Joseph's sweet voice, 'so extremely musical, that it rather allured the birds than terrified them', occasioned his withdrawal from the fields to the dog kennels, where his voice prevented him from being a useful whipper-in, 'the dogs preferring the melody of his chiding to all the alluring notes of the huntsman' (I, 2). Indeed the reunion of Fanny and Joseph takes place by way of a song which Fanny overhears (II, 12).

But the central figure, and the commanding interest, of *Joseph Andrews* is Parson Adams. Fielding himself recognized this fact, which is so obvious that it would not be worth underscoring if he were the chief titular as well as the actual hero. But the reader knows from the preface of his central importance. Adams, Fielding writes there, is 'designed a character of perfect simplicity'. Surely his outstanding characteristic, and the hallmark of his heroism, is simplicity; and when Fielding says that this character 'is not to be found in any book now extant', he is not so much claiming originality for himself as he is repudiating the mendacious romance writers. Adams belongs very much to his era, as recourse to Dr Johnson shows. In his *Dictionary*, Johnson lists five senses of the word 'simplicity', all but the last favourable, and even the last is at worst venial. Adams personifies in every particular these five senses of the word 'simplicity'.

The first of Johnson's meanings for 'simplicity' is: 'Plainness; artlessness; not subtility; not cunning; not deceit'. That is to say, guilelessness in the most ameliorative sense of the word. Simplicity is a laudable naïveté. To this Parson Adams conforms, not in obedience to his will against contrary impulses, but because he is by nature a simple man. Fielding is explicit on this central point. Adams, he says,

> was . . . a man of good sense, good parts, and good nature; but was at the same time as entirely ignorant of the ways of this world as an infant just entered into it could possibly be. As he had never any intention to deceive, so he never suspected such a design in others. He was generous, friendly, and brave to an excess; but simplicity was his characteristic: he did, no more than Mr Colley Cibber, apprehend any such passions as malice and envy to exist in mankind. (I, 3.)

Johnson's second definition of 'simplicity' is: 'Plainness; not subtility; not abstruseness'. That is to say, uncomplicatedness – and again the sense of the word is ameliorative. Moses Primrose may be gulled into buying shagreen spectacles, and Dr Primrose may even more naïvely allow himself to be hoodwinked – but it is the Moseses and Dr Primroses who bear away the victory after all. Thus Adams fails to run away when he is apprehended as a thief; he 'trusted rather to his innocence than his heels' (II, 10); his uncomplicated certainty of his own innocence leads him into difficulty in the short run, and costs him the trouble and embarrassment of his encounter with the analphabetic country justice, the ignorant pedant, and the pretentious (and equally ignorant) clergyman; but justice at last prevails, Adams being recognized as a gentleman – and uncomplicatedness succeeds.

Johnson's third definition of 'simplicity' applies to dress: 'Plainness; not finery', and it is an understatement to call Adams's dress plain, though plain it surely is – owing not merely to conviction but also to poverty and to forgetfulness. Adams's dress begins by being plain enough, and it is never fine. But it is often mussed, and fussed, more complicated in impact and effect than in intention. The narrator, with comic despair, repeatedly undertakes the description of this truly emblematic failure to be fine:

> It is not perhaps easy to describe the figure of Adams; he had risen in such a violent hurry, that he had on neither breeches nor stockings; nor had he taken from his head a red spotted handkerchief, which by night bound his wig, that was turned inside out, around his head. He had on his torn cassock, and his greatcoat; but as the remainder

of his cassock hung down below his greatcoat, so did a small stripe of white, or rather whitish, linen, appear below that; to which we may add the several colours which appeared on his face, where a long piss-burnt beard served to retain the liquor of the stone-pot, and that of a blacker hue which distilled from the mop. (III, 12.)

Adams's appearance is dégagé because he neglects the things of this world. Furthermore, he becomes entangled in and confused by worldliness, just as he does by and in his clothes. And it is perhaps a wonder that instead of being revulsed by this picture of the stained and dirt-covered parson, we are moved to laugh. But it is a wonder carefully designed; that is to say it is ridiculously larger than life, and so elicits our pleased laughter rather than the wish that the man could have a bath and that his clothes could be washed.

Johnson's fourth definition of 'simplicity' is: 'Singleness; not composition; state of being uncompounded'. In an age which celebrated the nobility of the savage, on account of his lack of exposure to civilizations' corrupting complexity, this 'state of being uncompounded' was certain to have an appeal. Such is Adams's classical learning: it is uncompounded with the experience or on the whole with the literature of the present day. Thus he uses his knowledge of the classics (and though it is thorough it is also simple) to combat the greater simplicity of the gentleman who discourses on courage but at first fright runs away (II, 9). His other use of classical learning is to wax philosophical when it is necessary to accept the inevitable. So when he discovers that his sermons have been left behind and that consequently the whole purpose of his journey is also left behind, he says to Joseph, ' "This disappointment may perhaps be intended for my good." He concluded with a verse out of Theocritus, which signifies no more than, "that sometimes it rains, and sometimes the sun shines" ' (II, 2).

'Weakness; silliness': this is the only pejorative sense in which 'simplicity' is defined by Johnson. Yet Parson Adams, though he is depicted as silly, also is revealed as the more amiable for this very silliness. Johnson, anyway, has a more stringent attitude toward weakness of the simple sort than does Fielding; the *Dictionary's* example under 'Simple. 3' from Proverbs demonstrates this point: 'The *simple* man believeth every word; but the prudent man looketh well to his going'.

It is, I think, fair to say that the direction in which simplicity leads is toward the dark: one of the chief hallmarks of Adams's character is opacity. 'O Mr Adams,' says Madam Slipslop 'people that don't see all, often know nothing' (II, 3). She is remarking on his ignorance of Lady Booby's real character, but within the context the exclamation ironically underscores Adams's ignorance of Slipslop's own character – for she has been criticizing Lady Booby for having stooped to try to conquer a footman, meanwhile striving to give the impression that she herself is above that sort of thing. Adams may be more subtle here than I am supposing, he may merely be remaining quiet about what Joseph has said to him about her. But this, I think, is unlikely; I suspect Joseph himself has been reticent: there was good reason for Joseph to explain his departure from Lady Booby's household, and this he could do by hinting at her importunities; but to mention Slipslop's as well would have been to boast. All the reader positively knows about what Joseph has revealed is said when Adams questions Joseph at the Dragon Inn. 'It would', the narrator says, 'be impertinent to insert a discourse which chiefly turned on the relation of matters already well known to the reader' (I, 14). The important fact is the opacity itself, an aspect of the simplicity which makes Parson Adams succeed where successful people fail.

Stuart M. Tave mistakes the significance of Adams, as it seems to me, when he remarks of the parson:

Not to apprehend the existence of such passions as malice and envy is a considerable imperfection, weakening, as it does, the effectiveness of virtue; the innocence that is unaware of the conflict between its own ideal motives and the resistant reality of the world in which it must act is in a continual state of blind confusion. Adams, moreover, is unaware of the conflict between his ideals and some of his own moral limitations, particularly vanity. And Fielding, whose heart is not so soft as many of his later readers who fell in love with the parson believed, subjects his man to a variety of ignoble, physical punishments to make the lesson quite clear.[8]

To argue thus is to scamp the fact that in eighteenth-century terms Adams's opaque simplicity was something to be not merely condoned but approved – and, by Fielding, celebrated. Adams, Fielding tells us, 'never saw farther into people than they desired to let him' (II, 10). This is commendable; here the deception is most innocent; Fanny only keeps Adams from finding out about her passion for Joseph. For, and this is merely the other side of the coin, to see far, to be profound, to be clever – these are to go down the paths of trickery and deceit; vanity and hypocrisy have an easier time establishing themselves on such soil. The armour of a good man is, to a certain extent, his very inability to see.

One of the first examples of Adams's opacity surely shows him in an entirely innocent light. When he and Joseph commence their journey by the method of ride and tie, Adams walks through 'a large water', wetting himself up to the middle, 'but was no sooner got to the other side than he perceived, if he had looked over the hedge, he would have found a footpath capable of conducting him without wetting his shoes' (II, 2). It would be hard indeed to convict Adams of any very great moral lapse here. His failure to be observant is caused directly by his concern for Joseph, of whom he can see no sign – and the reason why the young man does not appear is that Adams has forgotten to pay the horse's board. Again, when the promissory gentleman unfolds before Adams's quickly bedazzled eyes the prospect of a £300 living, lodging, and the loan of horses – this is, as the chapter heading puts it, 'a much greater instance of the honest simplicity of his heart, than of his experience in the ways of this world' (II, 16). Again his blindness is not only innocent, it is also charming. There is a good measure of adverse moral judgment in this chapter, but it is delivered against the gentleman, not against Adams, who is better off blind. Were he ocularly more powerful, he would be morally weaker.

In *Joseph Andrews* Fielding is not attempting to draw a picture of an ideal clergyman. As a man of God, Adams is superb; as a parson he is inadequate by many standards, including Fielding's. And this novel, 'written in the manner of Cervantes', centres on a clergyman not in order that Fielding can in Adams delineate the priesthood, but because, as the preface has it, 'no other office could have given him so many opportunities of displaying his worthy inclinations'. The office is subordinate to the man: Adams is Adams before he is a parson, and a good man whose goodness does by nature exceed the boundaries of his office. In fact, it is a fine achievement of *Joseph Andrews* altogether that this deeply contemplative man, this learned scholar, this preacher of impracticalities, should invariably, automatically, and unthinkingly act first and think afterwards. Nowhere is this fact more stunningly exemplified than when Fanny faints on hearing Joseph's song; Adams, in an ecstasy of concern, 'jumped up, flung his Aeschylus into the fire, and fell a roaring to the people of the house for help' (II, 12). Is not this the act of an Aeschylean hero comically transmogrified: is not this the portrait of a comic Prometheus?

TOM AS REFLECTED IN THE PEOPLE OF HIS WORLD

Freedom belongs to the realm of tragedy. The tragic hero can choose, and being human he makes the choice that brings the world crashing down about him; from the wreckage comes a vision of order in which freedom can be nourished and even sustained; it is, however, the vision rather than the actuality upon which the final curtain is rung down. But the comic hero, exhibiting a different idea of character, leads a more restricted life. The worst he can do is make a mistake; the best he can do is shed a layer or two of the self-deceptive skin that preoccupation with the self has encouraged. Tragedy centres on a character who becomes fully human only at the moment when he has destroyed himself. Comedy's focus is upon a character who abandons rather than nourishes his eccentricities, who discovers in the last chapter or the last act that self-love and social are the same. To be sure, order is the last word of tragedy as it is of comedy: Tom Jones's Somerset will probably be as restoratively orderly as the Denmark of Fortinbras. For order is the hope as it is the consolation of art. But the tragic order rises out of the luminous fires of self-destruction; the comic order is established in the light of common day. And the mistake to which every one at least occasionally succumbs is to use 'tragedy' and 'comedy' as though in life they were mutually exclusive. It is a mistake not simply because it involves a failure of generosity but because it underestimates human capacity. Tragedy, as Shakespeare shows us, need not rule out its opposite: the gravediggers, in fact, have notions of human life which Hamlet cannot despise; and comedy at its greatest – comedy, that is, in *The Tempest* – is for ever shaded with the threat of disaster, at sea in a storm, or on land through the agency of a Caliban.

But it is true that the comic writer leans upon the conviction that character is static. 'This world', Horace Walpole wrote in a celebrated letter to the Countess of Upper Ossory on 16 August 1776 (and as he often said), 'is a comedy to those that think, a tragedy to those that feel'.[9] An emblem of neo-classical thinking on the make-up of personality, this usefully exhibits the classifying impulse of the resolute amateur. Coming so late in the century, it displays a prejudice on the side of tragedy; but it also draws a line which Fielding himself tried to establish not between art and art but between art and life. Walpole, for some understandable personal reasons as well as because of temperamental preference, disliked Fielding and his work.[10] Fielding himself rigorously and deliberately eschews in his novels the possibility of freedom that leads to tragic consummation; even *Amelia* has a happy ending, though it is achieved at fatal artistic expense. In *Joseph Andrews* and in *Tom Jones*, however, he makes the comic assumption that bad men are irremediable but inferior to and controllable by good men: and good men behave in accordance with their 'nature', which is all that is necessary. I have already pointed out that Fielding is very far from viewing ordinary life with the comic assurance that he brings to his novels: art offered him an alternative to the bleak truths he observed in Bow Street and elsewhere. But the alternative was not that of comedy to tragedy. It was comedy or despair.

Within the splendid comedies of *Joseph Andrews* and *Tom Jones* there are, accordingly, moral statements that must be regarded as deliberately and exuberantly frivolous. When Fielding says in chapter 8 of Book XII of *Tom Jones* that Sophia's disapprobation of Tom is founded not on his freedoms 'with the person of another woman', but on the 'freedoms which she thought (and not without good reason) he had taken with her name and character', he himself – Fielding as narrator – pretends that this may cause his readers to be shocked. But, he says: 'I must remind such persons that I am not writing a system, but a history, and I am not obliged to reconcile every matter to the received notions concerning truth and nature'. Fielding then draws some possible lessons out of the Upton incident and its consequences:

> Wise and good men may consider what happened to Jones at Upton as a just punishment for his wickedness with regard to women, of which it was indeed the immediate consequence; and silly and bad persons may comfort themselves in their vices by flattering their own hearts that the characters of men are rather owing to accident than to virtue. Now, perhaps the reflections which we should be here inclined to draw would alike contradict both these conclusions, and would show that these incidents contribute only to confirm the great, useful, and uncommon doctrine, which it is the purpose of this whole work to inculcate, and which we must not fill up our pages by frequently repeating, as an ordinary parson fills his sermon by repeating his text at the end of every paragraph.

Yet it has been necessary for me to give this reminder about the moral status of *Tom Jones* by way of preface.

Allworthy is the first among the principal characters to claim attention – not because, as is so often and mistakenly supposed, he is the moral centre of *Tom Jones*, but because he is not. The assumption that Allworthy is the ideally prudential person to whose standards Tom finally learns how to conform – this assumption rests on the solid groundwork of Fielding's own statement of the theme of the novel, in chapter 7 of Book III, to which I have already made reference.[11] On the strength of such internal evidence – which is certainly not made ironically: Fielding indeed calls himself a chorus in the making of this utterance – it is tempting to suppose that here is the moral heart of *Tom Jones*, and that Allworthy is its exemplar and prophet.

Obviously, this is at most a half truth; and I now wish to face squarely the moral position of Allworthy, in order to locate his moral position and assess his moral stature. My argument has three parts: first, that Fielding repeatedly draws a line between

Allworthy's intention and the novel's meaning; second, that Allworthy behaves with an unconventionality which marks him out not as an ideally conforming country squire but as one whose comportment is fearlessly individual, if not always clear-sighted; third, that he lacks the vitality which Fielding values for itself.

When, at the beginning of the novel, Squire Allworthy lectures Jenny Jones on chastity and on love as a rational passion there is, built into the structure of the chapter and in the strong wording of the discourse itself, the qualificatory intent of Fielding. The most prominent evidence of this intent is announced in the title of the chapter: 'Containing such grave matter, that the reader cannot laugh once through the whole chapter, unless peradventure he should laugh at the author' (I, 7). In order to substantiate my case in detail, I should have to cite the whole chapter – and I do so; but a glance will, I think, confirm my argument. I want only to extract two small examples: the overstatement of Allworthy's address to Jenny about chastity – 'a crime, however lightly it may be treated by debauched persons, very heinous in itself, and very dreadful in its consequences'. The other example has to do with Allworthy's definition of love. 'Love,' he says,

> however barbarously we may corrupt and pervert its meaning, as it is a laudable, is a rational passion, and can never be violent but when reciprocal; for though the Scripture bids us love our enemies, it means not with that fervent love which we naturally bear towards our friends; much less that we should sacrifice to them our lives, and what ought to be dearer to us, our innocence.

I submit that this is, in Fielding's terms, the wisdom of excessively advanced maturity.

On the same point – that is, of the line drawn between All-worthy's intention and the novel's meaning – there is the fact of Allworthy's credulousness. Like Heartfree and Parson Adams before him, he is far too easily duped by the clever and malicious Blifil, and by others: the Squire's credulity, however lovable, separates him from the more perceptive and practical author, who locates 'reality' elsewhere. In the introduction to the Modern Library edition of *Tom Jones*, Professor Sherburn writes: 'The Good Man cannot . . . be suspicious, since he is innocent of any knowledge of evil; and thus such persons as Heartfree and Squire Allworthy are somewhat too easily duped. They seem to be constructed on a formula rather than from actual knowledge of men such as one might expect.'[12] But it seems to me that Allworthy – like both his predecessors in Fielding's work – is both formulary and realistic: he is that special combination which Fielding manages to achieve in his art: the character founded on actual observation who is transfigured by his incorporation into an artistic fabric, the design of which gives it a different status from that of the day-to-day world.

And yet, for all his conformity to expectation, Allworthy is unconventional. He has, for instance, a spiritual generosity which transcends the 'rules' that prudence must dictate the direction of courtship. Evidence of this trait occurs as early as chapter 12 of Book I, when he is entirely willing to accept the marriage between his sister and Captain Blifil: 'I see', he tells the incredulous Dr Blifil, 'no reason why I should object to her choice of her own happiness'. Nor – to put the shoe on the other foot – will he attempt to force the marriage between Blifil and Sophia: 'I will never give my consent to any absolute force being put on her inclinations, nor shall you ever have her unless she can be brought freely to compliance' (XVI, 6). So far as Allworthy's attitude to marriage is concerned, the argument can be made that his unconventionality is the sign of his heroism, and an indication that a centre (that is, at least one of the loci) of the novel's meaning is in the character of the squire. I accept that argument.

But there is one particular in which Squire Allworthy fails to measure up to *Tom Jones*'s moral demands. He lacks vitality. And for Fielding moral health is so closely related to physical stamina that this lack – he becomes so ill that he is thought to be dying – must tell against him. When he is speaking of the great quality of Sophia, he says (to Squire Western):

'I must use negatives on this occasion. I never heard anything of pertness, or what is called repartee, out of her mouth; no pretence to wit, much less to that kind of wisdom which is the result only of great learning and experience, the affectation of which, in a young woman, is as absurd as any of the affectations of an ape. No dictatorial sentiments, no judicial opinions, no profound criticisms. Whenever I have seen her in the company of men, she hath been all attention, with the modesty of a learner, not the forwardness of a teacher'. (XVII, 3.)

But the strongest of all reasons for thinking that Squire Allworthy is not the moral centre of *Tom Jones* is the existence of his opposite number, his neighbour and friend Squire Western. For all the moral blindness which Western suffers from, for all the barbarous and ignorant dislike of Tory, town, France, and nobility, he remains an attractive and indeed lovable character. Wilbur Cross traces his genesis and development in the Sir Positive Trap of *Love in Several Masques* and in the Squire Badger of *Don Quixote in England*[13]: that is to say, as a character Western is a persistent interest. He is not only full of vitality, he is also playful: and this combination Fielding finds irresistible. He delightedly describes Western as 'a little too apt to indulge that kind of pleasantry which is generally called rhodomontade' (IV, 11). This is by way of explaining Western's declaration that Allworthy in his youth was 'as arrant a whoremaster as any within five miles o' un' (IV, 10). Several pages later, the narrator wryly and delightedly remarks, 'there is much reason to imagine that there was not the least truth in what Mr Western affirmed, especially as he laid the scene of those improprieties at the university, where Mr Allworthy had never been' (IV, 11).

Squire Western, then, has a robust and exuberant temper: so highly valued by Fielding that its possession excuses the extravagances into which it impels him. When old Capulet treats his daughter with scornful barbarity, the audience's sympathy is entirely with Juliet; when Squire Western locks up his daughter, the reader's sympathy is certainly not withheld from Sophia; but the straightforward and unexamined way of Western requires that disapprobation be thinned with tolerance. The violent suddenness with which the illiterate squire acts, serves him not merely in bad but also in good stead. It is indeed culpable in him that he should speak to his daughter with such savage incomprehension, but toward the end of the novel his temperamental predilection for violent activity serves him well. He does, after all, rescue his daughter from the importunities of Lord Fellamar (XV, 5); and as soon as Tom's actual parentage is revealed, he changes his mind about the youth. 'Men over-violent in their dispositions are, for the most part, as changeable in them. No sooner then was Western informed of Mr All-worthy's intention to make Jones his heir, than he joined heartily with the uncle in every commendation of the nephew, and became as eager for her marriage with Jones as he had been before to couple her with Blifil' (XVIII, 9). A measure of the success of Fielding's characterization of Western is that we understand the Squire's assent to be based not on merely in-terested and prudential motive, but on inflexible, unmeditated, and therefore not inexcusable conviction.

Allworthy and Western are the elders among the principals of *Tom Jones*, and, much though it may delight the elderly, it is not an old man's book. In considering the hero of the novel against the characterization of his uncle and of father-in-law to be, one is tempted to think that Tom is to represent the golden mean, Tom 'was indeed a thoughtless, giddy youth, with little sobriety in his manners and less in his countenance, and would very often impudently and indecently laugh at his com-panion [Blifil] for his serious behaviour' (III, 5). Such is the young Tom, and there is no question but that at this point Tom less resembles his uncle than the father of Sophia. In truth Tom is remembered for his careless and utterly spontaneous gener-osity, his uncogitated bravery. The adventures with Black George, with Molly Seagrim, with Mrs Waters, and Lady Bellaston; the sale of the pony, the attempt to rescue Sophia's bird, the redoubtable encounter with Ensign Northerton: in all of these memorable adventures the reader is dared to make a moral judgment against Tom. When the reader takes the dare, he does so at the risk of being found ungenerous himself.

Tom's coeval and half-brother Blifil provides another yard-stick against which measurement is invited. The contrast is explicit. In chapter 2 of Book III, after Fielding tells us that Tom has long been regarded as 'certainly born to be hanged', there follows a list of the three robberies of which he has already been convicted. There follows also this important paragraph:

The vices of this young man were, moreover, heightened by the disadvantageous light in which they appeared when opposed to the virtues of Master Blifil, his companion; a youth of so different a cast from little Jones, that not only the family but all the neighbourhood resounded his praises. He was, indeed, a lad of remarkable disposition, sober, discreet, and pious beyond his age; qualities which gained him the love of every one who knew him: while Tom Jones was universally disliked; and many expressed their wonder that Mr Allworthy would suffer such a lad to be educated with his nephew, lest the morals of the latter should be corrupted by his example.

But in the famous poaching incident, which takes place in the same chapter (III, 2), Tom is unhelped and unhindered by Blifil, who has 'gone abroad on a visit with his mother'. Yet Tom's whole demeanour and comportment are to be contrasted to Blifil's. It is Tom's enthusiasm which persuades Black George, not altogether in opposition to the gamekeeper's wishes, to poach; and it is Tom's constancy, even despite the brutal beating he receives at the hands of Thwackum, which stands out in the boy's successful determination not to implicate Black George, even though the neighbouring squire – Western – has declared that *two* shots were fired.

Significantly, Blifil is arraigned for his devotion to justice, while Tom is exculpated for his merciful instinct. In chapter 10 of Book III – 'In which Master Blifil and Jones appear in different lights' – Fielding is appealing implicitly to the authority of a 'natural' justice (which Tom exhibits) as against the all too sublunary ideas held by Blifil, and taught by Thwackum and Square. In this chapter, which retails with heavy irony Blifil's successful effort to bring Black George under the cloud of Squire Allworthy's disfavour, Blifil's devotion to justice is demonstrated to be mere vindictive hypocrisy, while Thwackum and Square, though espousing mercy, reject it, 'for though they would both make frequent use of the word mercy, yet it was plain that in reality Square held it to be inconsistent with the rule of right; and Thwackum was for doing justice, and leaving mercy to Heaven'.

Partridge is ostentatiously stylized, operatic, literary. The connection to *Don Quixote* is, in the title of chapter 4 of Book

VIII, explicit: 'In which is introduced one of the pleasantest barbers that was ever recorded in history, the barber of Bagdad, or he in Don Quixote, not excepted'. A demi-learned pedant of a schoolmaster turned barber, a pusillanimous adventurer, a wildly impractical believer in practicality, a self-interested man with the saving grace of generosity, a thoroughly experienced and equally thoroughly credulous man whose convictions always adjust themselves to circumstance – Partridge stands in the same relation to Tom Jones as does Sancho Panza to Don Quixote.

Partridge has been expelled by Mr Allworthy because the Squire believes him to have cohabited with Jenny Jones and to have caused her to become pregnant and then to produce the child that is called Tom Jones. Partridge knows better, but he does not see his way to restoration in Mr Allworthy's favour until the chance encounter – years later – with Tom: and the schoolmaster-turned-barber for his part supposes Tom to be Allworthy's son. Partridge, is, however, a man of intellect, a man of masks – and in these two respects different from his Cervantine analogue. This is made explicit by Partridge himself, who is an exuberant barber, but a solemn surgeon. After applying some salve to Tom he says:

'Now I will, if you please, resume my former self; but a man is obliged to keep up some dignity in his countenance whilst he is performing these operations, or the world will not submit to be handled by him. You can't imagine, sir, of how much consequence a grave aspect is to a grave character. A barber may make you laugh, but a surgeon ought rather to make you cry!' (VIII, 6.)

Partridge sees in others the image of himself; he is utterly unable to comprehend the response of righteous indignation because he himself has never known it. Equally, he has had to fend for himself so long and so assiduously that he supposes others – even the well-placed squire – to respond and behave as he does. And yet Partridge is irresistibly attractive, because he is so undisguisedly human in the pursuit of his fulfilments: when he wrongly thinks that he can make love without penalty to a gypsy woman (XII, 12), none is more straightforwardly amorous than he. There is another reason for his attractiveness, and that is his perfectly unexpungable naïveté, the most blatant exhibition of which occurs at the performance in London of *Hamlet* (XVI, 5). It is Partridge's glory that he betrays – indeed trumpets forth – 'the simple dictates of nature, unimproved, indeed, but likewise unadulterated, by art'. His participation in the play, after the first skeptical moment (he will not at the beginning believe that the ghost is a ghost) is entire. 'And during the whole speech of the ghost, he sat with his eyes fixed partly on the ghost and partly on Hamlet, and with his mouth open; the same passions which succeeded each other in Hamlet succeeding likewise in him'.

The difference between Partridge and his creator is that Fielding knows how to distinguish between life and art; and in the championship of art for art's sake – which is to say, art for civilization's sake – Fielding is making, and he knows it, a contribution to civilization. Partridge is less sophisticated, so far less so that he mistakes Garrick's high art for life ('Anybody may see he is an actor'). Failure to distinguish between appearance and ostentation, between essence and pretence – this is what makes Partridge a delight to encounter and to contemplate: the more so in a novel which insists upon drawing just this line.

On the title page of *Tom Jones* appears the familiar Horatian tag, 'Mores hominum multorum vidit' (*Ars Poetica*, 142): this phrase – a translation from the opening of the *Odyssey* – invites the reader to take the novel panoramically rather than as a closet drama, and it is correct to appreciate in *Tom Jones* the generosity of scope. The hero's connection with the epigraph is twofold: in the first place, Tom is a man of the world, a man among men, a man whose selfhood is social; this fact is demonstrated nowhere more precisely than in the wholeness which he achieves through the discovery of his actual parenthood. In the second place, because he is a naturally good man, Tom exhibits correspondingly good manners: he is in himself a personification of the sentiment which gives life to Horace's dictum: the belief that good manners are the outward and visible sign of inner moral health.

In the first edition of *Tom Jones*, there is I think, an important feature that is obscured by omission in modern editions. In the first edition, each book is entitled 'THE HISTORY OF A FOUNDLING', and the running title throughout the novel is (verso): '*The History of*' (recto): 'a FOUNDLING'. Tom is a natural waif, a romantic figure because he is a foundling; only the most credulous reader will (with Allworthy) suppose him to be the son of Partridge and Jenny Jones. As the story goes forward the mystery deepens, especially with the appearance of Dowling. But when Tom's actual parentage is revealed, the romance appreciates. Bridget's liaison with a young man named Summer – 'A finer man', Mrs Waters says, 'the sun never shone upon; for, besides the handsomest person I ever saw, he was so genteel, and had so much wit and good breeding' (XVIII, 7) – this makes a fine, and still somewhat obscured, heritage: for little is told about the deceased Summer. And at the end of the novel, though he has been reconciled to his uncle and though he gets his heart's desire, Tom remains a natural son, born outside the boundaries of wedlock, and existing – freely and triumphantly – above the moral plane of the ordinary life.

AMELIA AND THE ULTIMATE CHARACTERIZATIONS

The art of fiction consists in the illusion of singularity. But the principals in *Amelia* are Fielding's ultimate development of characters – characters rather than ideas – in whom he has always been interested. Amelia, Will, Serjeant Atkinson, and Dr Harrison do not by any means set the limits to Fielding's interest in character, but they do indicate his major preoccupations: and each of these figures has an analogue in *Joseph Andrews* and *Tom Jones*. Amelia is a cousin to Sophia Western, who in turn is a development of the sketch which is Fanny Goodwill. Will Booth, though I have argued that he is far from being a mature Tom Jones, is surely related to him in some important ways, these previously having been rather lightly adumbrated in the depiction of Joseph Andrews himself. It is equally possible to see a close relationship between Joseph Andrews, Partridge, and Joe Atkinson. Finally, Dr Harrison is a paler version of Squire Allworthy and Parson Adams. Behind ᴉhese main portraits can be seen, in *Jonathan Wild*, the crude sketches of three of the principals: Mrs Heartfree the resolute and passive female, Mr Heartfree as a forerunner of the Adams-Partridge-Harrison innocence figure, Wild himself as a diabolical profiguration of the heroism to be realized best in the character of Tom Jones.

Since I have already discussed Amelia fairly thoroughly in Chapter 2, I can be brief here. But an additional remark ought to be made now. Amelia is a cruder and stronger version – an ancestor, if you will – of Fanny Price in *Mansfield Park*. Her role, like Fanny's, is that of strong passivity, of indomitable resistance, of the ability to endure. None the less she is imperfectly drawn; a small example of this occurs in chapter 6 of Book IV, wherein Amelia is described as 'a woman of great humour'. But she is never shown to be so, and therefore the reader will not take Fielding's assertion on faith. Her foil is Mrs Bennet, the principal contrast being that of the latter's erudition. Fielding has good sport guying female learning, but this, unfortunately, casts little light upon the character of Amelia.

And the characterization of Will Booth well demonstrates the fatal bifurcation of Fielding's aim in *Amelia*. A useful example, which occurs quite early in the novel, is Booth's courtship of Amelia Harris. The very shape of the courtship is not only significantly imprudent, but extravagant in incident – including the hamper. When Booth begins to dare to hope, he hobbles himself, and makes Amelia miserable, by pretending to be in love with her bitterest enemy – and I can find no justification for this gratuitously cruel usage of the woman he loves except in so far as it gives Amelia an opportunity to demonstrate her gullibility: always, as the earlier novels show, the sign of goodness of character. As Booth says here in so many words, 'A good heart will at all times betray the best head in the world' (II, 2). There is no question in my mind about Fielding's commitment to this judgment. Everything he writes tends to justify this conviction, and whereas it is a source of strength in the writing of *Joseph Andrews* and *Tom Jones* – and also that satiric blast, *Jonathan Wild* – it measures the weakness of *Amelia*, an explicitly didactic novel by a writer who does not believe that lessons can be taught, or learned.

Atkinson shares with Joseph Andrews not only a Christian name but a devotedness, a faithfulness, a bravery that bring the eponymous hero of Fielding's first novel very often to mind. Foster-brother to Amelia, Atkinson is Booth's servant. Although his companionage parallels that of Joseph to Parson Adams and Partridge to Tom, the comparison cannot be pressed too far: Joseph Andrews, though a servant by vocation, stands in a devoted but not servile relation to Adams, who regards him as one of the children of his parish rather than as a servant. Again, Partridge as a failed schoolmaster with ideas cannot contain himself within or be contained by his role as servant to Tom; besides, he is delineated in the roles of schoolmaster and barber, as well as in the role of Tom's Sancho. Atkinson is more senti- mentally or at least straightforwardly the faithful servant.

Dr Harrison is a major weakness in *Amelia* because he is seen too little to be anything much more than a half-deified *deus ex machina*, whereas he is obviously meant to occupy a position of the same order of centrality as does Squire Allworthy in *Tom Jones*. The good doctor is the proponent, one is almost tempted to say the champion, of prudence. Thus Dr Harrison for pru- dential reasons advises Booth to remain with his old regiment, which is going to Gibraltar. But Dr Harrison's is a prudence gone sour:

'As the malicious disposition of mankind is too well known, and the cruel pleasure which they take in destroying the reputations of others, the use we are to make of this knowledge is to afford no handle to reproach; for, bad as the world is, it seldom falls on any man who hath not given some slight cause for censure, though this perhaps is often aggravated ten thousand-fold: and when we blame the malice of the aggravation we ought not to forget our own imprudence in giving the occasion.' (III, 1.)

Parson Adams constantly gives advice which is so wildly at odds with common sense as to be hilarious; Squire Allworthy's judiciousness is more firmly based, but he is often wrong because he shares with Parson Adams an ineradicable innocence, a failure to see the world in any but his own benevolent image.

Dr Harrison, though he can be deceived, even self-deceived, is the victim of a myopia founded not on blinkered benevolence but on excessive suspiciousness. Thus when Booth is arrested at the suit of Dr Harrison, the reason is the misconstruction by the doctor of the toys (given by the noble lord) which are to be seen in Spring Gardens).

Of all the beliefs shared by Dr Harrison's forebears none is stronger than the faith in mankind's fundamental amiability. Even the most direct and painful experience of the harsh truth of the matter makes for little or no alteration in this faith. Evidence against mankind's goodness washes off before it can be absorbed or assessed. To negative evidence, these men are generally impermeable. But not Dr Harrison. Toward the end of the novel, Dr Harrison's neighbour, a peer, asks, 'Do you really believe any man upon earth was ever a rogue out of choice?' And Dr Harrison's reply is, 'I am ashamed to answer in the affirmative; and yet I am afraid experience would almost justify me if I should' (XI, 2).

When Will Booth, in prison, is telling his story to Miss Matthews he looks back to the temporary perfection of life in Dr Harrison's parish, with its trout stream, meadows, downs, and the plain house of Dr Harrison himself. It is, explicitly, an 'earthly paradise'. For a year Booth and his family lived in exquisite happiness in this parish, Booth having been set up as a farmer by Dr Harrison. It was, as Booth tells Miss Matthews, 'one continued series of love, health, and tranquillity. Our lives resembled a calm sea'. Even in the face of Miss Matthews's comment that this is 'the dullest of all ideas', Booth persists in detailing its perfection:

'Who can describe the pleasures which the morning air gives to one in perfect health; the flow of spirits which springs up from exercise; the delight which parents feel from the prattle and innocent follies of their children; the joy with which the tender smile of a wife inspires a husband; or lastly, the cheerful, solid comfort which a fond couple enjoy in each other's conversation? All these pleasures and every other of which our situation was capable we tasted in the highest degree. Our happiness was, perhaps, too great; for fortune seemed to grow envious of it.' (III, 12.)

Fortune, however, plays only a minor role in the destruction of this paradise.[14] To be sure, Dr Harrison is called away from the parish 'to attend the young lord in his travels as his tutor' (III, 12). In the absence of this benevolent mentor, Booth improvidently sets up an equipage and brings himself so near the edge of ruin that he must take himself and his family to London, on a rear-march in disgrace. But what strikes the reader so forcefully is how quickly his friends and neighbours are transmogrified. Their savagery to Booth is thoroughly ignoble. Yet Booth has described them in glowing terms, as Dr Harrison's 'children'; and they in their turn regard Dr Harrison

'as their common father. Once a week he constantly visits every house in the parish, examines, commends, and rebukes, as he finds occasion. This is practised likewise by his curate in his absence; and so good an effect is produced by this their care, that no quarrels ever proceed either to blows or law-suits; no beggar is to be found in the whole parish; nor did I ever hear a very profane oath all the time I lived in it.' (III, 12.)

From weal to woe is a short step – and it is the woe which dominates *Amelia* to the very end, when the worldly fortune of the Booths alters very considerably for the better, and when Booth is converted from such indifference as Claudian describes (in several lines from *In Rufinum*: these appear in I, 3 of *Amelia*) to the more positive religious commitment celebrated in Isaac Barrow's sermons. None the less, the mood of *Amelia* is solemn, and dark. Toward society Fielding exhibits distaste: there is a radical discontent with things as they are. In some respects, the world is ruined beyond hope of cure.

Chapter 5

LANGUAGE AND PLAY

'Many objects, natural as well as artificial, may be distinguished by the epithet of *risible*, because they raise in us a peculiar emotion expressed externally by *laughter*. This is a pleasant emotion; and being also mirthful, it most successfully unbends the mind and recruits the spirits.'

LORD KAMES, *Elements of Criticism*

'THERE is no branch of criticism', Fielding writes, 'in which learning, as well as good sense, is more required than to the forming an accurate judgment of style, though there is none, I believe, in which every trifling reader is more ready to give his decision'.[1] For style, as W. K. Wimsatt says, is 'the last and most detailed elaboration of meaning'.[2] No doubt – and yet this truth is so often ignored or ruled out that it must be insisted upon here. And surely the reader of Fielding quickly teaches himself that the honest plainness which the narrator affects is itself affectation, for even when he is at his most ostentatiously straightforward, Fielding refuses to stop smiling at himself and at his plainness; over against this is the almost bewildering variety of styles, ranging from the rococo to the spare, and including superb representation of class and occupational speech: taken altogether the kaleidoscope of Fielding's styles indicates that the meaning which he wishes to elaborate is nothing less than the consolations, the joys, and even the ontological doubts of 'art' as opposed to 'life'. This is especially borne home by the realization that except in his plays and in the novels Fielding fails to exhibit such versatility. When he is writing to say something straightforwardly, he can be straightforward – as he is, for instance, in his legal writings.[3] But in *Joseph Andrews* and *Tom Jones*, deployment of facts, arrangement of argument, development of a thesis: none of these is Fielding's aim. In his first two novels his purpose is more subtle. It is to be playful. But lest this sound as though Fielding wishes to turn his back on commitment to the responsibility of meaning what he says, let me assert

172

that I have no intention of trying to sustain such a thesis. My hope is to show that in this aspect of his work, as in the others with which I have dealt, Fielding's versatility exhibits the choice of a false world in which festivity is the hallmark of civilization founded on but superior to the squalor of the day-to-day.

In *Amelia*, however, Fielding betrays his failing powers, or perhaps one should rather say his failing confidence in the ability of language to communicate with the precision that he took for granted in *Joseph Andrews* and in *Tom Jones*. There is an alteration in aesthetic also, clearly discernible in the ambiguities of linguistic aim – a drift, to put the matter in other words, toward satire, which (for Fielding) is if not second childishness, at best retrogression to the rhetorical imperatives of *Jonathan Wild*, that precursor (perhaps in time as well as in immaturity) of the earlier novels. To be sure, the Fielding hallmarks are readily observable and identifiable. In the first chapter I dealt with the most central of the stylistic aspects, that is, the stance of the teller of the tale. No reader of *Joseph Andrews* and *Tom Jones* would mistake *Amelia's* authorship. None the less, there is, as I say, a declining confidence. There is also, though intermittently, an angrier tone. Altogether, there is a diffuseness of aim apparent in the diffuseness of achievement. Plain English, as a formulary invocation, almost disappears in *Amelia* – because, no doubt, it is necessary to be perfectly certain whom you are addressing if you want to make this appeal to common sense. Metaphor becomes far more thoroughly trusted, or at least far more heavily depended upon, than ever before. About the grand style there is, instead of a certain ambiguity behind which clear intention can be discerned, a kind of soft ambivalence that represents a sad decline. Class and occupational jargon is, by comparison to that in *Amelia's* predecessors, severely limited in scope. Finally, the satiric mode becomes open and raw: the festive intention of the author of *Joseph Andrew* and *Tom Jones* has given way to the severities of angry hope, and angry despair.

In the first chapter of Book II of *Joseph Andrews* – 'Of divisions in authors' – Fielding gives some instruction on how to interpret his chapter titles: 'In these inscriptions I have been as faithful as possible, not imitating the celebrated Montaigne, who promises you one thing and gives you another; nor some title-page authors, who promise a great deal, and produce nothing at all'. Fielding's practice, however, is not so ingenuous. For the chapter headings are almost always archly ironic whenever Fielding allows himself to go beyond mere description.[4] Thus chapter 5 of Book I is entitled: 'The death of Sir Thomas Booby, with the affectionate and mournful behaviour of his widow, and the great purity of Joseph Andrews'. The tag-name, together with the explicit parody of *Pamela*, and the information in the foregoing chapter of Lady Booby's 'innocent freedoms' with Joseph – these make the slyness of the title patent. Thenceforward the reader is on the lookout for the title that will mock expectation by showing man as he really is rather than as he pretends to be. So the chapter titles help sustain the promise which Fielding makes in the Preface, that he will expose the Ridiculous. The chapter titles, that is to say, do their job by pointing to the affectation behind which lies either vanity or hypocrisy.

Accordingly, 'Sayings of wise men' (I, 7) satirizes by the device of vague attribution a kind of wisdom that happens not to be true. The generalization, indeed, looks unexceptionable: 'It is the observation of some ancient sage, whose name I have forgot, that passions operate differently on the human mind, as diseases on the body, in proportion to the strength or weakness, soundness or rottenness, of the one and the other'. Yet when application to a particular instance is made, 'the different operations of this passion of love in the gentle and cultivated mind of the Lady Booby, from those which it effected in the less polished and coarser disposition of Mrs Slipslop', the reader learns that the generalization will not serve – and the reason lies in the affectations of the two women: the ironic assumption here is, the higher the class the finer the person. But the chapter title points the way to the humbler truth that *affection* in a waiting-gentlewoman is precisely comparable to that of a squire's lady, and that their *affectations* of difference are ridiculous.

It is not necessary to point to all the chapter headings which contain oblique and artful – sometimes, indeed, elephantine – claims that will fail to materialize, promises that are broken, ironies that betray themselves. 'A surprising instance of Mr Adams's short memory' (II, 2) is anything but surprising by the time one has known Parson Adams so far. That he should have left his sermons behind is a fact far far more surprising to Parson Adams than it is to the reader. 'A chapter very full of learning' (II, 12) is certain to be full of ignorance pretending to be learned. 'A scene of roasting, very nicely adapted to the present taste and time' (II, 7) is bound to characterize the present taste and times pejoratively. Adams's exhortations, 'calculated for the instruction and improvement of the reader', are sure to divert rather than to inform. And so forth. In short, the chapter headings (too often, I think, overlooked by the present-day reader) sustain, exhibit, and indeed in part embody a pattern of festivity consonant with the intention of the chapters themselves.

As I have thought about Fielding's style I have kept constantly in mind the question dictated by common sense: how does Fielding write when he means what he says? Unfortunately there is no clear-cut answer to this question. The obvious answer, for all its circularity, is that when Fielding wishes to be plain he uses plain English. But Fielding's notion of plainness fails to stand up to the most exacting analysis, because Fielding himself, as I shall hope to show, distrusts plainness's ability to be other than plain (and that he approves the panegyric style is evident from the dedication of *Tom Jones* to Lyttelton, from his descriptions of his heroines, and from the proposals of marriage). Besides, Fielding in his art was interested not in communicating in fictional form a simple truth about human existence, he was not aiming to teach young men how to preserve their virtue. In fact, as I have been arguing all along, Fielding's interest as a novelist was in providing for a cultivated audience cultivated delight. Therefore the answer to my question of common sense must be plural, so far as stylistic devices and levels are concerned. And I want to proceed by way of considering Fielding's attitude toward a number of stylistic topics, as well as his exploitation of various levels of usage available to him because of his good education, accurate ear, wide experience, and amused curiosity.

A good point of departure is metaphor. Obviously, the epic similes of his mock heroic flights are common form – they express a certain amount of delight in the elaborateness of classical diction, and an equal amount of skepticism about the ability of such language to do a plain job of work; not that he was, like Jane Austen, radically distrustful of figurative language as a whole. But on the one hand he felt that figurative extravagance was suitable for playful purposes; on the other hand he knew himself to be a master of the language which he employed, and as master perfectly free to make it his playful instrument. A classical education hardly discourages a writer from essaying metaphor. In the eighteenth century, however, and for a number of reasons which Reuben Brower and others have already made abundantly clear,[5] the characteristic employment of heroic language was by way of mockery.

When he is reflecting on the mixed emotions in Lady Booby's breast, Fielding summons up a number of personifications: 'She was a thousand times on the very brink of revoking the sentence she had passed against the poor youth. Love became his advocate, and whispered many things in his favour. Honour likewise endeavoured to vindicate his crime, and Pity to mitigate his punishment' (I, 9). In its neat juxtaposition of high language and low living, this is fine comic epic romance style. Fielding then goes on to make another comparison, this time again to exploit the ridiculousness of Lady Booby's emotional situation. He compares her conflict to that between two lawyers in a courtroom. Finally, in mock-despair he writes: 'If it was our present business only to make similes, we could produce many more to this purpose; but a simile (as well as a word) to the wise. We shall therefore see a little after our hero, for whom the reader is doubtless in some pain' (I, 9).

There is also the epic simile, impure and simple:

As when a hungry tigress, who long has traversed the woods in fruitless search, sees within the reach of her claws a lamb, she prepares to leap on her prey; or as a voracious pike, of immense size, surveys through the liquid element a roach or gudgeon, which cannot escape her jaws, opens them wide to swallow the little fish; so did Mrs Slipslop prepare to lay her violent amorous hands on the poor Joseph. (I, 6.)

Such linguistic humour may nowadays seem to be more trouble than it is worth, more elaborate than the proprieties of good jokes will now permit. But at least Fielding does not often construct this sort of simile; there is in fact only one other instance in *Joseph Andrews* in which the full panoply of mock-heroic simile is employed, and that is toward the end of the fourth book when Parson Adams climbs into Fanny's bed, thinking it his own: 'As the cat or lap-dog of some lovely nymph, for whom one thousand lovers languish, lies quietly by the side of the charming maid, and, ignorant of the scene of delight on which they repose, meditates the future capture of a mouse, or surprisal of a plate of bread and butter: so Adams lay at the side of Fanny' (IV, 14). In *Tom Jones*, Fielding is equally mischievous. Thus the title of chapter 6 of Book I is, in part, 'Mrs Deborah is introduced into the parish with a simile'. The simile verges on the mock-heroic. Mrs Deborah Wilkins, an elderly maid-servant at Squire Allworthy's, goes into the village, and to the house where the supposed mother of Tom Jones dwells. 'Not otherwise than when a kite, tremendous bird, is beheld by the feathered generation soaring aloft, and hovering over their heads, the amorous dove, and every innocent little bird, spread wide the alarm, and fly trembling to their hiding-places. He proudly beats the air, conscious of his dignity, and meditates intended mischief'. The image exists, in part at least, as a splendid divertissement in despite of life. 'The sagacious reader will not from this simile imagine these poor people had any apprehension of the design with which Mrs Wilkins was now coming towards them; but as the great beauty of the simile may possibly sleep these hundred years, till some future commentator shall take this work in hand, I think proper to lend the reader a little assistance in this place'. Fielding then explains, altogether gratuitously, what he might (except for his festive aim) have said plainly in the first place. 'It is my intention, therefore, to signify that, as it is the nature of a kite to devour little birds, so it is the nature of such persons as Mrs Wilkins to insult and tyrannize over little people'. The truth is that plain speaking of this sort is hardly consonant with the festive intent.

Again, when Mrs Partridge suspects her husband of infidelity, she is mock-heroically compared to a cat and her husband to a mouse, in an ample paragraph beginning, 'As fair Grimalkin . . .' There follows in a separate paragraph the deflationary actuality. 'Not with less fury did Mrs Partridge fly on the poor pedagogue. Her tongue, teeth, and hands fell all upon him at once. His wig was in an instant torn from his head, his shirt from his back, and from his face descended five streams of blood, denoting the number of claws with which nature had unhappily armed the enemy' (II, 4). More elaborate is the description of Molly Seagrim's fight in the churchyard (IV, 8). Here the invocation to his muse, the inverted sentence structure, the catalogue of names are put at the service of a motley group of rustics; and the contrast between sonorous language and humble fact is (as in the country scenes in Shakespeare) irresistible. Especially delightful are the names of the persons involved in the battle, including Jemmy Tweedle, John Giddish, Nan Slouch, Esther Codling, and Will Spray. Even more elaborate is the mock-heroic preliminary to the discovery of Tom by Thwackum and Blifil in the bushes with Molly Seagrim (V, 11). The chapter title itself leans upon the master of mock-heroics: 'In which a simile in Mr Pope's period of a mile introduces as bloody a battle as can possibly be fought without the assistance of steel or cold iron'.

Finally, I should like to call attention to the most thoroughly contrived stretch of mock-heroism in the whole length and breadth of Fielding's work. This treats of Mrs Waters's seduction of a far from unwilling Tom Jones (IX, 5). Fielding begins with a grave sobriety that is very often the signal for mirth in prospect. The narrator commences with a quasi-scientific philosophical disquisition on the nature of heroes, the point of which is that they feel the pangs of hunger the same as anyone else. This opening has a triple purpose: it reduces the hero to the level of ordinary men and thus is in itself anti-heroic; it introduces the subject of food which is to be the playful alternative to love in the encounter to follow; it is a feint, for the central matter of this chapter is not food but love.

Then, having developed the preliminary possibilities further than in any other mock-heroic passage in *Tom Jones*, Fielding soars to the level of invocation of the muses, and the splendid contrast between the sophistication of the courtly love tradition and the humble interference of food and drink with the exalted purposes of Mrs Waters.

First, from two lovely blue eyes, whose bright orbs flashed lightning at their discharge, flew forth two pointed ogles; but, happily for our hero, hit only a vast piece of beef which he was then conveying into his plate, and harmless spent their force. The fair warrior perceived their miscarriage, and immediately from her fair bosom drew forth a deadly sigh. A sigh which none could have heard unmoved, and which was sufficient at once to have swept off a dozen beaus; so soft, so sweet, so tender, that the insinuating air must have found its subtle way to the heart of our hero, had it not luckily been driven from his ears by the coarse bubbling of some bottled ale, which at that time he was pouring forth. Many other weapons did she assay; but the god of eating (if there be any such deity, for I do not confidently assert it) preserved his votary; or perhaps it may not be *dignus vindice nodus*, and the present security of Jones may be accounted for by natural means; for as love frequently preserves from the attacks of hunger, so may hunger possibly, in some cases, defend us against love. (IX, 5.)

Like all writers Fielding is against the sin of the cliché and he frequently takes stale metaphor to task. 'Those who have read any romance or poetry, ancient or modern, must have been informed that Love hath wings: by which they are not to understand, as some young ladies by mistake have done, that a lover can fly; the writers, by this ingenious allegory, intending to insinuate no more than that lovers do not march like horse-guards; in short, that they put the best leg foremost' (*Joseph Andrews*, I, 11). This is a familiar parodic device, to take literally a figure of speech until it stands convicted on its own terms of absurdity. Certainly one reason for employing this device is that Fielding did not want language to be abused, as it is always abused by half-dead metaphor. And yet the passage also invites amused response. Surely, Fielding means not simply to criticize but also to delight.

The same kind of usage also occurs somewhat later, where the narrator is describing the relationship between Mr and Mrs Tow-wouse, in order to explain Mr Tow-wouse's eagerness in his relationship with Betty the chambermaid:

for, as the violence of his passion had considerably abated to Mrs Tow-wouse, so, like water, which is stopt from its usual current in one place, it naturally sought a vent in another. Mrs Tow-wouse is thought to have perceived this abatement, and probably it added very little to the natural sweetness of her temper; for though she was as true to her husband as the dial to the sun, she was rather more desirous of being shone on, as being more capable of feeling his warmth. (I, 18.)[6]

Here the two figures of speech, one about water and the other the sun, linked ridiculously by the understatement about the natural sweetness of Mrs Tow-wouse's temper – these strike me as having the purpose of rejoicing in the follies which language is capable of, rather than as condemning the impure or inaccurate use of language. Again, mixture of half-dead metaphors is used to indicate the hypocritical thinking of such pretentious characters as Lady Booby when she speaks to Mrs Slipslop about Joseph. 'I believe indeed thou dost not understand me. – These are delicacies which exist only in superior minds; thy coarse ideas cannot comprehend them. Thou are a low creature, of the Andrews breed, a reptile of a lower order, a weed that grows in the common garden of creation' (IV, 6).

As a man of wide experience, a countryman who lived in the town, an aristocrat who when Bow Street Magistrate came in contact with the hopeless dregs of London humanity, a true-born Englishman whose university experience was at Leyden – and moreover as a man whose powers of intelligence, observation, and imitation were both acute and profound – Fielding was superbly equipped to separate out the characteristic styles of the professions and also of the various social classes. In *Joseph Andrews* alone, when his powers had not yet reached the heights that produced the wonderful versatility and variegation of *Tom Jones*, there are unforgettable encapsulations of the legal, the medical, and the parsonical styles.[7] Thus the perfect circularity of Parson Barnabas's line of argument is transparently exhibited in syntax, as he tells Joseph to forgive the thieves who have robbed him:

'Doubtless . . . it is lawful to kill a thief; but can you say you forgive them as a Christian ought?' Joseph desired to know what that forgiveness was. 'That is,' answered Barnabas, 'to forgive them as—as – it is to forgive them as – in short, it is to forgive them as a Christian.' Joseph replied, 'He forgave them as much as he could'. – 'Well, well,' said Barnabas, 'that will do'. (I, 13.)

As for class usages in *Joseph Andrews*, the most outstanding examples are those of Lady Booby (I, 8 and IV, 3), some of the passion of her utterance prefiguring that of Lady Catherine de Bourgh in *Pride and Prejudice*; the French-English Bellarmine, whose French-English letter is entirely heartless (II, 4); the analphabetic justice of the peace (IV, 5); and, most original of all, Mrs Slipslop who as a waiting gentlewoman has half-literate pretensions of gentility that are nothing short of hilarious. Mrs Slipslop's solecisms are oblique utterance. She says what she thinks a lady ought to mean, but actually means what a waiting gentlewoman says: the fact of dramatic irony therefore makes her speeches the more amusing to the readers of *Joseph Andrews*. 'If we like a man, the lightest hint *sophisticates*' (I, 6), she says with a perfection of accuracy which she is not by any means clever enough to intend. 'Is it not enough,' she asks Joseph, 'ungrateful as you are, to make no return to all the favours I have done you; but you must treat me with *ironing*?' (I, 6). She means that Joseph is being cruel and inflexible to her, but the word 'irony' gleaming through the solecism makes for a level of meaning superbly unintentional but also deliciously just.

Tom Jones abounds in examples of the jargon which is the disease of the pretentious among the professional classes. Thus there occurs the combination of portentous Latin and self-congratulatory obfuscation which is the mark of the surgeon:

'Of wounds, indeed, it is rightly and truly said, *Nemo repento fait turpissimus*. I was once, I remember called to a patient who had received a violent contusion in his tibia, by which the exterior cutis was lacerated, so that there was a profuse sanguinary discharge; and the interior membranes were so devellicated, that the os or bone very plainly appeared through the aperture of the vulnus or wound. Some febrile symptoms intervening at the same time (for the pulse was exuberant and indicated much phlebotomy), I apprehended an immediate mortification'. (VII, 13.)

There is also in *Tom Jones* the fine variety of jargons of which samples appear in *Joseph Andrews*. Thus philosophical jargon is spouted by Square (e.g. V, 2), parsonical jargon is uttered by Roger Thwackum (e.g. V, 2) and Mr Supple the curate (e.g. IV, 11), academic jargon by Partridge (e.g. VIII, 5), fop's jargon by Watson (the Man of the Hill's college mate – e.g. VIII, 12), and – last but not least – servant's jargon by Mrs Honour (e.g. VI, 6). In *Joseph Andrews* Mrs Slipslop's solecisms are a delight. Nothing in *Tom Jones* quite rises to those heights. None the less, this inventiveness is copious in *Tom Jones*. Honour's letter to Tom Jones is a case in point. Illiteracy and solecism happily combine to make what the good servant says highly amusing. For instance, 'I wish ure Onur all thee gud luk in the wurld; and I don't cuestion butt thatt u will haf Madam Sofia in the end; butt ass to miself ure onur nose I kant bee of ani farder sarvis' (XV, 10).

About the grand style Fielding often betrays skepticism, but it is the doubt of a lover rather than the mistrust of an unbeliever. For all his invocation of plain English, Fielding uses the grand style when, in his view, grandeur is called for – as, for instance, in the description of a heroine: in *Joseph Andrews* Fanny's

complexion was fair, a little injured by the sun, but overspread with such a bloom, that the finest ladies would have exchanged all their white for it: add to these a countenance in which, though she was extremely bashful, a sensibility appeared almost incredible; and a sweetness, whenever she smiled, beyond either imitation or description. To conclude all, she had a natural gentility, superior to the acquisition of art, and which surprised all who beheld her. (II, 12.)

In *Joseph Andrews* there are a few but only a few other occasions on which propriety calls for panegyric language: dedications; declarations of passion, such as Wilson's to Harriet (III, 3);

proposals of marriage, such as Horatio's to Leonora (II, 4) –
(and compare the exchange of letters in the same chapter);
conclusions, such as that contained in the final paragraph of
Joseph Andrews. All these must be taken straight, or nearly
straight. They are common form.[8] And yet the characteristic
hard wit which is seldom absent in Fielding manifests itself even
here. It is for this reason, I think, that Fielding cannot in the
final lines of *Joseph Andrews* resist what Maynard Mack calls
'a last flick at the author of *Pamela*'.[9] 'The happiness of this
couple is a perpetual fountain of pleasure to their fond parents;
and, what is particularly remarkable, he declares he will
imitate them in their retirement; nor will be prevailed on by
any booksellers, or their authors, to make his appearance in
"high-life".'[10] That is to say, the grand style is usable, and far
more capacious than it is today; thus the dedications, descriptions, declarations, proposals, and conclusions which Fielding
invests in this style now seem to us overdone and therefore dated.
They stand out; we must make an effort of sympathy if we are
to understand them as Fielding meant them to be understood.
None the less, often though not invariably, he allows a few drops
of irony to roughen the surface of the panegyric. Thus, everyone believes the pedlar's story, 'except Pamela, who imagined,
as she had never heard either of her parents mention such an
accident, that it must certainly be false; and except the Lady
Booby, who suspected the falsehood of the story from her ardent
desire that it should be true; and Joseph, who feared its truth
from his earnest wishes that it might prove false' (IV, 13). The
perfection of the balance here provides that mirth-inducing
overbalance which is the eternal tendency and frequent outcome of Fielding's use of the grand style.

Indeed, there is often in Fielding's employment of the
panegyric a touch or more than a touch of the mocking, and
here Fielding anticipates the romantic irony of such writers as
Eichendorff who in *Aus dem Lebens eines Taugenichts* mocks and
approves simultaneously. So in *Tom Jones*, when Sophia is
introduced (IV, 2) there is a preliminary quartet of paragraphs
as sentimental as anything Sterne ever wrote. Fielding, that is
to say, has no one plain style that can do all his work for him.

Grandeur of sentiment calls for grandeur of language, and if Fielding occasionally betrays himself so far as to smile when he is writing panegyrically, he certainly does not intend his meaning to be upset by the operation of simple irony. 'Hushed be every ruder breath', he writes at the beginning of chapter two of Book IV:

May the heathen ruler of the winds confine in iron chains the boisterous limbs of noisy Boreas, and the sharp-pointed nose of bitter-biting Eurus. Do thou, sweet Zephyrus, rising from thy fragrant bed, mount the western sky, and lead on those delicious gales, the charms of which call forth the lovely Flora from her chamber, perfumed with pearly dews, when on the first of June, her birthday, the blooming maid, in loose attire, gently trips it over the verdant mead, where every flower rises to do her homage, till the whole field becomes enamelled, and colours contend with sweets which shall ravish her most.

In such a passage, which comes so close to self-parody, can be seen the confidence of a man who is, in Tennyson's phrase, a lord of language.

Elsewhere the grand style is also used entirely straightforwardly as it is in Tom's letter to Sophia in chapter 12 of Book VI. It can also be used – so completely is Fielding in control of his medium – in such a way as to betray insincerity of sentiment. Thus Lord Fellamar plainly desires to have Sophia for himself: that is, he is straightforwardly lustful; and he rightly supposes that the correct style of address is panegyric. But he so manages himself as to betray his violent purpose. 'I doat on you,' he says, 'to the highest degree of distraction. O most adorable, most divine creature! what language can express the sentiments of my heart?' (XV, 5). Two inadvertencies betray Lord Fellamar here: first the alliteration – 'dote . . . degree . . . distraction . . . adorable . . . divine'. And second, his asking for language instead of supplying it. By comparison, Tom in another letter to Sophia (XVI, 3) is no less elevated but much more effectively controlled and articulate.

Can the most perfect admiration, the most watchful observance, the most ardent love, the most melting tenderness, the most resigned submission to your will, make you amends for what you are to sacrifice to my happiness? If they can, fly, my lovely angel, to those arms which are ever open to receive and protect you; and to which, whether you bring yourself alone, or the riches of the world with you, is, in my opinion, an alternative not worth regarding.[11]

The panegyric style is used as appropriate for tenderness in *Amelia*, as it also is in *Tom Jones*. There is nothing to be laughed at in chapter 3 of Book IV, when Booth exclaims to his wife in the following way:

'O, my Amelia, how much are you my superior in every perfection! how wise, how great, how noble are your sentiments! why can I not imitate what I so much admire? Why can I not look with your constancy on those dear little pledges of our loves? All my philosophy is baffled with the thought that my Amelia's children are to struggle with a cruel, hard, unfeeling world, and to buffet those waves of fortune which have overwhelmed their father.'

The triads of the opening phrases, the antithesis of the first question, above all the highly charged diction: these are quite obviously meant to be taken as read, without any coloration of irony.

On the other hand, and somewhat discomfortingly, there appears an elevated style in chapter 1 of Book VI. Here the beauty of Amelia is described in high style: 'Exercise had painted her face with vermilion; and the highest good-humour had so sweetened every feature, and a vast flow of spirits had so lightened up her bright eyes, that she was all ablaze of beauty'. Thus far, the panegyric strikes one as belonging quite comprehensibly within the framework of Fielding's linguistic habits. But then he over-extends himself. Immediately after the sentence which I have cited occurs reference to Milton's Eve, together with quotation; and reference as well to Waller and to Suckling's Cupid. It is too much: Fielding's intention topples under the weight of his own rhetoric. For *Amelia*, as its style so undoubtedly reveals, veers away from the novel and edges toward the instrumental end of satire. In the sixth chapter of Book VIII Colonel James arranges for Booth to be bailed, and Bondum – the bailiff – is recalcitrant until it is revealed to him that James is a Member of Parliament, after which Bondum becomes all obsequiousness. The matter of this chapter could be made into the stuff of comedy but Fielding gives his intention away in the very chapter title itself. The title of the chapter is: 'Which rather inclines to satire than panegyric'.

In the earlier novels Fielding has a clear idea of the uses to which the grand style should be put. Rotundity of style makes for an elevated and often appropriate sonorousness; magniloquence is laughable – and the twain occasionally meet in such a way as to produce in the utterance of Parson Adams and Squire Allworthy portraits of innocent vanity. But by the time he comes to write *Amelia* Fielding's purpose has become blunted, and this fact is as demonstrable in his use of the grand or panegyric style as it is in the employment of other stylistic – and indeed other novelistic devices.

In chapter 10 of Book III Dr Harrison writes to Booth and Amelia (who are in Paris) a fairly long and heavily sententious letter. The news it contains is that Amelia's mother has died, and that she has left her entire fortune to Betty, Amelia's disagreeable elder sister. Obviously we are meant to understand the letter to be oppressively full of platitudinous appeals to endure the news which the good clergyman withholds until very near the end of the letter. But the letter is discomforting because we are left with a disagreeable fact that can be brought into no comic focus within the narratives. Fielding makes some fun of Dr Harrison, but it is pointless fun, the half-joke of an author no longer in firm command of things.

Implicit in Fielding's very approach to language is an ideal of plainness which, however, vanishes at the onset of straightforward appeal. Again and again in the course of the novels Fielding produces the phrase 'plain English' or some equivalent as a bridge between consequentially inaccurate and sparely straightforward utterance.[12] This is a matter which demands attention for several reasons. The most important is that what is offered as the plain alternative is nearly always hedged by irony. The second reason is that Fielding never establishes, except by implication, a norm of plainness. And the third is that the variety of styles in evidence throughout the novels (with the usual qualification so far as *Amelia* is concerned) seems to me to point not to an attempt to achieve plainness as such, but to a highly sophisticated effort to establish realms of artistic being.

LANGUAGE AND PLAY

I begin with an easy and uncomplicated example, from *Joseph Andrews*.

> Slipslop, who knew the violence of her lady's temper, and would not venture her place for any Adonis or Hercules in the universe, left her a third time; which she had no sooner done, than the little god Cupid, fearing he had not yet done the lady's business, took a fresh arrow with the sharpest point out of his quiver, and shot it directly into her heart: *in other and plainer language*, the lady's passion got the better of her reason. (I, 7; italics mine.)

The effect of elevating Lady Booby's passion to an heroic level is clear enough. Again, Fielding brings forward Hesperus, Thetis, and Phoebus, only to send them back again with: '*In vulgar language*, it was in the evening when Joseph attended his lady's orders' (I, 8; italics mine). Fielding, it seems to me, has no discernible critical motive – he is not trying to find a way to write plainly: he is playing.

But I confess that – also in *Joseph Andrews* – it is less easy to interpret Fielding's twice-given description of Leonora's abandonment of the faithful Horatio in favour of Bellarmine. 'Thus, what Horatio had by sighs and tears, love and tenderness, been so long obtaining, the French-English Bellarmine with gaiety and gallantry possessed himself of in an instant. *In other words*, what modesty had employed a full year in raising, impudence demolished in twenty-four hours' (II, 4; italics mine). The first part of this utterance is interesting in that it uses 'gaiety and gallantry' as ironic ballast. That the adjectives applied to Bellarmine are to be understood ironically is foreshadowed in the dual nationality he possesses and underscored by the alliteration of the phrase itself. So Fielding is using grand language to deflate; it is gratuitous to put the matter 'in other words' – or would be gratuitous if Fielding consistently used the panegyric style in this way. Francophobia was a popular disease in the eighteenth century; the terms and methods have changed but little since Fielding's day. But this contrast between French nonsense and English sense can point the way to a narrower contrast which Fielding occasionally affects – the contrast between poetic language and the language of prose. Adams fights with a man who has been trying to rape Fanny;

the ruffian 'belaboured the body of Adams till he was weary, and, indeed, till he concluded (to use the language of fighting) "that he had done his business"; or, in the language of poetry, "that he had sent him to the shades below"; *in plain English*, "that he was dead" ' (II, 10; italics mine). It is certain that the spare four-word statement is useful dramatically; it helps to frame the scene. The affectation of simplicity is appealing; but the alternatives call attention to themselves; they are self-consciously literary, diverting, artificial. They prevent us even here from confusing this comic epic romance with actual life. Once again artifice precludes not judgment itself, but judgment's sting. Such is Fielding's final choice so far as the novel is concerned: the novel's function is to nourish the festive sense and, by presenting civilization, perform a civilizing role. This is not didacticism but it is communication of knowledge of a kind and quality that requires hope and charity: the reader willing to meet Fielding so far along the road between the writer and himself will be rewarded by an accretion of faith, not in man but in art.

Equally flexible, and equally sophisticated, is the use of the appeal to plainness in *Tom Jones*. In the concluding chapter of Book I, Dr Blifil, having acted as go-between in his brother's courtship of Bridget, is now discarded; the book ends with the Doctor's removal to London, 'where he died soon after of a broken heart'. Toward the beginning of this chapter there occurs the following paragraph relating to Captain Blifil's treatment of his brother. 'One of the maxims which the devil, in a late visit upon earth, left to his disciples, is, when once you are got up, to kick the stool from under you. *In plain English*, when you have made your fortune by the good offices of a friend, you are advised to discard him as soon as you can' (I, 13; italics mine). Assuredly there is no lack of plainness in the first half of this paragraph; and it is clear that the application of the quality of Captain Blifil's gratitude to his brother would be easy to make without the 'explanation' that follows the phrase 'in plain English'. The phrase is used here, it seems to me, as a device to make repetition palatable and also as a device to draw attention to the literary aspect of the story.

Exuberance for the sake of exuberance, richness for the sake of decorative endowment: such seems to me to be the motive for the following passage.

The shadows began now to descend larger from the high mountains; the feathered creation had betaken themselves to their rest. Now the highest order of mortals were sitting down to their dinners, and the lowest order to their suppers. *In a word*, the clock struck five just as Mr Jones took his leave of Gloucester; an hour at which (as it was now mid-winter) the dirty fingers of Night would have drawn her sable curtain over the universe, had not the moon forbid her, who now, with a face as broad and as red as those of some jolly mortals, who, like her, turn night into day, began to rise from her bed, where she had slumbered away the day, in order to sit up all night. (VIII, 9; italics mine.)

The passage begins with an orotundity which perhaps needs deflating but certainly does not require clarification. Therefore, instead of repeating 'in a word' what he has already said, Fielding says two other things: first that the clock struck five, and second, that Jones departed. But, not content with his sideswipe at fancy language, he then goes on to mix the grand and the grubby ('dirty fingers of night') in a double relative clause the periodicity of which is breathtaking.

In truth, Fielding is skittish about language. At the same time, however, he knows what he wants to say, and he knows how to say it in such a way as to be entirely clear. This is even truer of *Tom Jones* than of *Joseph Andrews*: the maturer work shows Fielding to be supremely confident. Chapter 2 of Book IX begins as follows: 'Aurora now first opened her casement, *Anglice* the day began to break. . . .' Fielding writes thus in a high-spirited invitation – implicit in the orotundity and in the gratuitous clarification – to take what he says and what he presents as having a mode of existence that is high spirited. It is especially appropriate in this chapter, for it provides a framework to the rescue by Tom of the screaming woman whom he discovers to be a certain Mrs Waters. Thus the pall is removed even from the scene of attempted rape.

The Battle of Upton, which takes place in the following chapter (IX, 3), offers Fielding rich opportunity for exploitation of the playful possibilities of language; I should like to call attention only to the arch paragraph which describes Tom's pusillanimous response to the belabourings of the landlady's tongue: 'he could not be provoked to make any resistance; but in a most cowardly manner applied, with many entreaties, to his antagonist to desist from pursuing her blows; *in plain English*, he only begged her with the utmost earnestness to hear him' (IX, 3; italics mine). Ian Watt, as I have already remarked,[13] writes of the double audience which Fielding and his contemporaries addressed, the ordinary reader, and the learned man. Here, however, he is pretending that some readers will need to have explained to them the fact that the landlady's weapon is her tongue. He is thus flattering the ignorant reader by pretending that others are more opaque than is in fact humanly probable.

Wherever, in *Tom Jones*, the moral pressure threatens to destroy the light and festive tone of the novel as a whole, Fielding interposes in one or more of several ways and, by the act of linguistic prevention through embellishment, preserves the tone entire. Thus when it is becoming clear in Book XIV that Nightingale has engaged irresponsibly in a dalliance with Nancy Miller, the moral situation is portentous. And Tom as a responsive and sympathetic youth perceives what threatens. He lies awake at night. 'Sleep, however, at length got the better of all resistance; and now, as if he had already been a deity, as the ancients imagined, and an offended one too, he seemed to enjoy his dear-bought conquest. *To speak simply, and without metaphor*, Mr Jones slept till eleven the next morning' (XIV, 6; italics mine). This is, it seems to me, an excellent example, since what is mocked is hardly more orotund than the 'translation'.

Near the beginning of *Amelia* occurs a reassuringly familiar example of the two modes of utterance, the fancy and the plain. Assessing the quality of the venal Jonathan Thrasher, J.P., the narrator writes:

He perfectly well understood that fundamental principle so strongly laid down in the institutes of the learned Rochefoucault, by which the duty of self-love is so strongly enforced, and every man is taught to consider himself as the centre of gravity, and to attract all things thither. *To speak the truth plainly*, the justice was never indifferent in a cause but when he could get nothing on either side. (I, 2; italics mine.)

But this exhibition of contrasts almost disappears in the course of *Amelia*: it is a formula which Fielding abandons for less self-confident weapons. At best the example which I have just cited represents some considerable loss of power: the multiple negations of the plain-English phrase are the ordinary weapons of irony in the armoury of every writer of satire. Playfulness, that self-contained and unambitious delight in language which irradiates the earlier novels, has all but disappeared.

In that wise and illuminating series of lectures which she has published as *The Business of Criticism*, Helen Gardner speaks of 'the necessity of learning the author's own personal language, the idiom of his thought'.[14] Of course she is right, but the critic – as Miss Gardner well realizes and always, in her own criticism, demonstrates – must attend to the idiom employed in the particular work under consideration; the critic must be sufficiently generous and sufficiently pertinacious to realize that his author may easily be at least as complicated and as multivalent as himself. Fielding was a novelist and he was a magistrate; the characteristics that he exhibited in the one field of competence doubtless overlap the characteristics exhibited in the other – but it is a different thing to write a novel from what it is to sit in judgment in Bow Street. Historians, biographers, and critics all tend to oversimplify – to find a single characteristic, a single motive, a single ruling passion, to explain what is perhaps more accurately understood as but one strand in the fabric of a vision. For a literary critic style is not the man, it is the artifact; my study is founded upon the belief that the 'rhetoric of fiction' is for ever what needs attending to; and Fielding's three novels have seemed to me worth examining because he found even in an evil and corrupt world, modes of existence that were for him and are perhaps for all time a saving glory.

NOTES

Chapter 1

1. That very useful phrase resuscitated by Kathleen Tillotson, and employed by Wayne Booth in *The Rhetoric of Fiction* (Chicago, 1961), p. 71. Booth's book is a landmark in the history of criticism. A more usual and less helpful way of looking at Fielding's narrative method is that of E. A. Baker in *The History of the English Novel* (10 vols., London, 1924-39). Baker remarks that Fielding 'discarded both Defoe's method of the conscientious reporter and Richardson's subterfuge of authentic letters. Without making any elaborate pretences, he stationed himself at the point of view of the omniscient spectator, and launched straightway into his prose epic. It was the first time in English fiction that the performers in the story evoked the sense of life by their dramatic self-sufficiency. Even Richardson had wasted our time and his by accumulating superfluous details to assure us that he was retailing fact; Defoe had been driven into downright fraud. Fielding flung all these tricks aside, and attended to the real business. He tells you he is giving you fiction and he lets fiction speak for itself' (IV, 102). Behind Baker's sentence is an idea of the novel which did not establish itself until near the end of the nineteenth century. Fielding's second self does indeed tell us he is giving us fiction – so far, so good; but to say, 'he lets fiction speak for itself' is to disjoin the connection between comment and action. Fortunately, Wayne Booth has blown away a great many cobwebs from this important area. See also E. D. Hirsch, Jr., 'Objective Interpretation', *PMLA*, LXXV (1960), 478.

2. *The Mirror and the Lamp* (New York, 1953), p. 16.

3. An impressively detailed consideration of this important aspect of Fielding's life is contained in B. M. Jones's *Henry Fielding: Novelist and Magistrate* (London, 1933), pp. 113-245.

4. Reprinted in Scott Elledge, ed., *Eighteenth-Century Critical Essays* (Ithaca, N.Y., 1961), II, 838-47. The passage cited is on p. 847.

5. Ford Maddox Ford, one of Fielding's most unfriendly critics, takes him to task for just this failure to be realistic: 'The trouble with the English novelist from Fielding to Meredith is that not one of them cares whether you quite believe in their characters or not. If you had told Flaubert or Conrad in the midst of their passionate composings that you were not convinced of the reality of Homais or Tuan Jim, as like as not they would have called you out and shot you, and in similar circumstances Richardson would have showed himself extremely disagreeable. But Fielding, Thackeray, or Meredith would have cared relatively little about that, though any one of them would have knocked you down if they could, supposing you had suggested that he was not a "gentleman" ' (*The English Novel* [Philadelphia,

1929], p. 96). Booth cites this passage in *The Rhetoric of Fiction*, and makes devastating comment on it, pp. 40, 41.

6. Martin C. Battestin, ed., *Joseph Andrews & Shamela* (Boston, 1961), p. 307.

7. Ian Watt finds it natural that Fielding should have tried to rub some of the epic's dignity on to the novel. Nevertheless, as Professor Watt points out (and as Fielding no doubt realized): 'the epic is, after all, an oral and poetic genre dealing with the public and usually remarkable deeds of historical or legendary persons engaged in a collective rather than an individual enterprise; and none of these things can be said of the novel' (*The Rise of the Novel* [London, 1957], p. 240). Fielding himself is plain enough as to the purpose of the comic epic poem in prose. In the preface to *David Simple* he writes as follows: 'This fable hath in it three difficult ingredients, which will be found on consideration to be always necessary in works of this kind, viz., that the main end or scope be at once amiable, ridiculous, and natural' (Henley ed., XVI, 11).

8. The celebrated roasting scene of Book III, chapter 7, is among the most amusing in the novel because Fielding has distanced it sufficiently to take the moral sting out, or almost out, of the incident, and thus to make it conform to the festive intent of the novel as a whole. But in *The Champion* for 13 March 1739-40 Fielding wrote as follows of roasting: 'If we consider this diversion in the worst light, it will appear to be no other than a delight in seeing the miseries, misfortunes, and frailties of mankind displayed; and a pleasure and joy conceived in their sufferings therein. A pleasure, perhaps, as inhuman, and which must arise from a nature as thoroughly corrupt and diabolical, as can possibly pollute the mind of man' (Henley ed., XV, 243).

9. Several years later, in the issue of *The Jacobite's Journal* in which he announces that he is going to abandon the mask of irony (No. 17, 26 March 1748), Fielding renounces also the weapon of ridicule against the Jacobites: their threats to the throne and the constitution are too grave: 'To consider such Attempts as these in a ludicrous Light, would be as absurd as the Conceit of a Fellow in *Bartholomew-Fair*, who exhibited the comical Humours of *Nero* ripping up his Mother's Belly; and surely a man who endeavours to rip up the Bowels of his Country, is altogether as improper an Object of Ridicule'. This issue of *The Jacobite's Journal* is not reprinted in the Henley edition.

10. In the introduction to *A Journey from this World to the Next*, Fielding delightedly mocks the stratagems by which authors hope to make an aura of verisimilitude. He pretends to have found *A Journey* through having discovered that a bundle of pens, bought of a stationer in the Strand, was wrapped in a sheet of paper on which writing appeared. 'I therefore perused this sheet with wonderful application, and in about a day's time discovered that I could not understand it'. He then proceeds to write a solemn account of the recovery of the rest of the sheets, the decipherment, and so forth. And then, lest the fictive nature of the work itself be lost sight of, he mock-

pedantically writes footnotes, such as the following, which appears as a note to the date 1741: 'Some doubt whether this should not be rather 1641, which is a date more agreeable to the account given of it in the introduction: but then there are some passages which seem to relate to transactions infinitely later, even within this year or two. – To say the truth, there are difficulties attend either conjecture; so the reader may take which he pleases' (Henley ed., II, 212, 215). By directing our attention to the apparatus of his fiction, he reminds us of its fictive quality. Hence – in *Joseph Andrews* itself – the confidence of such an intrusion as the following, which is the narrator's comment on a dishonest constable's protestations of innocence on the escape of the thief (I, 16): 'But, notwithstanding these and many other such allegations, I am sufficiently convinced of his innocence; having been positively assured of it by those who received their informations from his own mouth; which, in the opinion of some moderns, is the best and indeed only evidence'. This is a sideswipe at the followers of Shaftesbury, but the passage is less significant for that reason than for its demonstration of assumed complicity between narrator and readers – they will know what to think of 'some moderns' without further argument.

11. Wayne Booth's warning is useful here: 'We too easily fall into the habit of talking as if the narrator who says, "O my good readers!" were Fielding, forgetting that for all we know he may have worked as deliberately and with as much detachment in creating the wise, urbane narrator of *Joseph Andrews* and *Tom Jones* as he did in creating the cynical narrator of *Jonathan Wild*' (*The Rhetoric of Fiction*, pp. 82, 83). I myself use the word 'Fielding' to mean Fielding in his role as narrator – or rather, in his roles, because they change from novel to novel.

12. Henry Knight Miller, *Essays on Fielding's 'Miscellanies': A Commentary on Volume One* (Princeton, 1961), p. 373. This is an indispensable study of Fielding's ideas; it is of far wider application than the title indicates.

13. Cohen translation, Penguin edition (London, 1950), p. 581.

14. James Sutherland cites a useful example and makes a sensible comment on p. 250 of his *Defoe* (London, 1938).

15. 'Towards Defining an Age of Sensibility', originally published in *ELH*, reprinted in James L. Clifford, ed., *Eighteenth-Century English Literature: Modern Essays in Criticism* (New York, 1959), p. 312.

16. For the reader of Cibber's *Apology* there is additional cause for mirth; here as elsewhere Fielding is making fun of Cibber's predilection for gastronomical figures of speech. For instance, 'If, indeed, to our several Theatres we could raise a proportionable Number of good Authors to give them all different Employment, then perhaps the Publick might profit from their Emulation: But while good Writers are so scarce, and undaunted Criticks so plenty, I am afraid a good Play and a blazing Star will be equal Rarities. This voluptuous Expedient, therefore, of indulging the Taste with several Theatres, will amount to much the same variety as that of a certain Oeconomist, who, to enlarge his Hospitality, would have two Puddings and

two Legs of Mutton for the same Dinner. – But to resume the Thread of my History' (*An Apology for the Life of Colley Cibber*, ed. Robert W. Lowe [London, 1889], I, 93). The editor appends the following: 'Fielding ("Champion", 6th May, 1740): Another Observation which I have made on our Author's Similies is, that they generally have an Eye towards the Kitchen. Thus *page 56, Two Play-Houses are like two* PUDDINGS *or two* LEGS OF MUTTON. *224. To plant young Actors is not so easy as to plant* CABBAGES. To which let me add a Metaphor in *page 57*, where *unprofitable Praise can hardly give Truth a* SOUP MAIGRE'.

17. 'The Ironic Tradition in Augustan Prose from Swift to Johnson', *Restoration & Augustan Prose* (Los Angeles, 1956), p. 22.

18. In *The Champion* for 5 July 1740 Fielding wrote: 'It is a bold Assertion, and yet, I believe, a true one. That all Men of Sense are of one Mind. Here we must understand, Men whose Minds are strong enough to throw off all ridiculous Prejudices of Education, whose Eyes, if I may so express myself, are able to behold Truth without a Glass, such I believe will be very seldom found to maintain any gross Error, or to depart from the Way of Truth, where some private Passion or interest is not immediately concerned'. This issue was not reprinted in the Henley edition.

19. Nor was Fielding reluctant to laugh at protestation. *Tom Thumb* is, of course, a burlesque of conventional tragedy, and the preface to the revised version – *The Tragedy of Tragedies* – contains a solemn, detailed, and lunatic 'justification' of the play in Aristotelian terms. In addition – and also by extension – *The Tragedy of Tragedies* is a burlesque of pedantic scholarship. The play is filled with footnotes drawing attention to the sources and analogues which in fact Fielding wishes to caricature.

20. These have been edited by S. J. Sackett and collected in the Augustan Reprint Society's Publication Number 67, *The Voyages of Mr Job Vinegar from the Champion* (Los Angeles, 1958). Explicitly imitative of *Gulliver's Travels*, these 'papers' are bitterly condemnatory of things-as-they-are. Here are some samples of the laws of the Ptfghsiumgski, the Inconstants: 'All great Vices as Drinking, Gaming, injuring their Neighbour by walking over his Land, or taking away a Cock or a Hen from him, &c. are very severely punished, but for little Foibles, and which may rather be called Weaknesses than Crimes, such as Avarice, Ingratitude, Cruelty, Envy, Malice, Falsehood, and the rest of this Kind, they are entirely overlooked. . . . Beside their written Laws, they have several Customs which by long Usage have obtained great Force, and established several Offences which are punished by what they call Contempt: Such are Poverty, Poetry, Modesty, Good-nature, Charity, and other of the like Kind' (*p.* 11).

21. In *Pasquin* (1736), a play about plays – art about art – the comic play-wright Trapwit says to the tragic playwright Fustian: 'Do you think I am like your shallow writers of comedy, who publish the banns of marriage between all the couples in their play in the first act? No, sir, I defy you to guess my couple till the thing is done, slap, all at once; and that too by an incident arising from the main business of the play, and to which everything conduces' (I, i – Henley ed., XI, 177, 178).

22. E. A. Baker begs the question by dilution, it seems to me. 'There is no Sancho Panzo in *Joseph Andrews*; but his matter-of-fact stolidity, his sensuality, his greed, his horse-sense, are, as it were, distributed among a vulgar rabble who provide the necessary contrast' (*History of the English Novel*, IV, 95).

23. The great care which Fielding took in writing *Joseph Andrews* is abundantly and incontrovertibly documented in Martin C. Battestin's 'Fielding's Revisions of *Joseph Andrews*', *Papers of the Bibliographical Society of the University of Virginia*, XVI (1963), 81-117. This essay discusses and records the differences in substance among the first five editions of the novel. Chiefly the alterations take place in the second edition, and these make the utterance more precise, the scene more vivid, the speech more idiosyncratic, the action clearer. Thus in chapter 2 of Book II there appears in the first edition this sentence: 'This Accident was no other than the forgetting to put up the Sermons, which were indeed left behind'; in the second edition, Fielding adds a detail, and invites his audience to become more closely implicated: 'This Accident was, that those Sermons, which the Parson was travelling to *London* to publish, were, O my good Reader, left behind'. Another example demonstrates Fielding's wish to underscore Parson Trulliber's hypocrisy: In the first edition, Book II, chapter 15, appears this sentence: 'Now Mr *Trulliber* had by his Piety, Gravity, Austerity, Reserve, and the Opinion of his great Wealth . . .'. The second edition reads: 'Now Mr *Trulliber* had by his Professions of Piety, by his Gravity, Austerity, Reserve, and the Opinion of his great Wealth . . .'.

24. *The Novels of Fielding* (London, 1925), p. 84. 'Il montrera impitoyablement le secret égoisme qui nous décide à choisir tel parti plutôt que tel autre' (*Les Romans de Fielding* [Paris, 1923], p. 110).

25. See, for instance, that formidable document, *An Enquiry into the Causes of the Late Increase of Robbers* (1751). Or see, in *Joseph Andrews* itself, Joseph's observation to Parson Adams: 'It is strange that all men should consent in commending goodness, and no man endeavour to deserve that commendation; whilst, on the contrary, all rail at wickedness, and all are as eager to be what they abuse' (III, 6).

26. This issue of *The True Patriot* is not reprinted in the Henley edition.

27. *The Moral Basis of Fielding's Art* (Middletown, Conn., 1959), *passim*. But Donald J. Greene will not accept Battestin's argument: 'The "latitudinarianism" referred to seems to be another construct of literary historians, very different from the historical latitudinarianism that Macaulay, say, describes' (*Studies in English Literature*, I (1961), 136).

28. Author's Preface. William B. Coley's erudite and elegant 'The Background of Fielding's Laughter', *ELH*, XXVI (1959), 229-52, traces the genealogy of Fielding's comic postures.

29. Compare Wayne Booth: 'Much as Fielding and Dickens, Trollope and Thackeray may talk about their passion for truth to nature or the real,

they are often willing, as some modern critics have complained, to sacrifice reality to tears or laughter' (*The Rhetoric of Fiction*, p. 57).

30. Wilbur Cross, in *The History of Henry Fielding*, II, 104, 105, points out that this first chapter elaborates on a letter written by Fielding in *The True Patriot* for 3 December 1745.

31. See Ian Watt on the neo-classical idea of requiring and reconciling both verisimilitude and the marvellous (*The Rise of the Novel*, pp. 252, 253).

32. Henry James writes approvingly of Fielding ('he handsomely possessed of a mind') as narrator of *Tom Jones*: 'Fielding's fine old moralism, fine old humour and fine old style . . . somehow really enlarge, make every one and every thing important' (Preface to *The Princess Casamassima*, reprinted in *The Art of the Novel* [New York, 1934], p. 68).

33. 'The Augustan Conception of History', in J. A. Mazzeo, ed., *Reason and the Imagination* (London, 1962), p. 214.

34. In this sense also Fielding was a man of his own time, since as historian he wished to extend the boundaries of history beyond the realms to which it had been confined, the realms of politics and morals. See Professor Davis's essay, p. 229.

35. Ian Watt is, it seems to me, writing autobiography rather than criticism when he says: 'Sophia never wholly recovers from so artificial an introduction, or at least never wholly disengages herself from the ironical attitude which it has induced' (*The Rise of the Novel*, pp. 254, 255). But it is Fielding who induces the ironical attitude, openly and deliberately, in the first chapter of the book; Sophia appears, with all the rhetorical flourishes for which Fielding has prepared us, in chapter 2.

36. 4 February 1813, in R. W. Chapman, ed., *Jane Austen's Letters to Her Sister Cassandra and Others* (2nd ed., London, 1952), pp. 299, 300.

37. *The Rhetoric of Fiction*, p. 217.

38. 'Fielding's *Amelia*: An Interpretation', *ELH*, III (1936), 1-14.

39. A handful, anyway, comparatively speaking: it is difficult to know how to count the number of characters in a novel – whether to include those who are dead before the action is presumed to have begun, whether to reckon characters who have no names, and so forth – but by any scheme there are far fewer characters in *Amelia* than there are in *Tom Jones*. (My own way of reckoning is to include all characters given either surnames or Christian names – including nicknames, and to apply a common-sense rule of relative importance for other characters. Thus I include the keeper of the prison in which Booth and Miss Matthews are incarcerated, but I exclude many other unnamed characters, including some ostlers and others who appear only momentarily. By this flexible system, I count 43 characters in *Amelia*, as compared to 38 in the far shorter *Joseph Andrews* and 69 in *Tom Jones*.

40. In 'The Background of Fieldings' Laughter', William Coley cites this passage in support of his argument that Fieldings' last novel manifests some

important changes in attitude, including the 'anti-comic notion of a new verisimilitude' (*ELH*, XXVI (1959), 251, 252).

41. To demonstrate that the distance covered by Booth is short I would point (as does Professor Sherburn in the essay to which I have referred) to the lines from Claudian's *In Rufinum* cited by Fielding in chapter 3 of Book I, to describe 'the wavering condition' of Booth:

> labefacta cadebat
> Relligio, causaeque viam non sponte sequebar
> Alterius; vacuo quae currere semina motu
> Adfirmat magnumque novas per inane figuras
> Fortuna, non arte, regi; quae numina sensu
> Ambiguo, vel nulla putat, vel nescia nostri.

'... then in turn my belief in God was weakened and failed, and even against mine own will I embraced the tenets of that other philosophy [Epicureanism] which teaches that atoms drift in purposeless motion and that new forms throughout the vast void are shaped by chance and not design – that philosophy which believes in God in an ambiguous sense, or holds that there be no gods, or that they are careless of our doings' (Claudian, *In Rufinum*, I: 14-19. Loeb translation quoted by Sherburn, 'Fielding's *Amelia*: An Interpretation', p. 6).

42. Wayne Booth is not so harsh about the narrator of *Amelia*, but he does underscore the fact that there is a radical difference from what might have been expected of the narrator of *Joseph Andrews* or *Tom Jones*: 'The author who greets us on page one of *Amelia* has none of that air of facetiousness combined with grand insouciance that we meet from the beginning in *Joseph Andrews* and *Tom Jones*. . . . Though the author of *Amelia* can still indulge in occasional jests and ironies, his general air of sententious solemnity is strictly in keeping with the very special effects proper to the work as a whole' (*The Rhetoric of Fiction*, pp. 72, 73).

43. *Tom Jones* was published in February 1749, but Millar the printer issued a receipt for the nearly completed MS. in June 1748; the dedication was written, Cross says, in October or early November. *Amelia* was begun in January 1751 and published in the following December. Wilbur L. Cross, *The History of Henry Fielding* (New Haven, Conn., 1918), II, 108, 304, 311.

44. Cross argues that *Jonathan Wild* was written in 1742, *op. cit.*, I, 409-12; but Dudden argues that some sections were written about 1740, and some others in 1742 and 1743. F. Homes Dudden, *Henry Fielding: His Life, Works, and Times* (Oxford, 1952), I, 80-3.

45. Swift, *Correspondence*, ed. F. E. Ball (London, 1910-14), IV, 216.

Chapter 2

1. *Aspects of the Novel* (London, 1927), p. 156.

2. See Charles B. Woods, 'The Authorship of *Shamela*', *PQ*, XXV (1946), 248-72; see also Ian Watt's introduction to the Augustan Reprint

Society's reproduction of the William Andrews Clark Library copy of the second edition (Augustan Reprint Society Publication Number 57, Berkeley, 1956).

3. For an account of the furore which the appearance of *Pamela* occasioned, see Frederic T. Blanchard, *Fielding the Novelist: A Study in Historical Criticism* (New Haven, 1926), pp. 1-4.

4. *The Novels of Fielding*, p. 53. 'Cette volte-face apparente a généralement surpris les critiques. Ils expliquent que Fielding s'est lui-même laissé prendre par l'histoire qu'il contait, et s'y est intéressé suffisamment pour oublier de parodier Richardson. Je me méfie d'une explication qui s'appuie sur une faiblesse d'un si grand écrivain. Le vérité me parait plus simple. Si Fielding cesse de développer la donnée première de son oeuvre, c'est peut-être, tout uniment, parce qu'elle ne comportait pas en elle-même un plus long développement' (*Les Roman de Fielding*, p. 74).

5. Letter II.

6. John Middleton Murry makes the sensible point that a straight parody of *Pamela* would bring Lady Booby to marry Joseph. 'Not only would this have made Joseph a character thoroughly uncongenial to Fielding, but, because nature would insist on breaking in, Joseph's character had already, in the Lady Booby scenes, been so presented that such a development was impossible' ('In Defence of Fielding', *Unprofessional Essays* [London, 1956], p. 27).

7. *Novels of Fielding*, p. 58. 'Or il construit son roman comme nos écrivains classiques construisaient leurs pièces, suivant un plan régulier, solide et sûr. Les quatre livres sont comme quatre actes, dont le premier contient l'exposition et le noeud, le deuxième et le troisième des péripéties, le quatrième le dénoument' (*Les Romans de Fielding*, p. 79).

8. At this point it is necessary to say something about the word 'structure' itself. In *The Business of Criticism* (Oxford, 1959, p. 23) Helen Gardner wisely says that 'structure' is inadequate as applied to a work of literature because it does not allow for the aspect of time. She prefers the word 'movement', and I do too. None the less, I find it difficult to use, because 'movement' does not without explanation convey the idea of structure. So I am going to continue to use the older word, but I would be understood to mean structure *and* movement. I should like to be able to use the phrase 'dynamic structure'; the curative phrase, however, is worse than the disease. But despite the difficulties of terminology I shall want to consider *Joseph Andrews* developmentally.

Irvin Ehrenpreis, in an excellent essay on *Joseph Andrews*, makes a spirited if perhaps not altogether persuasive description of the novel's characteristic movement as follows: 'When Fielding is not advancing by retreats, he is generally continuing by interruptions. One scene commonly breaks in upon its predecessor rather than develops it. Almost every turn of events is due to some unexpected meeting of characters with one another.

These encounters are the beginning of a sequential formula which normally stops short of completion. In the proper sequence, a meeting is followed by a second step, conversation. This leads eventually to disagreement, and the fourth stage is an intense verbal argument. If the sequence is permitted to proceed, the final tableau is a ferocious mock-heroic scuffle, uproarious but causing no permanent injury' ('Fielding's Use of Fiction: The Autonomy of *Joseph Andrews*', in Charles Shapiro, ed., *Twelve Original Essays on Great English Novels* [Detroit, 1960], pp. 26, 27). Although Professor Ehrenpreis gives several examples of this method of construction, and perfectly sound examples, he is – I think – stretching things a bit: the 'modifications' of this pattern are such as to make differences in kind; the novel cannot be reduced so far.

9. In making this Table, I have used the Rinehart edition, ed. Martin C. Battestin.

10. For some remarks about which, see p. 65.

11. Nor is this the only evidence of care. Wilson tells of the strawberry birthmark on his abducted son's breast while Joseph is asleep – but the fact that he is asleep is not disclosed until after Wilson has revealed this fact. See the first two paragraphs of chapter 4. Furthermore, the fact that Fanny is a foundling is revealed very incidentally by Parson Adams in chapter 9, when he wishes to assure the captain that she is not suspiciously high-born.

12. The imitation of Cervantes here is patent. Throughout *Don Quixote* this device is used – for instance, in chapter 23 of Part II, when Don Quixote is relating his adventures of the cave of Montesinos, he mentions a stiletto. ' "That stiletto", put in Sancho, "must have been made by Ramon de Hoces of Seville." ' Don Quixote responds: ' "I do not know," continued Don Quixote. "But it could not be that stiletto-maker, because Ramon de Hoces was living yesterday, and the fight at Roncesvalles, where this tragedy occurred, was many years ago. But inquiry into that is of no importance, for it does not disturb or alter the truth and sequence of the history" ' (Cohen translation [Penguin edition, London, 1950], p. 616).

13. The time has come when critics are ready to acknowledge that the interpolated tales (Leonora's, Wilson's, and little Dick Adams's tale of Leonard and Paul) belong, are made to belong. I. B. Cauthen, Jr., for instance, argues that the three tales – which are, as he says, 'placed at almost regular intervals throughout the novel' – are intrinsic in that each deals with 'the exposure of ridiculous human frailty and folly. . . . The novel, therefore, is designed both to entertain and, more importantly, to instruct by laying bare the "only true source of the ridiculous" – affectation' ('Fielding's Digressions in *Joseph Andrews*', *College English*, XVII [1956], 379). My own analysis of these tales, as they fit into the plot of *Joseph Andrews* as a whole, leads me to the conclusion that the instructive aspect of these tales is subordinate to the festive intent; but I certainly do agree that the tales are intrinsic. Nor am I alone (see Martin C. Battestin on Wilson's tale in *The Moral Basis of Fielding's Art*, pp. 118-29). But Mr Battestin also

emphasizes the instructive aspect of this tale. Irvin Ehrenpreis defends the inclusion of the tale on sheerly structural grounds. 'The common charges', he says, 'against this story are that it has only a weak connection with Fielding's main plot and that it contains too many particulars. Neither charge is sound. From a "plot" which marches by reversals, interruptions, and digressions, the sagacious reader quickly learns not to expect causal coherence. Similarly, the details are no more crowded or minute than in the rest of the novel' ('Fielding's Use of Fiction: The Autonomy of *Joseph Andrews*', p. 34).

14. For instance, 'Doubtless the narrative of Mr Wilson . . . is fiction, but doubtless also it contains some autobiography' (Howard Mumford Jones, introduction to *Joseph Andrews* (Modern Library College Edition) [New York, 1950] p. viii).

15. 'There is a generous element of earth and soil in this man, but it is sweet, pungent, and fertile, nurturing the things that grow up towards the light. He has a discerning sense and warm adoration of that which is noble and lovely in human nature, and presents it always in some vital relation to the gross and muddy elements of life beneath it. Critics liken him to out-of-doors, its invigorating fresh air, its daylight of reality, with the teeming earth beneath, and above the enduring sun and stars and sky' (C. G. Osgood, *The Voice of England* [2nd ed., New York, 1952], p. 338). Or: 'He was, indeed, Taine's "good buffalo": a man with no knack and hence no use for the subtle or the complex – which is why his novels, aside from their fine portrayal of manners, are so thin; and a man who, though he might denounce injustice and corruption, never dreamt of questioning the conditions that produced them. He too had not a rebellious mind, only a satiric nature; and as a good buffalo, a sturdy Englishman who could take his misfortunes without whimpering, he took the world's without deep scrutiny' (Louis Kronenberger, *Kings and Desperate Men* [New York, 1942], pp. 304, 305).

16. The pedlar who helps unravel the lines of Joseph's and Fanny's parentage says of himself, 'I was a drummer in an Irish regiment of foot' (IV, 12). This identifies him as the selfsame saviour of Adams in chapter 15 of Book II. Fielding's attachment to Irish drummers is reflected earlier in *Pasquin* (1736), in which there is but one soldier in the army of Queen Common-Sense: a 'poor Drummer who was lately turned out of an Irish regiment' (V, i).

17. Thomas Middleton Raysor, ed., *Coleridge's Miscellaneous Criticism* (Cambridge, Mass., 1936), p. 437.

18. *The Times*, 2 September 1840. Thackeray drew on this for his lecture on 'The English Humourists' (Cross, III, 214).

19. 'The Concept of Plot and the Plot of *Tom Jones*', in R. S. Crane, ed., *Critics and Criticism Ancient and Modern* (Chicago, 1952), p. 639; cf. p. 642. At this point, Dr Leavis's demurrer must be cited: 'The conventional talk

about the "perfect construction" of *Tom Jones* . . . is absurd. There can't be subtlety of organization without richer matter to organize, and subtler interests, than Fielding has to offer. He is credited with range and variety and it is true that some episodes take place in the country and some in Town, some in the churchyard and some in the inn, some on the high-road and some in the bed-chamber, and so on. But we haven't to read a very large proportion of *Tom Jones* in order to discover the limits of the essential interests it has to offer us. Fielding's attitudes, and his concern with human nature, are simple, and not such as to produce an effect of anything but monotony (on a mind, that is, demanding more than external action) when exhibited at the length of an "epic in prose" (*The Great Tradition* [London, 1948], pp. 3, 4). In my view, Fielding is not so simple as Dr Leavis thinks he is; and one of the arguments of this book is that a proper understanding of Fielding's masks as narrator makes clear the distinctions among roles, none of which is simple, except by design.

20. *The Rhetoric of Fiction*, pp. 218, 219.

21. Crane, pp. 633-5. The threefold division of the novel, as analysed by Mr Crane in the subsequent pages, is excellent.

22. Crane, p. 638.

23. 'HERE LIES, IN EXPECTATION OF A JOYFUL RISING, THE BODY OF CAPTAIN JOHN BLIFIL. LONDON HAD THE HONOUR OF HIS BIRTH, OXFORD OF HIS EDUCATION. HIS PARTS WERE AN HONOUR TO HIS PROFESSION AND TO HIS COUNTRY: HIS LIFE, TO HIS RELIGION AND HUMAN NATURE. HE WAS A DUTIFUL SON, A TENDER HUSBAND, AN AFFECTIONATE FATHER, A MOST KIND BROTHER, A SINCERE FRIEND, A DEVOUT CHRISTIAN, AND A GOOD MAN. HIS INCONSOLABLE WIDOW HATH ERECTED THIS STONE, THE MONUMENT OF HIS VIRTUES AND OF HER AFFECTION.'

24. The first chapter of this book contains an assertion which quite gives away, it seems to me, Fielding's own view: 'It is a more useful capacity to be able to foretell the actions of men, in any circumstances, from their characters, than to judge of their characters from their actions. The former, I own, requires the greater penetration; but may be accomplished by true sagacity with no less certainty than the latter' (III, 1).

25. Page 35.

26. There is support elsewhere for my contention that Fielding's admiration for withdrawal to the country was not unqualified. In a poem written in the style of Pope's epistles, 'Of True Greatness' (first published in 1741, and reprinted in the *Miscellanies*, but 'writ several years ago' – i.e. before January 1741 [Cross, I, 289]), Fielding considers the Hermit's claims to greatness.

THE HERMIT

. . . flies society, to wilds resorts,
And rails at busy cities, splendid courts.
Great to himself, he in his cell appears,
As kings on thrones, or conquerors on cars.

O thou, that dar'st thus proudly scorn thy kind,
Search, with impartial scrutiny, thy mind;
Disdaining outward flatteries to win,
Dost thou not feed a flatterer within?
While other passions temperance may guide,
Feast not with too delicious meals thy pride.
On vice triumphant while they censures fall,
Be sure no envy mixes with thy gall.
Ask thyself oft, to power and grandeur born,
Had power and grandeur then incurr'd thy scorn?

Henley ed., XII, 250

27. William Empson is certainly correct to insist on the central importance of the Man of the Hill. 'All critics call the recital of Old Man irrelevant,
though Saintsbury labours to excuse it; but Fielding meant to give a survey
of all human experience (that is what he meant by calling the book an epic)
and Old Man provides the extremes of degradation and divine ecstasy
which Tom has no time for; as part of the structure of ethical thought he is
essential to the book, the keystone at the middle of the arch' ('*Tom Jones*',
Kenyon Review, XX (1958), 228).

28. 'This [the Bellaston intrigue], in truth, is the most heinous of his
offences, and has been brought up against Fielding and his hero by genera-
tions of critics. Fielding, whose ethics were in advance of his time, in this
case was only too true to its prevailing standards. . . . If he had known more
of life, it he had been as wise as his author, Jones would have expressed his
shame and humiliation more feelingly. But he was only a raw country lad,
learning by experience in a world that was not our world' (Baker, *History of
the English Novel*, IV, 130, 131).

29. Coleridge, however, would have liked something more explicit! An
'additional paragraph, more fully and forcibly unfolding Tom Jones's
sense of self-degradation' as a result of the Bellaston affair (*Coleridge's
Miscellaneous Criticism*, ed. T. M. Raysor [Cambridge, Mass., 1936], p. 304).

30. *The Early Masters of English Fiction* (Lawrence, Kansas, 1956), p. 119.

31. Fielding defends himself at an imagined court of 'Censorial Enquiry':
' "If you, Mr Censor, are yourself a Parent, you will view me with Com-
passion when I declare I am the Father of this poor Girl the Prisoner at the
Bar; nay, when I go farther, and avow, that of all my Offspring she is my
favourite Child. I can truly say that I bestowed a more than ordinary Pains
in her Education; in which I will venture to affirm, I followed the Rules of
all those who are acknowledged to have writ best on the Subject" ' (*Convent-
Garden Journal* (28 January 1752), ed. Gerard Edward Jensen [New Haven,
1915], I, 186).

32. *Macbeth*, IV, 2.

33. In 'The Background of Fielding's Laughter', William B. Coley makes
the following point: 'The assumed "reader" of *Amelia* differs from those of
earlier Fielding novels. No longer is he jestingly referred to as "sagacious",

"ingenious", or "sensible". The dedication of *Amelia* speaks, apparently directly, to a "good-natured reader", who, "if his heart should be here affected, will be inclined to pardon many faults for the pleasure he will receive from a tender sensation". And when ever this novel presumes to find fault with its readers, it does so with "readers of a different stamp", hardened souls knowing nothing of tenderness. In short, the deliberate ironic discrepancy between the assumed identities ("author" and "reader") and their implied, "real" counterparts (Fielding and his audience) is in *Amelia* considerably reduced. At the expense, it may be presumed of comic effect' (pages 249, 250).

34. The discussions occur in the following chapters: I, 10; V, 1; VI, 7; VIII, 5; VIII, 10; IX, 3; IX, 8; IX, 10; X, 1; X, 2; X, 4; XI, 2 (V, 1 was excised from the second and most subsequent editions, although it appears in the 1930 Everyman reprint).

35. Walter Raleigh says, 'Captain Booth, like the earlier hero, is a man "of consummate good nature", with perhaps a truer and deeper repentance for his faults than the buoyant Mr Jones ever succeeded in experiencing, and is saved, like his prototype, by the warmth of his feelings and the virtues of his wife' (*The English Novel* [New York, 1896], p. 176). Compare Taine, who speaks of Booth and Jones as 'brothers' (*History of English Literature*, trans. Henry Van Laun [New York, 1900], II, 426).

36. A phrase used by Professor Richmond Lattimore in the first of his Northcliffe Lectures at University College, London, on 1 May 1961.

Chapter 3

1. See Robert Etheridge Moore, *Hogarth's Literary Relationships* (Minneapolis, 1948), especially chapter 4.

2. In chapter 13 of Book II of *Joseph Andrews*, for instance, he mocks the journalistic fidelity of which Defoe, among others, was fond; there is presented a balance-sheet in which Adams and his companions are schematically shown to be six shillings, five and one-half pennies short of being able to pay a total reckoning of seven shillings.

3. In his excellent essay on Fielding, Professor Butt makes this point with specific reference to *The Letter Writers* (1731), in which a character named Rakel hides under the table. John Butt, *Fielding*, revised ed. (London, 1959), p. 11.

4. Wayne Booth analyses part of this incident in order to show that Fielding the narrator is never absent, even when the scene is 'dramatic'. 'If to be dramatic is to show characters dramatically engaged with each other, motive clashing with motive, the outcome depending upon the resolution of motives, then this scene is dramatic. But if it is to give the impression that the story is taking place by itself, with the characters existing in a dramatic relationship vis-à-vis the spectator, unmediated by a narrator and decipherable only through inferential matching of word to word and word to deed, this is a relatively undramatic scene' (*The Rhetoric of Fiction*, p. 162).

5. As Howard S. Babb points out in *Jane Austen's Novels: The Fabric of Dialogue* (Columbus, Ohio, 1962), *passim*.

6. Because, for one thing, Jane Austen never stoops so low. The nearest one comes in Jane Austen to this kind of figure is the Augusta Hawkins who becomes Mrs Elton, in *Emma*.

7. *Anatomy of Criticism* (Princeton, 1957, pp. 309-12).

8. The genealogy, by way of Cervantes and Marivaux, of these night adventures is economically set forth by Irvin Ehrenpreis in 'Fielding's Use of Fiction', *loc. cit.*, pp. 29-31.

9. Mark Spilka says that the comic night adventures in *Joseph Andrews* indicate that 'Fielding has put a kind of comic blessing upon the novel; he has resolved the major themes and passions through benevolent humour' ('Comic Resolution in Fielding's *Joseph Andrews*', *College English*, XV [1953], 19).

10. See Cross, III, 390, for a series of references.

11. 'Now it required no very blamable degree of suspicion to imagine that Mr Jones and his ragged companion had certain purposes in their intention, which, though tolerated in some Christian countries, connived at in others, and practised in all, are however as expressly forbidden as murder, or any other horrid vice, by that religion which is universally believed in those countries' (IX, 3).

12. See Sheridan Baker, 'Fielding's *Amelia* and the Materials of Romance', *PQ*, XLI (1962), 437-49.

Chapter 4

1. *The Rise of the Novel*, p. 272.

2. *The Nude* (London, 1956), p. 9.

3. Compare Wilson's view. In his tale he speaks with special distaste of those 'whose birth and fortunes place them just without the polite circles; I mean the lower class of the gentry, and the higher of the mercantile world, who are, in reality, the worst-bred part of mankind' (III, 3).

4. See George Sherburn, 'Fielding's Social Outlook', *Philological Quarterly*, XXV (1956), 1-23; reprinted in James L. Clifford, ed., *Eighteenth-Century English Literature: Modern Essays in Criticism* (New York, 1959), 251-73.

5. See *Aspects of the Novel* (London, 1927), pp. 103-11; and Northrop Frye's comment in *Anatomy of Criticism*, pp. 168, 169.

6. 'I conceive, the passions of men do commonly imprint sufficient marks on the countenance; and it is owing chiefly to want of skill in the observer that physiognomy is of so little use and credit in the world' ('An Essay on the Knowledge of the Characters of Men', Henley ed., XIV, 284). Actually, Fielding is, even in this essay, less consistent than the assertion

indicates. As Henry Knight Miller points out in his useful analysis of this work, 'Fielding . . . concludes with some doubts as to the ultimate efficacy of his guide' (*Essays on Fielding's 'Miscellanies'*, pp. 192, 193).

7. Martin Battestin (in his edition of *Joseph Andrews*, p. 364) persuasively identifies the original of Didapper as Lord Hervey: the 'truth' of the portrait is, however, that of a cartoon, of low rather than high relief.

8. *The Amiable Humorist* (Chicago, 1960), p. 141.

9. *Letters*, ed. Mrs Paget Toynbee, IX (1904), 403.

10. See, for instance *Letters*, XIII (1905), 281.

11. In Chapter 1, p. 35.

12. Pages x, xi.

13. *History of Henry Fielding*, I, 70, 71.

14. 'Symptomatic of a change of mode in *Amelia* is the emphasis on Prudence rather than on Fortune as the guiding principle of the action' (William B. Coley, 'The Background of Fielding's Laughter', p. 250).

Chapter 5

1. Preface to the *Familiar Letters between the Principal Characters in David Simple and Some Others*, Henley ed., XVI, 19.

2. *The Prose Style of Samuel Johnson* (New Haven, 1941), p. 63.

3. 'A Charge to the Grand Jury' is a good example.

4. The author of *An Essay on the New Species of Writing Founded by Mr Fielding* (1751) – authorship never discovered – remarks of Fielding's chapter titles: 'These little Scraps, if rightly manag'd, conduce more to his [the reader's] Entertainment than he is at first aware of' (Reprinted by Augustan Reprint Society [No. 95 – Los Angeles, 1962], p. 22).

5. See, for instance, Brower's *Alexander Pope: The Poetry of Allusion* (Oxford, 1959), pp. 152-62.

6. This is, of course, a cliché. See Barton Booth's, 'Song', *The Oxford Book of 18th Century Verse* (Oxford, 1926), p. 234.

7. For legal mumbo-jumbo, see I, 12 and IV, 3; for medical, I, 13, 14; for parsonical, I, 13.

8. And thus the grand style accommodates itself to hackney purposes, such as the dedication of *The Modern Husband* to Robert Walpole. Fielding's hack work and attitude to it are given authoritative treatment by Martin C. Battestin in 'Fielding's Changing Politics and *Joseph Andrews*', *PQ*, XXXIX (1960), 39-55.

9. In the Rinehart edition of the novel (New York, 1948), p. 347.

10. Fanny, that is to say, is what Pamela pretends to be.

11. Nor is the successful use of the panogyric style limited to addresses to Sophia and patrons (see the dedication of *Tom Jones* to Lyttelton): Tom, when heated, speaks with fine elevation to Dowling (XII, 10). See also the final paragraph of the novel.

12. In this connection, see Wimsatt, *The Prose Style of Samuel Johnson*, p. 101.

13. In Chapter 1, p. 24.

14. Oxford, 1959, p. 52.

BIBLIOGRAPHICAL NOTE

ANYONE wanting to undertake the study of Fielding should obtain two excellent works: first of all, John Butt's *Fielding* (Writers and their Work: No. 57: Bibliographical Series of Supplements to 'British Book News', revised edition, London, Longmans, 1959). Professor Butt gives a short and just account of Fielding's life, and he appends an extremely useful bibliography. Second, under the editorship of Ronald Paulson, *Fielding: A Collection of Critical Essays* (Twentieth Century Views, Englewood Cliffs, New Jersey, Prentice-Hall, 1962). This compilation contains essays by John S. Coolidge, Aurélien Digeon, William Empson, André Gide, A. R. Humphreys, Arnold Kettle, Maynard Mack, John Middleton Murry, Winfield H. Rogers, George Sherburn, Mark Spilka, and Ian Watt. Professor Paulson's collection also includes a selective and critical bibliography of much usefulness: here are listed works by Martin Battestin, Wayne C. Booth, Sheridan Baker, William B. Coley, Ronald Crane, A. D. McKillop, Henry Knight Miller, Charles B. Woods, and James Aiken Work. All of these ought to be read.

Further Fielding study should begin with the lists in the *Cambridge Bibliography of English Literature* and its 1957 *Supplement*. This can be used in conjunction with the appropriate volume of the new (i.e. since 1960) Photolithographic Edition of the Reading Room copy of the British Museum *General Catalogue of Printed Books*; and these bibliographies should be supplemented by the bibliography 'English Literature, 1660-1800', appearing annually in *Philological Quarterly*. The issues of this bibliography for 1925-60 are collected in Louis A. Landa *et al.*, *English Literature, 1660-1800: A Bibliography of Modern Studies*, 4 vols., Princeton, 1950-52, 1962.

INDEX

(Fielding's works are indexed alphabetically by title)

Kritzer, Hyman,
acknowledgment, 7

Landa, Louis A., bibliography
of the Restoration and
eighteenth century, 192
Lattimore, Richmond, on the
'rights of the story', 205
Lazarillo de Tormes, 28
Leavis, F. R., on *Tom Jones*,
202, 203
Lesage, Alain René, as
fictional biographer, 25
Licensing Act of 1737, 60
Locke, John, epistemology, 49
Lombardo, Agostino,
acknowledgment, 7
Lucian, imitated by Fielding,
21

McKillop, A. D., on the
artificiality of *Tom Jones*, 104,
204; on Fielding, 192
Mack, Maynard, on *Joseph
Andrews* and *Pamela*, 183, 192,
207
Mandel, Jerome,
acknowledgment, 7
Mariana, Juan de, compared
by Fielding to Cervantes, 26
Marivaux, Pierre Carlet de
Chamblain de, as fictional
biographer, 25
Masquerade, The, 15
Miller, Henry Knight,
compares Lucian and
Fielding, 21, 195; on
Fielding, 192, 206, 207
Milton, John, imitated by
Fielding, 23, 43; referred to
in *Amelia*, 185
Miscellanies, 203, 204
Modern Husband, The, 148, 207

Molière (Jean Baptiste
Poquelin), *L'Avare*, 59; *Le
Médecin malgré lui*, 59
Moore, Robert Etheridge, on
Hogarth and Fielding, 205
Murry, John Middleton, on
Fielding, 192, 200

Ohio State University,
acknowledgment, 7
Osgood, C. G., on Fielding, 202

Pasquin, 148, 196
Paulson, Ronald, editor of
Fielding criticism, 192
Pope, Alexander, *Essay on Man*,
49

Radcliffe, Ann, *The Mysteries of
Udolpho* and the Man of the
Hill, 86
Raleigh, Walter, on *Amelia*, 205
Richardson, Samuel,
didacticism in *Amelia*
Richardsonian, 48, 49; as
false biographer, 25; *Joseph
Andrews* and *Pamela*, 57-59,
70, 148; knowledge of
audience, 24; method of
Pamela, 28; as moralist, 16,
17; *Pamela* mocked by
Fielding, 20; *Pamela* as
'testament to prurience', 15;
reception of *Pamela*, 200;
unctuousness, 92;
verisimilitude, 19; see also
under *Shamela*
Rogers, Winfield H., on
Fielding, 192

Sackett, S. J., editor of
Fielding, 196

Walpole, Sir Robert,
dedication of *The Modern
Husband*, 207; Licensing Act,
60, 148
Watt, Ian, on the epic and the
novel, 194; 'formal realism',
19, 192, 198; on the reading
public, 24, 196; on
Richardson and Fielding,
146, 147, 206; on *Shamela*,
199, 200; on verisimilitude
and the marvellous,
198

Wesleyan University Press,
edition of Fielding, 9
Wimsatt, W. K., on style, 172,
207
Woods, Charles B., on Fielding,
192, 199
Work, James Aiken, on
Fielding, 192
Wright, Virginia, acknowledg-
ment, 7; dedication, 5

Zola, Emile, naturalism of
Fielding compared to, 116